CodeWarrior™

Software Development using PowerPlant™

LIMITED WARRANTY AND DISCLAIMER OF LIABILITY

ACADEMIC PRESS, INC. ("AP") AND ANYONE ELSE WHO HAS BEEN INVOLVED IN THE CREATION OR PRODUCTION OF THE ACCOMPANYING CODE ("THE PRODUCT") CANNOT AND DO NOT WARRANT THE PERFORMANCE OR RESULTS THAT MAY BE OBTAINED BY USING THE PRODUCT. THE PRODUCT IS SOLD "AS IS" WITHOUT WARRANTY OF ANY KIND (EXCEPT AS HEREAFTER DESCRIBED), EITHER EXPRESSED OR IMPLIED, INCLUDING, BUT NOT LIMITED TO, ANY WARRANTY OF PERFORMANCE OR ANY IMPLIED WARRANTY OF MERCHANTABILITY OR FITNESS FOR ANY PARTICULAR PURPOSE. AP WARRANTS ONLY THAT THE MAGNETIC DISC(S) ON WHICH THE CODE IS RECORDED IS FREE FROM DEFECTS IN MATERIAL AND FAULTY WORKMANSHIP UNDER THE NORMAL USE AND SERVICE FOR A PERIOD OF NINETY (90) DAYS FROM THE DATE THE PRODUCT IS DELIVERED. THE PURCHASER'S SOLE AND EXCLUSIVE REMEDY IN THE EVENT OF A DEFECT IS EXPRESSLY LIMITED TO EITHER REPLACEMENT OF THE DISC(S) OR REFUND OF THE PURCHASE PRICE, AT AP'S SOLE DISCRETION.

IN NO EVENT, WHETHER AS A RESULT OF BREACH OF CONTRACT, WARRANTY OR TORT (INCLUDING NEGLIGENCE) WILL AP OR ANYONE WHO HAS BEEN INVOLVED IN THE CREATION OR PRODUCTION OF THE PRODUCT BE LIABLE TO PURCHASER FOR ANY DAMAGES, INCLUDING ANY LOST PROFITS, LOST SAVINGS OR OTHER INCIDENTAL OR CONSEQUENTIAL DAMAGES ARISING OUT OF THE USE OR INABILITY TO USE PRODUCT OR ANY MODIFICATIONS THEREOF, OR DUE TO THE CONTENTS OF THE CODE, EVEN IF AP HAS BEEN ADVISED OF THE POSSIBILITY OF SUCH DAMAGES, OR ANY CLAIM BY ANY OTHER PARTY.

Any request for replacement of a defective CD-ROM disc must be postage prepaid and must be accompanied by the original defective disc, your mailing address and telephone number, and proof of date of purchase and purchase price. Send such requests, stating the nature of the problem, to Academic Press Customer Service, 6277 Sea Harbor Drive, Orlando, FL 32887, 1-800-321-5068. APP shall have no obligation to refund the purchase price or to replace a disc based on the claims of defects in the nature or operation of the Product.

Some states do not allow limitation on how long an implied warranty lasts, nor exclusions or limitatiions of incidental or consequential damage, so the above limitations and exclusions may not apply to you. This Warranty gives you specific legal rights, and you may also have other rights which may vary from jurisdiction to jurisdiction.

THE RE-EXPORT OF UNITED STATES ORIGIN SOFTWARE IS SUBJECT TO THE UNITED STATES LAWS UNDER THE EXPORT ADMINISTRATION ACT OF 1969 AS AMENDED. ANY FURTHER SALE OF THE PRODUCT SHALL BE IN COMPLIANCE WITH THE UNITED STATES DEPARTMENT OF COMMERCE ADMINISTRATION REGULATIONS. COMPLIANCE WITH SUCH REGULATIONS IS YOUR RESPONSIBILITY AND NOT THE RESPONSIBILITY OF AP.

CodeWarrior™

Software Development using PowerPlant™

Jan L. Harrington

AP PROFESSIONAL

AP Professional is a division of Academic Press, Inc.

Boston San Diego New York
London Sydney Tokyo Toronto

AP PROFESSIONAL

An Imprint of ACADEMIC PRESS, INC.
A Division of HARCOURT BRACE & COMPANY

ORDERS (USA and Canada): 1-800-3131-APP or APP@ACAD.COM
AP Professional Orders: 6277 Sea Harbor Dr., Orlando, FL 32821-9816

Europe/Middle East/Africa: 0-11-44 (0) 181-300-3322
Orders: AP Professional 24-28 Oval Rd., London NW1 7DX

Japan/Korea: 03-3234-3911-5
Orders: Harcourt Brace Japan, Inc., Ichibancho Central Building 22-1, Ichibancho Chiyoda-Ku, Tokyo 102

Australia: 02-517-8999
Orders: Harcourt Brace & Co. Australia, Locked Bag 16, Marrickville, NSW 2204 Australia

Other International: (407) 345-3800
AP Professional Orders: 6277 Sea Harbor Dr., Orlando FL 32821-9816

Editorial: 1300 Boylston St., Chestnut Hill, MA 02167 (617)232-0500

Web: http://www.apnet.com/approfessional

This book is printed on acid-free paper. ∞

United Kingdom Edition published by
ACADEMIC PRESS LIMITED
24–28 Oval Road, London NW1 7DX

Library of Congress Cataloging-in-Publication Data
Harrington, Jan L.
CodeWarrior software development using PowerPlant / Jan Harrington.
p. cm.
Includes index.
ISBN 0-12-326422-7
1. Computer software--Development. 2. Macintosh (Computer)--Programming. 3. Object-oriented programming (Computer science) 4. PowerPlant. 5. CodeWarrior. I. Title.
QA76.76.D47H38 1996
005.26'2--dc20 96-13291
CIP

Printed in the United States of America
96 97 98 99 IP 9 8 7 6 5 4 3 2 1

Contents

Preface

Back in 1984, when many of us began programming for the Macintosh, we learned quickly that although the Macintosh user interface made life easy for the user, it placed an enormous burden on the software developer. Writing applications for a GUI environment is a lot tougher than writing simple text-based applications; there're no two ways about it.

If you happen to be working in C++, then the situation is a bit worse because the Macintosh environment is steeped in its Pascal heritage. The Macintosh ToolBox routines are Pascal functions and procedures and there's nothing object-oriented about them.

So, if you're committed to writing an object-oriented C++ Macintosh application, what do you do? You can start from scratch, writing all your own classes, a painstaking, lengthy, and largely unnecessary process. Why unnecessary? Because Metrowerks PowerPlant can do a lot of the work for you.

PowerPlant is a collection of C++ functions that provide an object-oriented framework for a Macintosh application. PowerPlant functions take care of tasks such as installing and updating the menu bar, managing the event loop, handling dialog box actions, and printing. Using PowerPlant can significantly speed up development time as well as give your application all the benefits of object-orientation.

In this book you will learn about the structure of PowerPlant—including how its many classes are related—and how to use PowerPlant classes to implement many common Macintosh application features. You will discover when you can create objects directly from PowerPlant classes, and when you need to first create a custom subclass. You will read about everything from menus, windows, and dialog boxes to QuickTime movies. You will discover where direct ToolBox calls are essential and where you can avoid them by taking advantage of the code provided by the PowerPlant classes.

Most of all, you *will* learn how PowerPlant works. We'll explore the sequences of function calls that implement basic elements of the Macintosh user interface to give you an in-depth understanding of the general principles behind the PowerPlant architecture.

What you *won't* find in this book is an exhaustive discussion of every PowerPlant class. There are two major reasons why this is the case. First, PowerPlant is *huge* (more than 2,000 functions) and you'd need a wheelbarrow to carry around a tome that attempted to cover all of them. Second, PowerPlant is always changing. As you probably know, Metrowerks releases three versions of the CodeWarrior development environment every year, and each of those releases includes changes to PowerPlant. Some classes become obsolete, others are added, and still others are modified.

Therefore, I think the most important thing you can do is become familiar with the general way in which PowerPlant works. Then you can explore classes on your own and also feel comfortable when Metrowerks presents you with modifications to the PowerPlant framework.

The Sample Program

When an author designs a programming book, he or she has a major choice to make about the size of the sample programs used for examples. Most introductory books tend to stick with relatively short programs, as I did in my first CodeWarrior book. However, PowerPlant isn't really intended for writing short programs that don't do much more than demonstrate a handful of techniques. It's intended for writing large, useful applications. In fact, it's very difficult to see the way in which the elements of a PowerPlant application work unless you are working with a large program.

Given that you need a large program to really understand the PowerPlant environment, this book is based on a single application rather than a collection of short ones.

The program that you will find on the CD-ROM that accompanies this book is designed to manage a video rental store (Penultimate Videos). The application isn't complete—there are many things that need to be added to make it truly usable by a retail outlet—nor is it guaranteed to be bug free. In addition, some of its features have been added just for demonstration purposes and probably wouldn't be part of a real-world video store management application. Nonetheless, the program is large enough and practical enough to demonstrate many PowerPlant techniques and to show you one way that an application of reasonable size can be put together.

What You Need to Know

Because PowerPlant is a complex programming environment, there are several areas of knowledge you should have before you begin working with this book:

- You should be fluent in object-oriented C++ programming, including an understanding of multiple inheritance, operator overloading, and the object-oriented way of implementing data structures such as linked lists. The program used for examples in this book also makes heavy use of binary trees, a data structure that isn't part of the PowerPlant environment. A discussion of binary tree algorithms and iterators can be found in the Appendix if you aren't familiar with them.
- You should be familiar with the structure and use of the Macintosh ToolBox. Although you can get a great deal from this book without an in-depth knowledge of the ToolBox, keep in mind that PowerPlant hides many ToolBox operations from the programmer. If you need to modify or debug PowerPlant behavior and you aren't familiar with the ToolBox, it may be difficult to understand what PowerPlant is doing.
- You should be familiar with the idea of resources and know how to use a resource editor or compiler (for example, ResEdit, Rez, or Resourcer). The examples in this book use ResEdit.
- You should be comfortable with using the Metrowerks CodeWarrior Integrated Development Environment (IDE), including the debugger. (Repeat after me: "The debugger is my friend, the debugger is my friend....") Penultimate Videos was begun using CW7 and completed with CW8. It therefore won't work with versions of the software prior to CW8.

Acknowledgments

As with any book, there is an entire cast of characters that makes the book possible. I'd therefore like to thank the following people for the valuable work on this project:

- Mike Williams, Assistant Acquisitions Editor at AP Professional.
- Peter Sullivan, Production Editor at AP Professional.
- Owen Hartnett, Technical Editor, who really knows his C++!
- Dave Mark, Publisher Liason at Metrowerks.
- Greg Combs, Metrowerks burnmaster who made the CD-ROM.

JLH

CHAPTER 1

Introducing PowerPlant

In this chapter you will read about the organization of the PowerPlant framework, including such diverse topics as the files you need to work with it, the major types of classes that are part of the framework (for example, commanders, broadcasters, and listeners), and the functions the classes have in common. You will also learn about application classes, which provide the foundation for a PowerPlant application, and a special resource type called a PowerPlant object. In addition, this chapter looks at some global PowerPlant features, including support for exception handling.

PowerPlant as an Application Framework

PowerPlant is what is called an *application framework*. It provides a program structure that supports the basic activities performed by most Macintosh applications. In this case, that structure is object-oriented.

Using PowerPlant gives a programmer several advantages:

- It provides an object-oriented structure for a Macintosh program, which—given its Pascal heritage—has no inherent object-oriented characteristics.
- It relieves the programmer from writing code for basic Macintosh program activities, such as managing the menu bar, the event loop, and a great deal of event trapping.
- It speeds application development because a great deal of code is already written.

Although PowerPlant does provide support for basic Macintosh program actions, that doesn't mean that you never need to write direct ToolBox calls. As you will see throughout this book, there are many things PowerPlant doesn't do. For example, the class LPrintout, which enormously simplifies printing a document, doesn't ensure that a line of text isn't split horizontally between two pages. If you want to adjust printed pages for complete lines of text, you will need to write the code yourself.

NOTE

While on the topic of ToolBox calls, this is as good a place as any to mention that you should place the unary scope resolution operator (::) in front of all ToolBox calls. This will ensure that they aren't confused with PowerPlant function calls.

PowerPlant is supplied as a collection of more than a hundred classes, just under half of which participate in a single class hierarchy. Unlike many class libraries, which are supplied to programmers only as object code, PowerPlant classes are provided as source code. This means you can study, copy, and modify the classes in any way you choose. Although you do need to compile the PowerPlant classes the first time you attempt to run any given project, the extra compile time is well worth the benefit of having access to that source code.

What You Need to Use PowerPlant

PowerPlant is supplied with the CodeWarrior package of development tools. To use its classes in a program, you need the following:

- The CodeWarrior Integrated Development Environment (IDE) for each platform for which you will be developing code.
- The C++ compiler for each platform for which you will be developing code.
- The CodeWarrior debugger. As mentioned in the Preface, you'll find CodeWarrior's excellent debugger one of your best allies in a PowerPlant development project.
- The source code for all PowerPlant classes.
- The application Constructor (a resource editor for special PowerPlant resources).
- A standard resource editor or compiler, such as Resourcerer, ResEdit, or Rez.

The easiest way to get all these files is to use the CodeWarrior installer and check all the appropriate parts (for example, Figure 1.1). Be sure to include the following along with the IDE and debugger you see selected in Figure 1.1:

- Metrowerks C/C++ for Mac OS: If you don't want all the C/C++ libraries (for example, if you don't want the ANSI libraries), be sure to select the specific compiler package you want rather than letting the installer copy them all.
- Metrowerks PowerPlant: Be sure to install all of PowerPlant, which includes Constructor.

Finally, you probably want to install at least some of the PowerPlant documentation, which is part of the CodeWarrior Documentation package.

PowerPlant Class Types

PowerPlant classes fall into one or more of four broad categories:

- Stand-alone classes: These classes don't participate in the large PowerPlant class hierarchy and can therefore usually be used in non-PowerPlant programs. Classes

Figure 1.1 Selecting parts of the CodeWarrior package to install

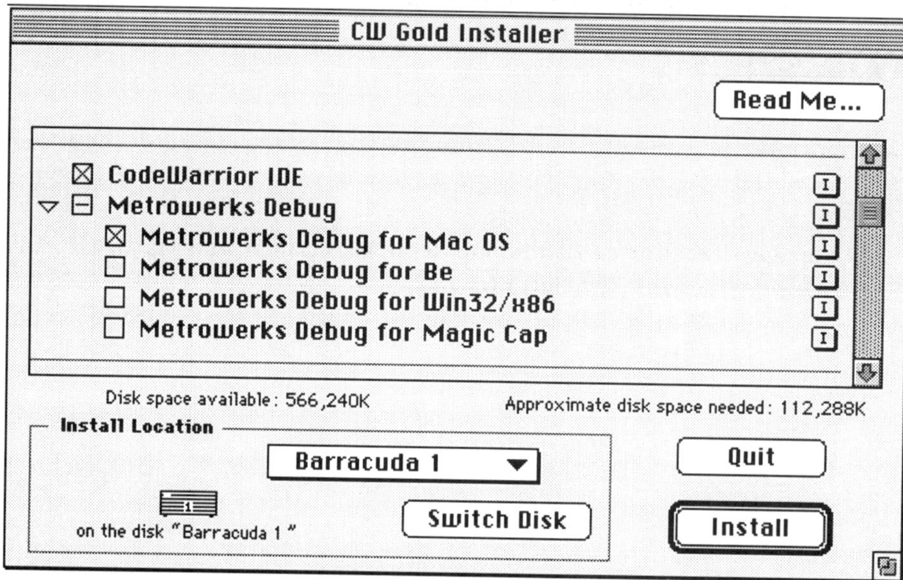

of this type include LFile (for handling basic File Manager file I/O) and LMenuBar and LMenu, which handle the menu bar and menus.

- PowerPlant-only classes: These classes participate in the large class hierarchy about which you will read in the next section of this chapter. Their use is restricted to PowerPlant programs.
- Mix-in classes: These classes are designed to be used as base classes to add functionality to other objects. You would never create an object directly from these classes. For example, the LBroadcaster class allows a class derived from it to broadcast a message. However, the derived class must have some additional functionality besides being able to send a message. LControl, a class that acts as a base class for many specific control classes (e.g., buttons, check boxes, and radio buttons), has LBroadcaster as one of its base classes. In addition, LControl also inherits from LPane, a base class that provides support for the drawing of most objects that appear on the Macintosh screen. LControl can use what it inherits from LPane to help it draw itself on the screen; it can use what it inherits from LBroadcaster to send a message whenever the user makes a change in the state of the control.
- Wrapper classes: These classes simplify access to many groups of ToolBox routines. For example, UPrintingMgr is a wrapper for ToolBox Manager functions, and LFile is a wrapper for File Manager functions.

The PowerPlant Class Hierarchy

In Figure 1.2 you can see the relationships between many of the most frequently used PowerPlant classes. Each box represents one class. The names of the classes generally suggest what the class is designed to support. For example, LDialogBox creates and manages dialog boxes, LStdPopupMenu takes care of a popup menu, and LStdButton supports standard push buttons.

The arrowheads in the diagram indicate the direction of inheritance. The different patterns and shadings of the lines have no significance other than to make it easier to follow the inheritance where the lines cross.

As you can see from the diagram, the PowerPlant classes aren't in a straight-line hierarchy. The structure of these classes uses a lot of multiple inheritance to ensure that classes inherit only exactly what they need. A straight-line hierarchy would mean that many classes would be expanded by functions and variables that would never be used. Although the multiple inheritance, broad hierarchy is conceptually more complex than a straight-line hierarchy, it does help keep individual classes as small as possible.

There are also some classes that aren't part of the hierarchy at all. For example, as you read earlier LMenu (used to implement one menu) and LMenuBar (used to manage the menu bar) are stand-alone.

You will be introduced to most of the classes in Figure 1.2 throughout this book. In some cases, you will be able to create objects from the classes without modification. Alternatively, you may need to either define a subclass or create a "clone" of a class, where you duplicate a PowerPlant class and make some custom modifications.

NOTE

As far as this writer knows, there is no official C++ term for "cloning" a class, although the term is used in object-oriented systems analysis to describe one way of reusing a class. Occasionally you may need to modify a PowerPlant class in such a way that subclassing isn't appropriate, but making a copy of the class and changing it slightly is. When that latter behavior is required, this book will call it cloning (for want of a better term).

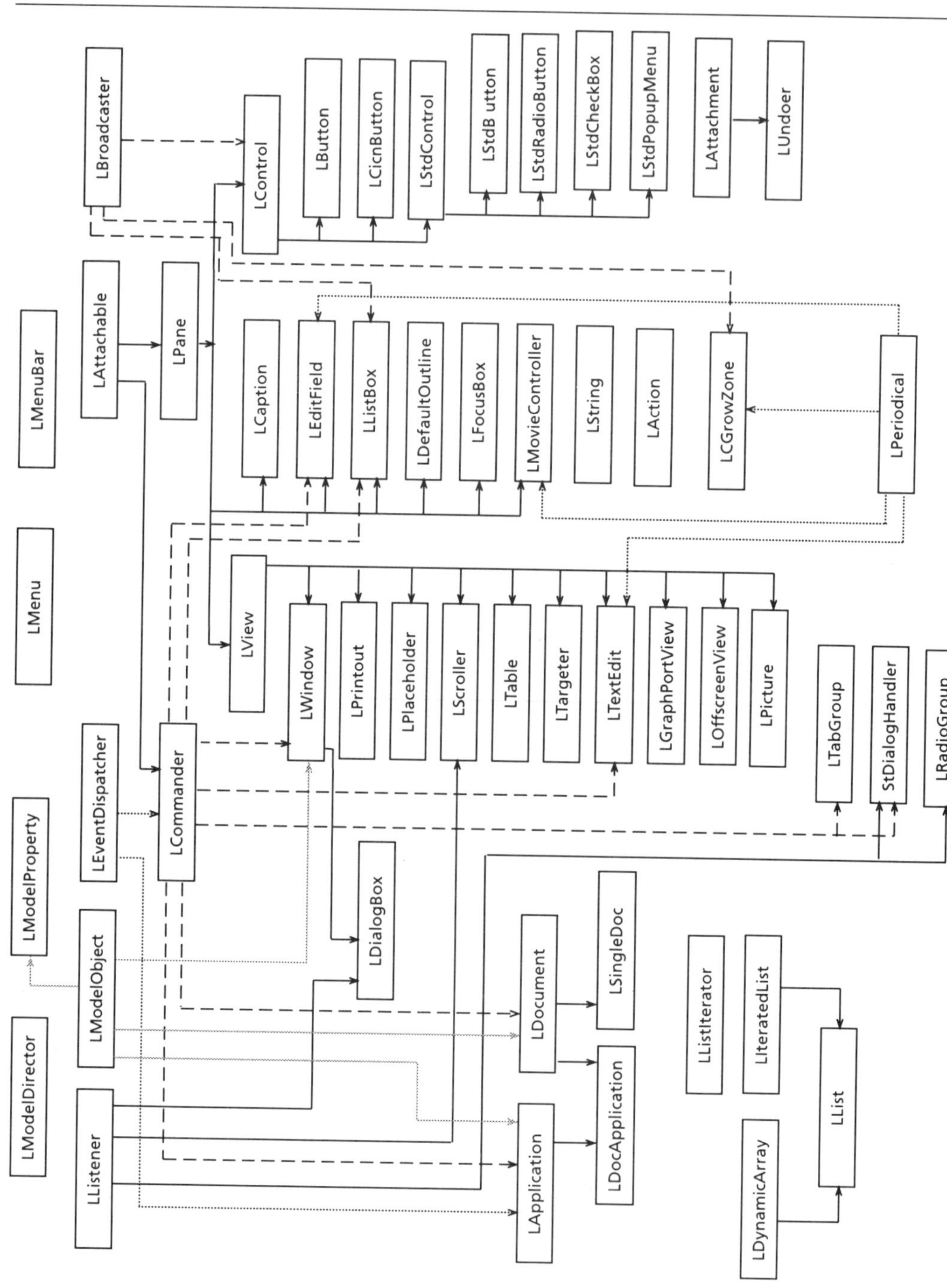

Figure 1.2 A portion of the PowerPlant class hierarchy

Class Naming Conventions

In Figure 1.2 almost all the classes are named beginning with "L." This isn't an accident. PowerSoft uses the following naming conventions for PowerPlant classes.

Class Name Prefix	Use	Sample
`L`	Precedes the name of PowerPlant library classes	`LMenu`
`U`	Precedes the name of PowerPlant utility classes	`UTextMenus`
`St`	Precedes the name of PowerPlant stack-based classes	`StDialog Handler`

As you explore PowerPlant files, you may also encounter classes whose names begin with `C`. These are subclasses created for use in the sample programs that accompany PowerPlant. You might want to use the prefix for the classes you declare yourself.

NOTE

Although PowerPlant classes are named using the preceding conventions, there is no hard and fast rule that says you must adhere to those conventions when naming your own classes. In fact, the Penultimate Videos program doesn't use PowerPlant rules for naming classes; this made it easier for the author to distinguish classes written specifically for the program from PowerPlant classes. Nonetheless, how you name files is a personal (or team, if you're working on a programming team) decision. Whatever you do, try to be consistent so that when you return to the program after a long weekend, you'll be able to figure out why you did what you did.

The Application Classes

The foundation of a PowerPlant application is one application object, which is created from a subclass of LApplication, LDocument, LSingleDoc, or LDocApplication. These classes take care of general program management activities such as implementing the event loop. They create a menu bar with , File, and Edit menus and handle events associated with all options in the menu and the Quit option in the File menu.

The difference between the four application classes can be found in the way in which they support documents:

- LApplication, the most basic of the four, provides no document support.
- LDocument is designed for programs that manipulate one or more document files. It therefore supports actions on documents such as Save, Save As, Revert, and Print.
- LSingleDoc is similar to LDocument but aimed at programs that work with only one document at a time.
- LDocApplication is designed for programs that display more than one window for a single document file.

Creating the Application Object

Just like any C++ program, a PowerPlant program must have a `main` function which, at the very least, creates the application object. A PowerPlant `main` function also usually performs some program setup operations. The code in Listing 1.1, the `main` function for the Penultimate Videos program, is typical. It sets the PowerPlant debugging options—you can remove that code when the program is ready to ship—and initializes the heap and the ToolBox. Then, it creates the application object and finishes by calling the object's `Run` function. The remainder of the application's actions are initiated by that call.

Listing 1.1 The Penultimate Videos main function

```
// ===========================================================================
//        • Main Program
// ===========================================================================

void main(void)
{
                                        // Set Debugging options
#ifdef Debug_Throw
     gDebugThrow = debugAction_Alert;
#endif

#ifdef Debug_Signal
     gDebugSignal = debugAction_Alert;
#endif

     InitializeHeap(4);
     UQDGlobals::InitializeToolbox(&qd);
     new LGrowZone(20000);

     CPPVideoStoreApp theApp;
     theApp.Run();
}
```

This statement creates the application object, calling the constructor

This function call initiates program actions

The Application and the Event Loop

One of the most important actions performed by an application object is to manage a program's event loop, which is initiated in the object's `Run` function. As you can see in Listing 1.2, the function contains a `while` that either calls a function named `ProcessNextEvent` or signals an exception.

Listing 1.2 An application object's Run function

```
void
LApplication::Run()
{
    SwitchTarget(this);
    ::InitCursor();
    UpdateMenus();

    mState = programState_ProcessingEvents;

    while (mState != programState_Quitting) {
        try {
            ProcessNextEvent();
        }

        catch(...) {
            SignalPStr_("\pException caught in LApplication::Run");
        }
    }
}
```

`ProcessNextEvent`, which is found in Listing 1.3, takes care of setting the cursor shape, and then calls the ToolBox routine `WaitNextEvent` to pull the next event record that belongs to the application off the event queue. To handle an event, the function first attempts to let PowerPlant's attachment mechanism handle the event.

An *attachment* is a class that modifies the way in which another class behaves while the program is running. You might, for example, use an attachment to draw a letterhead on every piece of output your program prints. Rather than modifying the classes that produce the output, you can "attach" some code that draws the letterhead to the appropriate classes. PowerPlant provides attachment classes for actions such as beeping the computer's speaker in response to an event and supporting the scrolling keys on the extended keyboard (page up, page down, and so on). Your program can certainly use any of the attachments provided by PowerPlant, or you can write your own attachments. You will find an example of using an attachment in

Listing 1.3 An application object's ProcessNextEvent function

```
void LApplication::ProcessNextEvent()
{
	EventRecord macEvent;

		// When on duty (application is in the foreground), adjust the
		// cursor shape before waiting for the next event. Except for the
		// very first time, this is the same as adjusting the cursor
		// after every event.

	if (IsOnDuty()) {

			// Calling OSEventAvail with a zero event mask will always
			// pass back a null event. However, it fills the EventRecord
			// with the information we need to set the cursor shape--
			// the mouse location in global coordinates and the state
			// of the modifier keys.

		::OSEventAvail(0, &macEvent);
		AdjustCursor(macEvent);
	}

		// Retrieve the next event. Context switch could happen here.

	SetUpdateCommandStatus(false);
	Boolean gotEvent = ::WaitNextEvent(everyEvent, &macEvent, mSleepTime,
							mMouseRgnH);

		// Let Attachments process the event. Continue with normal
		// event dispatching unless suppressed by an Attachment.

	if (LAttachable::ExecuteAttachments(msg_Event, &macEvent)) {
		if (gotEvent) {
			DispatchEvent(macEvent);
		} else {
			UseIdleTime(macEvent);
		}
	}

							// Repeaters get time after every event
	LPeriodical::DevoteTimeToRepeaters(macEvent);

							// Update status of menu items
	if (IsOnDuty() && GetUpdateCommandStatus()) {
		UpdateMenus();
	}
}
```

A call to the ToolBox routine WaitNextEvent

A call to the routine that identifies the event that has occurred

A call to handle events that should occur when the program receives a null event

Chapter 6, where attachments are used to implement the Undo operation in a text edit window.

There are two classes that support the attachments mechanism: LAttachable, from which classes that can accept attachments are derived, and LAttachment, which generates attachment objects. Notice in Listing 1.3 that once the application object has grabbed an event from the event queue, it calls the LAttachable function `ExecuteAttachments`. This function returns true if the application object should handle the event and false if the event was handled by an attachment and therefore requires no action by the application object.

When a null event occurs, `ProcessNextEvent` calls its own function `UseIdleTime` to give time to events that should be processed when the program isn't doing anything else. However, if anything other than a null event occurs (`gotEvent` is true), `ProcessNextEvent` calls `LEventDispatcher::DispatchEvent`.

The class LEventDispatcher exists to dispatch events to the correct object. Because LApplication is derived from LEventDispatcher, an application object created from this class has access to the event dispatching functions. As you can see in Listing 1.4, `DispatchEvent` identifies the event that has occurred and then branches to the LEventDispatcher function that handles the specific event. Typically the event handling functions process events that aren't related to other program objects. For example, LEventDispatcher takes care of mouse clicks in system windows and in the menu bar. However, when an event should be handled by another program object, LEventDispatcher passes the event to the appropriate object. The mechanism for determining which object receives an event is part of the class LCommander, which is discussed in the next section of this chapter.

Interclass Communication

Like objects in any other object-oriented program, those used in a PowerPlant program send messages to communicate with one another. Objects that listen to message and objects that send messages fall into three broad categories: commanders, broadcasters, and listeners. In this section you will be introduced to these three categories of objects and learn how they relate to one another when handling events.

Listing 1.4 Dispatching an event

```
voidLEventDispatcher::DispatchEvent(const EventRecord&inMacEvent)
{
    switch (inMacEvent.what)
    {
        case mouseDown:
            AdjustCursor(inMacEvent);
            EventMouseDown(inMacEvent);
            break;

        case mouseUp:
            EventMouseUp(inMacEvent);
            break;

        case keyDown:
            EventKeyDown(inMacEvent);
            break;

        case autoKey:
            EventAutoKey(inMacEvent);
            break;

        case keyUp:
            EventKeyUp(inMacEvent);
            break;

        case diskEvt:
            EventDisk(inMacEvent);
            break;

        case updateEvt:
            EventUpdate(inMacEvent);
            break;

        case activateEvt:
            EventActivate(inMacEvent);
            break;

        case osEvt:
            EventOS(inMacEvent);
            break;

        case kHighLevelEvent:
            EventHighLevel(inMacEvent);
            break;

        default:
            UseIdleTime(inMacEvent);
            break;
    }
}
```

COMMANDERS

Classes that listen for and respond to messages generated by keystrokes and menu choices are called *commanders*. At some point in their inheritance hierarchy, they are derived from LCommander. When you use a class derived from LCommander, or derive a class that includes LCommander in its inheritance hierarchy, you must override two member functions to customize the behavior of the derived class in response to events:

- The `FindCommandStatus` function determines whether menu options should be enabled or disabled. As you would expect, a program responds only to enabled menu options.
- The `ObeyCommand` function identifies which command has been chosen by the user—either with the mouse or a command-key equivalent—and takes action appropriate to that command. If the action requires just a few lines of code, you can include it as part of the `ObeyCommand` function. However, in most cases you will want to call another function to handle the command.

If you look back at Figure 1.2, you'll notice that there are a number of classes that are ultimately derived from LCommander, including LApplication, LDocument, LEditField (a text entry box in a window or dialog box), LTextEdit (an area for editable text in a window based on the ToolBox's TextEdit routines), LListBox (a scrolling list of items), LTabGroup (a group of items that are reached successively by pressing the Tab key), and LWindow (the base class for all windows). When you derive a class from one of these classes, the derived class will have its own `FindCommandStatus` and `ObeyCommand` functions. Those functions will contain code that is applicable to the specific class. As a result, a program contains a group of `FindCommandStatus` and `ObeyCommand` functions, each of which handles a distinct part of the program's keystroke and menu events.

As an example, consider the dialog box in Figure 1.3, which is used to enter data about a new movie title using the Penultimate Videos program. Each rectangular data entry area is an object created from LEditField and is therefore a commander. The dialog box itself (an object of class LDialogBox, which is derived from LWindow) is also a commander. In addition, the application is a commander. Finally, there is a commander that you can't see in the window: an object of class LTabGroup. All of the LEditField objects are part of a single tab group, which makes it possible for the user to move the cursor from one field to another by pressing Tab.

Figure 1.3 A dialog box from a PowerPlant program

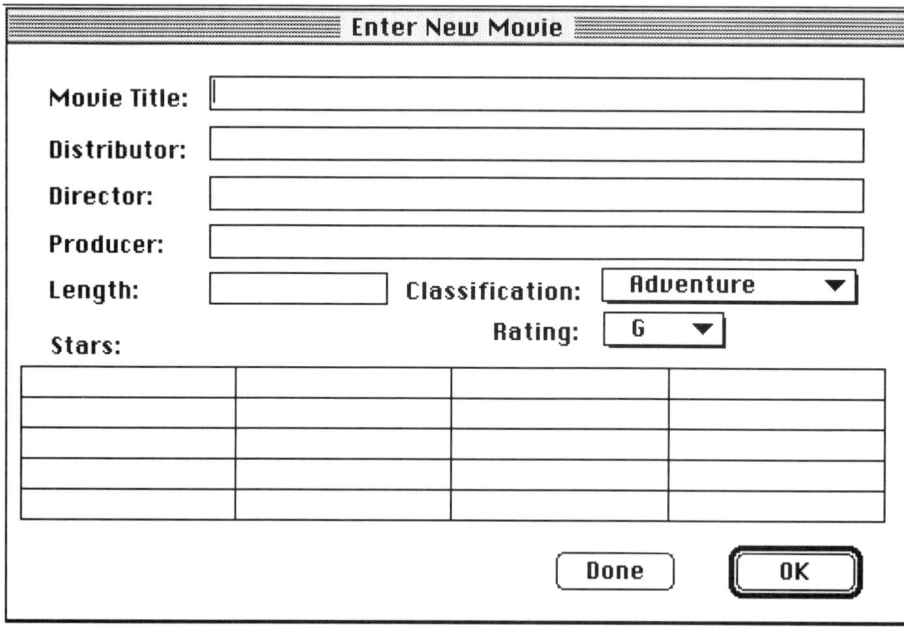

As well as the `FindCommandStatus` and `ObeyCommand` functions, commanders have several functions that work together to handle keypress events:

- `HandleKeyPress`: A member function that is part of each commander class to act directly on keypress events.
- `EventKeyDown`: The application object's member function that traps keypress events. It ultimately calls `HandleKeyPress` to allow the object in which the event occurred to take care of the keypress event. Because a keypress may be a menu selection, the event may either be passed to a commander or to a menu object.
- `CouldBeKeyCommand`: A member function of the menu bar that identifies whether a keypress included the ⌘ key, called by `EventKeyDown`.
- `FindKeyCommand`: A member function of the member bar that identifies the menu option that was selected by a ⌘ key equivalent, called by `EventKeyDown` when `CouldBeKeyCommand` identifies a command instead of a regular keypress.

The Chain of Command

Commanders are arranged in a hierarchy (the *chain of command*) that determines the order in which each commander is given the chance to decide whether it should handle an event or pass it up the hierarchy. The hierarchy of objects for the dialog box in Figure 1.3 appears in Figure 1.4, including the name of the class from which each object is created. Some of the objects—those created from the classes LStdPopupMenu, LCaption, and LStdButton—aren't in the chain of command because they aren't derived from LCommander. However, the LDialogBox, LTabGroup, and LEditField objects are derived from LCommander and therefore are in the chain of command. Those objects that are indented underneath other objects in Figure 1.4, such as the LEditField objects that have been placed on the dialog box, are lower in the hierarchy.

> **NOTE**
>
> *The hierarchy in Figure 1.4 was taken from Constructor, a resource editor about which you will read throughout this book.*

A commander has one *supercommander*, the commander that is above it in the chain of command. The only exception to this rule is the application object, which has no supercommander. A commander can also have many *subcommanders*, commander objects that are below it in chain of command.

When a keystroke or menu selection event occurs, the program first submits the event to objects lowest on the chain of command. If an object can't handle the event, it passes it up to its supercommander. As an example, look at the `ObeyCommand` function from the LTextEdit class in Listing 1.5. This function contains a `switch` statement that implements standard text editing operations such as Cut, Copy, Paste, and Clear. However, as you can see from the `switch` statement's `default` option, if the event isn't one that LTextEdit handles, the event is passed to the base class (in this case LCommander) `ObeyCommand` function (Listing 1.6), which in turn calls the supercommander's `ObeyCommand` function.

The Target

The current object that is available to listen for and handle a command is known as the *target*. In Figure 1.3, for example, there are 25 objects created from the LEditField class, all of which are subcommanders of the dialog box and on the same level of the chain of command. However, only one of those 25 is active at any given time. This object, which contains the flashing insertion point, is the current target. Although the dialog box has many objects created from the same class, the program has no

Figure 1.4 The object hierarchy for the dialog box in Figure 1.3

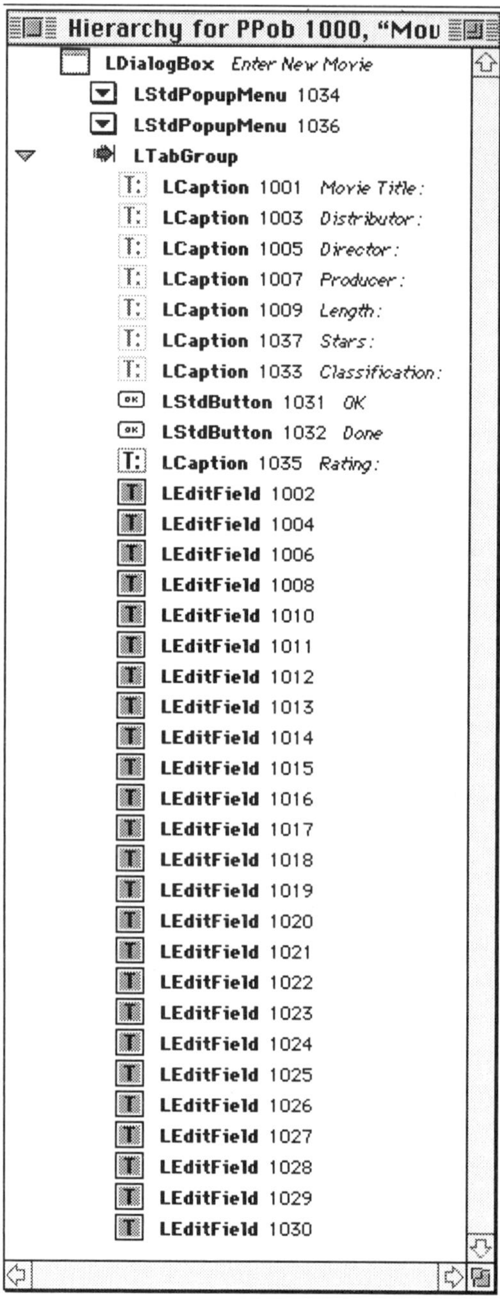

Listing 1.5 The ObeyCommand function from the class LTextEdit

```
Boolean LTextEdit::ObeyCommand( CommandT inCommand,void * ioParam)
{
    Boolean cmdHandled = true;
    switch (inCommand) {

        case cmd_Cut:
            ::TECut(mTextEditH);
            ::ZeroScrap();
            ::TEToScrap();
            AdjustImageToText();
            UserChangedText();
            break;

        case cmd_Copy:
            ::TECopy(mTextEditH);
            ::ZeroScrap();
            ::TEToScrap();
            break;

        case cmd_Paste:
            ::TEFromScrap();
            ::TEPaste(mTextEditH);
            AdjustImageToText();
            UserChangedText();
            break;

        case cmd_Clear:
            ::TEDelete(mTextEditH);
            AdjustImageToText();
            UserChangedText();
            break;

        case msg_TabSelect:
            if (!IsEnabled())
                cmdHandled = false;
                break;
            // else FALL THRU to SelectAll()

        case cmd_SelectAll:
            SelectAll();
            break;

        default:
            cmdHandled = LCommander::ObeyCommand(inCommand, ioParam);
            break;
    }

    return cmdHandled;
}
```

These cases take care of events that are appropriate for an object of the LTextEdit class to handle

This function call passes the event to the base class

Listing 1.6 LCommander's Obey Command function

```
Boolean
LCommander::ObeyCommand(
     CommandT inCommand,
     void    *ioParam)
{
     BooleancmdHandled = false;
     if (mSuperCommander != nil) {
         cmdHandled = mSuperCommander->ProcessCommand(inCommand, ioParam);
     }
     return cmdHandled;
}
```

Event is passed up the chain of command here

trouble deciding which LEditField object should receive an event: The event goes to the current target.

In this particular dialog box, the LEditField objects have been placed in a tab group (an object of class LTabGroup). The user can therefore switch the target in two ways: by pressing Tab to move to the next LEditField object in the group, or by clicking in an object with the mouse pointer. Although in this case the target switching behavior has been included in the PowerPlant code, there are circumstances under which you might want to explicitly make a particular object the target. For example, you might want to reset the contents of a dialog box without removing it from the screen and therefore want to make sure that the first LEditField object is the target. To do so, you use the `SwitchTarget` function. If you are working with a class you have derived, you may need to write your own `SwitchTarget` function.

Going on and off Duty

Like any other Macintosh program, a PowerPlant application must exist in the Macintosh Operating System's cooperatively multitasked environment. When a user switches from the PowerPlant application to another program, the PowerPlant application must suspend itself until it is reactivated. Suspension means that the application object goes "off duty"—it no longer responds to events.

In most cases, every commander in the chain of command is on duty when the application is active. When the application is suspended, the application object goes off duty. All other on duty commanders become "latent." This means that they would be on duty if their supercommander was on duty. On the other hand, if the application has explicitly taken a commander off duty (and consequently, all its subcommanders), suspension leaves the commander and all its subcommanders off duty.

Upon becoming active again, the PowerPlant application places the application object on duty. It then searches the chain of command for all latent commanders and places them on duty; any off-duty commanders are left in that state. The latent commander at the bottom level of the chain of command becomes the current target.

BROADCASTERS AND LISTENERS

In addition to commanders, there is another group of objects that responds to messages in the PowerPlant environment: *listeners*, which are at some point derived from LListener. Listeners wait for messages sent by *broadcasters*, objects derived at least in part from LBroadcaster. For example, in Figure 1.3, the dialog box is a listener; the Done and OK buttons are broadcasters. The dialog box waits until it receives a message from one of its buttons and then takes action based on the message.

The message sent by a broadcaster is known as its *value message*. Some value messages are arbitrary—you can set them as you like. Others have restrictions to which you must adhere if your program is to execute properly. For example, the button that closes a dialog box without processing the state of the dialog box's contents (the Cancel button, or in Figure 1.3, the Done button) must have a value message of 4. This is because the LDialogBox class has been written to expect this message as an instruction to close the dialog box. In addition, with the exception of the value message 4, LDialogBox only listens for negative messages.

Each listener has a list of broadcasters to which it listens. For example, by default a dialog box listens for its Cancel and OK buttons. If you want the dialog box to respond to anything else, such as an additional button, your program must add that button to the listener's list of broadcasters, using the `AddListener` function.

NOTE

The `AddListener` function has been known to give programmers heartburn because the broadcaster object calls it, saying to the listener "add me to your list of broadcasters," rather than the other way around.

If you look back at Figure 1.2 again, you'll notice that LControl is a broadcaster (because it inherits from LBroadcaster). LControl is the base class for classes that provide most of the Macintosh's standard controls (push buttons, radio buttons, check boxes, popup menus, and so on). In addition, the class LListBox is a broadcaster, which provides support for responding to double-clicking in a list of items.

LWindow, the base class for PowerPlant windows, is *not* derived from LListener. This means that if you want a window to respond to controls, you must explicitly link the controls to the window, using the function `UReanimator::LinkListenerToControls`. However, LDialogBox *is* derived from LListener and is therefore often the easiest class to use when you are creating windows that must contain buttons, check boxes, popup menus, and so on. Alternatively, you can create a subclass that inherits from both LWindow and LListener.

PowerPlant Objects

You can certainly create an object from a PowerPlant class the old fashioned way—by passing a constructor all the parameters it needs to define the object. In fact, lists, strings, and other non-graphic objects are created in just that way. However, when creating graphic objects (for example, windows and dialog boxes), it rather defeats the purpose of working with an application framework to hard code all the details of an object into a program or header file; you're back at a very primitive level worrying about such things as screen coordinates for windows and controls. Ideally, you should be able to find some easy way to create graphic objects, without having to fiddle with such details.

The answer lies in *PowerPlant objects*, resources named *PPob* that can be used as the basis for objects created from a number of PowerPlant classes. You create PowerPlant objects with Constructor, an application that is part of the CodeWarrior package. Constructor lets you draw windows, dialog boxes, and print formats and then saves them as resources that a PowerPlant program can use.

NOTE

Although you can also edit PowerPlant object resources with Rez or Resourcer, PPob resources are too complex for ResEdit to handle.

In most cases, you will find it easier to edit PowerPlant objects using Constructor rather than any other resource editor or compiler, simply because Constructor lets you draw the resources. It is therefore often convenient to keep at least two program-specific resource files, one for PowerPlant objects and one for all other resources you create for the program. You can then keep both resource files open at the same time.

NOTE

Constructor is quite easy to use. You will learn how to use it throughout this book as we explore the various classes that go into a PowerPlant program.

POWERPLANT OBJECT CLASSES

Top-level PowerPlant objects come from one of five classes:

- LWindow: Provides support for windows created with calls to the ToolBox Window Manager. Most document windows come from this class.
- LDialogBox: Creates dialog boxes with support for default OK and cancel buttons. As you read earlier in this chapter, a dialog box is a listener that can respond to messages broadcast by the controls it contains.
- LPrintout: Provides a layout for printing.
- LView: Provides a starting place for a chain of command of objects without associating them with a window. You will learn more about views and how they relate to other objects throughout this book.
- LGrafPortView: Provides support for objects that work with externals such as OpenDoc or applications that accept plug-ins (for example, HyperCard or Photoshop).

PowerPlant objects based on LWindow and LDialogBox have accompanying WIND resources that are created automatically when you create the PPob resource. If you decide to work with two program-specific resource files, you should leave the WIND resources in the same file as the PPob resources. This will ensure that the WIND resources are updated whenever the PPob resources are updated. You will probably never need to deal with them directly.

REGISTERING POWERPLANT OBJECTS WITH UREGISTRAR

Each PowerPlant class whose objects can be defined as PowerPlant objects has a four-character ID string. For example, LDialog box is known as *dlog*, LEditField as *edit*, and LStdPopupMenu as *popm*. When you derive PowerPlant classes whose objects can be defined as PowerPlant objects, you give each its own ID. For example, the class that Penultimate Videos uses to provide a printable, multistyled area for writing a simple note has an ID of *note*. The only restriction on class IDs is that they must be unique within the program.

One of the first actions a PowerPlant program takes is to figure out the classes from which PowerPlant objects are going to be created using a stream of data from an external source (usually a resource file). The program builds a table of class IDs and the names of the functions used to create objects from that class. This action is known as *registering* classes.

Class registration is handled by the class URegistrar. When you are first working developing a PowerPlant program, you can register all classes that will create PowerPlant objects by calling the global function `RegisterAllPPClasses`. This function (which can be found in the file *PPobClasses.cp*) contains multiple calls to `URegistrar::RegisterClass`. If you aren't using every class registered by `RegisterAllPPClasses`, your program will end up a bit larger than it needs to be. You may therefore want to replace the call to `RegisterAllPPClasses` with individual calls to `RegisterClass` just before shipping your program.

You must also register derived or cloned classes from which objects can be defined as PowerPlant objects. Such classes are registered directly with calls to `RegisterClass`. As an example, take a look at Listing 1.7, the constructor for the Penultimate Videos program's application object. Notice that there are six classes (IDs of *note*, *grph*, *rtab*, *stab*, *SWin*, and *Ther*) that have been created specifically for this program. They are handled by direct calls to `RegisterClass`. The function requires two parameters: the class ID and the name of the function used to create objects from an input stream. You will learn more about these stream input constructors throughout this book as we explore specific PowerPlant classes.

NOTE

The constructor in Listing 1.7 also performs some additional setup operations, including initializing the Font, Size, and Style menus, initializing counters and a flag used by program, and initializing QuickTime.

If a program attempts to create an object from a class that hasn't been registered, PowerPlant returns the following runtime error:

```
Signal raised
Condition: nil object created from tag
File: UReanimator.cp
Line #127
```

NOTE

The alert that presents the preceding message is generated by PowerPlant's exception handling mechanism, which is discussed at the end of this chapter.

Unfortunately, the message doesn't tell you which class isn't registered. You will need to use the debugger to step through the portion of code in which the signal is raised.

Listing 1.7 The constructor for the Penultimate Videos application object

```
CPPVideoStoreApp::CPPVideoStoreApp()
{
    // Register functions to create core PowerPlant classes

    RegisterAllPPClasses();

    // Register classes unique to this program
    // multistyled TextEdit note
    URegistrar::RegisterClass('note', Note::CreateNoteStream);
    URegistrar::RegisterClass('grph',Graph::CreateGraphStream); // pane for a graph
    URegistrar::RegisterClass('rtab',ReceiptTable::CreateReceiptTableStream);
        // table for rental receipt
    URegistrar::RegisterClass ('stab',StatsTable::CreateStatsTableStream);
        // table view for stats window
    URegistrar::RegisterClass ('SWin',StatsWindow::CreateStatsWindowStream);
        // statistics window
    URegistrar::RegisterClass ('Ther',Ther::CreateTherStream);
        // thermometer pane

    UFontMenu::Initialize (TRUE); // set up the font menu
    // zero indicates that there are no items that aren't sizes
    USizeMenu::Initialize (0, TRUE);
    UStyleMenu::Initialize (TRUE); // set up the style menu

    strcpy (FileName, "Video Data"); // give a default file name

    Movie_count = 0;
    Other_count = 0;
    Game_count = 0;
    Cust_count = 0;
    lastTitle_numb = 0;
    lastCopy_numb = 0;

    save_flag = TRUE;

    UQuickTime::Initialize();
}
```

Creating PowerPlant Objects

Some classes whose objects can be defined as PowerPlant objects have a function named `CreateX` (*X* being the name of the type of object) that returns a pointer to the new object. For example, LWindow has a function named `CreateWindow`. Other classes, such as LDialogBox, use a base class's `CreateX` function and typecast the returned pointer to the correct class. You might, for example, use the following to create a dialog box object from a PowerPlant object resource:

```
LDialogBox * theDialog;
theDialog = (LDialogBox *) LWindow::CreateWindow (DIALOG_BOX_RESOURCE_ID,
     this);
```

Like other functions for creating objects from PowerPlant resources, `CreateWindow` requires two parameters: the resource ID of the PowerPlant resource and a pointer to the supercommander. In the preceding example, the dialog box is being created in a member function of the application object, which becomes the supercommander by specifying its address with `this`.

Inside a `Create`*X* function, an object is actually created by the UReanimator class. The `CreateX` function calls `UReanimator::ReadObject`, which reads the data describing the PowerPlant object from the resource file. The `ReadObject` function then calls `UReanimator::ObjectsFromStream` (which calls `URegistrar::CreateObject`) to actually create the object and return a pointer to its main memory location. You will see this process in more detail in Chapter 5.

Even when you write your own subclasses, you won't need to write code to create objects from PowerPlant resources. All you need is a a constructor that creates an object from an input stream that can then call the appropriate base class constructor to do the work.

PANES AND VIEWS

Many of the PowerPlant classes in Figure 1.2 are derived from LPane and LView. These two classes, whose objects are typically defined as PowerPlant objects, underlie all drawing in a PowerPlant program.

A *pane* is an area in which a program can draw. A pane also can respond to clicks of the mouse pointer. Panes include, for example, controls, scrollable areas, and areas for entering text. You can place a pane in a window (even a non-PowerPlant window) and you can place it in a view.

A *view* is a container for panes, a pane that can contain other panes. The panes that are within a view are known as *subpanes*. A view that contains a pane is the pane's *superview*. For example, the dialog box in Figure 1.3 is a view. It contains subpanes for display text (objects of class LCaption), panes for entering text (objects of class LEditField), and panes for displaying popup menus (objects of class LPopupMenu). The dialog box is the superview for all the panes it contains.

As a second example, consider the window in Figure 1.5. This very simple window is actually a multistyled text editor. It lets the user enter and edit text, as well as change font, style, and type size. The contents of the window can be printed and saved in a text file. The resource that makes up the window contains three objects:

the window itself (an object of class LWindow), the scrollable area and the scroll bars (an object of class LScroller, and the text entry area (an object of a class cloned from LTextEdit). The window is a view that contains a second view (the scroller), which contains a pane (the text entry area). In other words, views can contain other views and panes; panes cannot contain views or other panes.

Figure 1.5 A window for entering and editing text

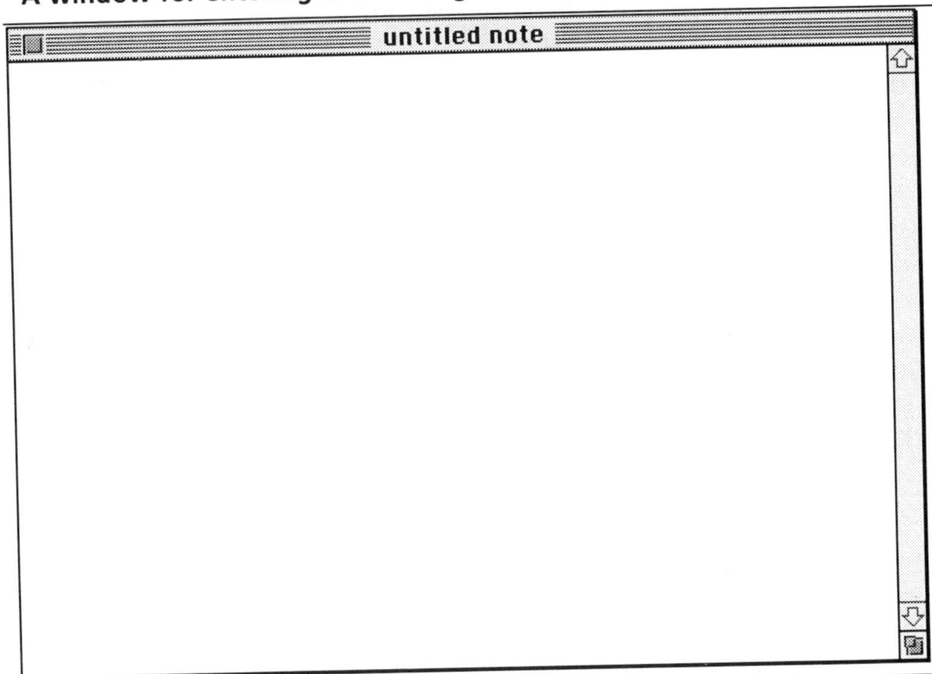

NOTE
The relationship between panes and views can be a bit confusing. Although LView is derived from LPane, a view is a container for panes, just the opposite of what you might expect.

Basic Pane and View Functions

Classes that include LPane or LView in their inheritance hierarchy have the following functions in common:

- `DrawSelf`: Uses QuickDraw routines to draw the contents of the pane.
- `ClickSelf`: Handles activities that occur when the user clicks the mouse pointer in the pane.
- `ActivateSelf`: Handles activities that occur when a pane becomes active. In this context, a pane is *active* if it is in an active window (usually the foreground window)
- `DeactivateSelf`: Handles activities that occur when a pane becomes deactive. In many cases, a program will redraw the contents of the pane, perhaps making its contents shaded rather than solid.
- `EnableSelf`: Handles activities that occur when a pane is *enabled*. (An enabled pane will respond to clicks of the mouse.)
- `DisableSelf`: Handles activities that occur when a pane is disabled.

You may need to override any of the these functions when a derived class should behave differently from the base class.

Pane Descriptors and Values

Panes have programmer-accessible data known as *descriptors* and *values*. A pane descriptor is a Pascal string whose precise contents depends on the class with which you are working. For example, the descriptor of an object of class LCaption is the display text itself. The descriptor of an object of class LEditField is the contents of the edit field, while the descriptor of an object of class LListBox is the currently highlighted item in the list.

Instead of using a pane's descriptor directly, you can retrieve its value, the integer equivalent of the descriptor. If you know that a descriptor will contain an integer and you need to handle that integer as a number rather than a string, requesting the value rather than the descriptor can save you a conversion step. Your program will access the descriptor, translate it to an integer, and return the integer to the program. Note that the pane only maintains the descriptor; the value is generated from the descriptor when needed.

A program accesses and modifies descriptors and values using the following four functions:

- `GetDescriptor`: Returns the Pascal string descriptor.
- `SetDescriptor`: Takes a Pascal string and makes it an object's descriptor.
- `GetValue`: Returns the integer equivalent of the descriptor.
- `SetValue`: Converts an integer to a Pascal string and makes the string an object's descriptor.

You will be introduced to panes in much greater depth beginning in Chapter 5. In addition, because panes are the basic display element for a PowerPlant program, we will be talking about them throughout the book.

Exception Handling

As well as managing the event loop, PowerPlant also provides an exception handling mechanism that now maps directly to the C++ `try/catch/throw` statements. PowerPlant provides a group of macros that not only set up `try` and `catch` blocks, but also provide `signal` and `throw` capabilities.

The exception macros are defined in *UException.h*. As you can see in Listing 1.8, the macros that set up `try` and `catch` blocks do indeed map to the C++ exception handling commands. These basic macros are accompanied by a set of macros that throw errors under some common error conditions, a sampling of which appear in Listing 1.9.

Listing 1.8 Exception handling macros

```
#define Try_                try
#define Catch_(err)         catch(ExceptionCode err)
#define EndCatch_
#define Throw(err)          throw (ExceptionCode)(err)
```

As an example of how you might use these exception handling macros, take a look at Listing 1.10. This code is part of a function that creates a new object of class Film. The code for creating the object is within a Try block. The Catch block below it throws an exception if any error occurs. If you don't want to use the generic `Throw_` macro to trap any error, use one of the specific error macros found in *UException.h*.

NOTE
If you are using ANSI C++ stream I/O, then there will be some duplication between console.stubs.c (the stream I/O support file) and UException.cp, causing the linker to warn you that it has discovered a duplicate definition of abort.c. Although the warning is harmless, if you find it annoying you can prevent it from occurring by removing UException.c from any project that includes console.stubs.c to support ANSI stream I/O. (You will read more about adding ANSI stream I/O support in Chapter 3.)

Listing 1.9 Some useful Throw macros

```
#define ThrowIfOSErr_(err)      \
    do {                        \
        OSErr__theErr = err;    \
        if (__theErr != noErr) {\
            Throw_(__theErr);   \
        }                       \
    } while (false)

#define ThrowIfError_(err)      \
    do {                        \
        ExceptionCode__theErr = err;\
        if (__theErr != 0) {    \
            Throw_(__theErr);   \
        }                       \
    } while (false)

#define ThrowOSErr_(err)Throw_(err)
#define ThrowIfNil_(ptr)        \
    do {                        \
        if ((ptr) == nil) Throw_(err_NilPointer);\
    } while (false)

#define ThrowIfNULL_(ptr)       \
    do {                        \
        if ((ptr) == nil) Throw_(err_NilPointer);\
    } while (false)

#define ThrowIfResError_() ThrowIfOSErr_(ResError())
#define ThrowIfMemError_() ThrowIfOSErr_(MemError())
```

Listing 1.10 Using exception handling macros

```
Try_
    {
        // Create new object and insert into binary tree
        newMovie = new Film (Title_numb, iTitle, iDistributor, iDirector,
            iProducer, iClass, iLen, numb_stars, istars, iRating, Items, ItemsByNumb);
        Movie_count++;

        // move cursor back to first edit field
        theFirstEditField->SwitchTarget (theFirstEditField);
        save_flag = FALSE; // flip this flag whenever data are modified
    }

    Catch_ (inErr)
    {
        Throw_ (inErr);
    } EndCatch_
```

CHAPTER 2

Penultimate Videos

In this chapter you will see the Penultimate Videos application from two viewpoints: the user's and the programmer's. The user's view includes an overview of menu options and the functions they provide. The programmer's view includes a discussion of the program's underlying data classes and the data structures that manage objects of those classes.

The User's View

The purpose of the Penultimate Videos application is to manage a video store's inventory as well as the rental and sales of items. The store's inventory contains video tapes, laser discs, and video game cartridges, all of which can be rented. Rental copies that are no longer needed can be sold.

Handling Inventory

Inventory management functions are gathered together in the Inventory menu (Figure 2.1). As you can see, this menu lets the user enter new inventory items as well as copies of those items. It also supports modifying and deleting items and copies.

Figure 2.1 The Penultimate Videos Inventory menu

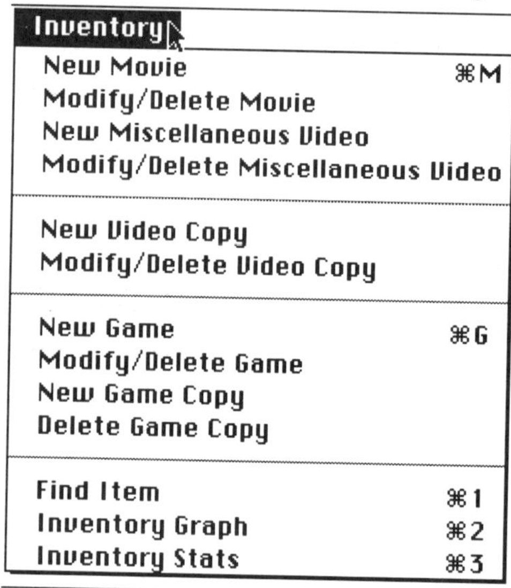

Entering new inventory items is handled through dialog boxes. For example, the dialog box in Figure 2.2 is used to enter data about a new miscellaneous video. A similar dialog box (Figure 2.3) is used to modify or delete items. The user reaches the dialog box in Figure 2.3 by double-clicking on a scrolling list of titles.

A video store doesn't rent "titles," it rents copies of those titles. Therefore, before Penultimate Videos can rent something, a user must record the copies of an item that the store has purchased. Each copy has an arbitrary unique inventory number that is generated automatically by the program. To enter a copy of a video, the user highlights the title in a scrolling list of titles and then uses the radio buttons, check boxes, and popup menu to enter data about the copy. For example, in Figure 2.4 the user is recording a letterboxed laserdisc copy of *Beauty and the Beast* in CAV format. When the user clicks the OK button, the program responds with the inventory number that should be attached to the new copy (Figure 2.5).

Figure 2.2 Entering a new title

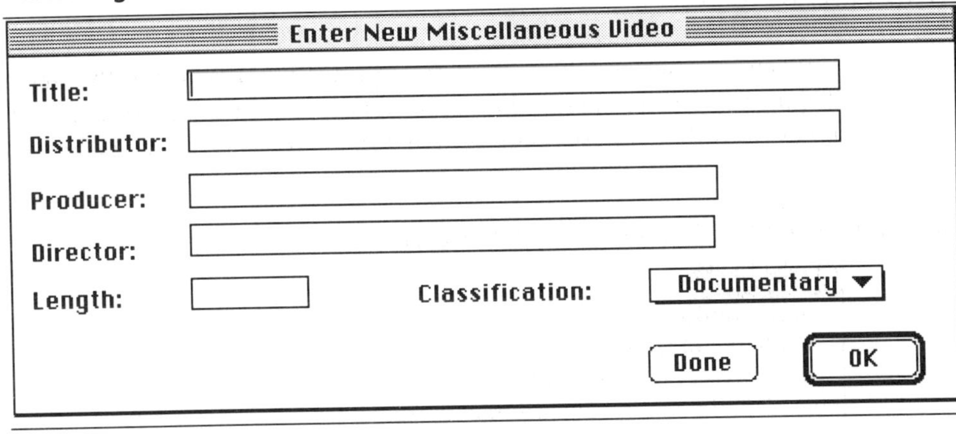

Figure 2.3 Modifying an item

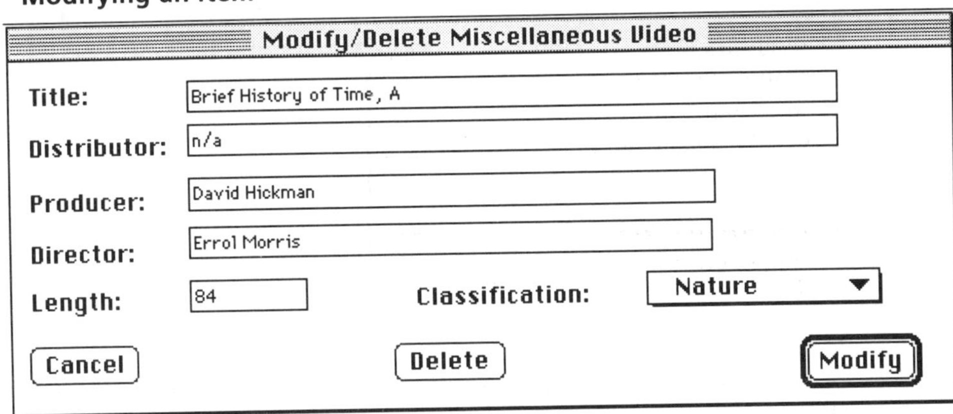

To delete a copy of an item, the user simply enters the copy's inventory number. The number can be typed on a keyboard or scanned by a bar code reader. As long as the input enters through the ADP port, the Macintosh doesn't know the difference between the two.

Figure 2.4 Entering a new video copy

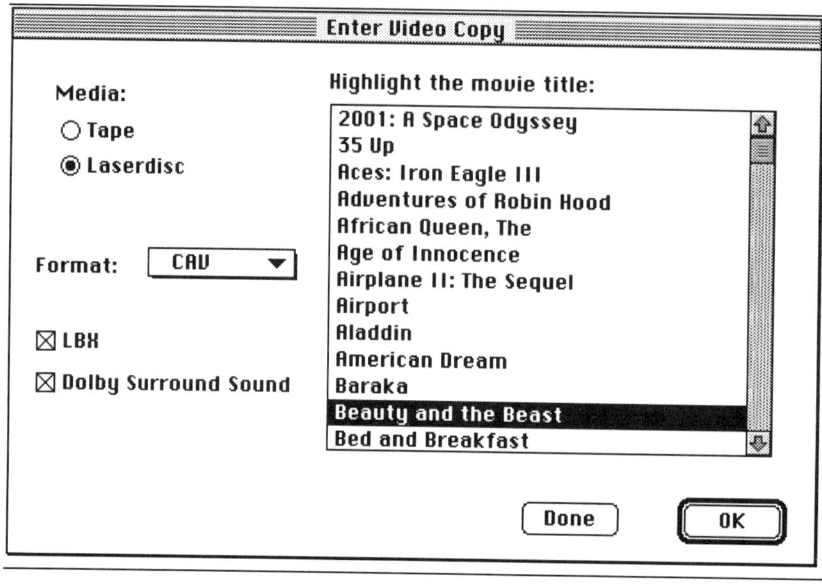

Figure 2.5 The inventory number for a new copy

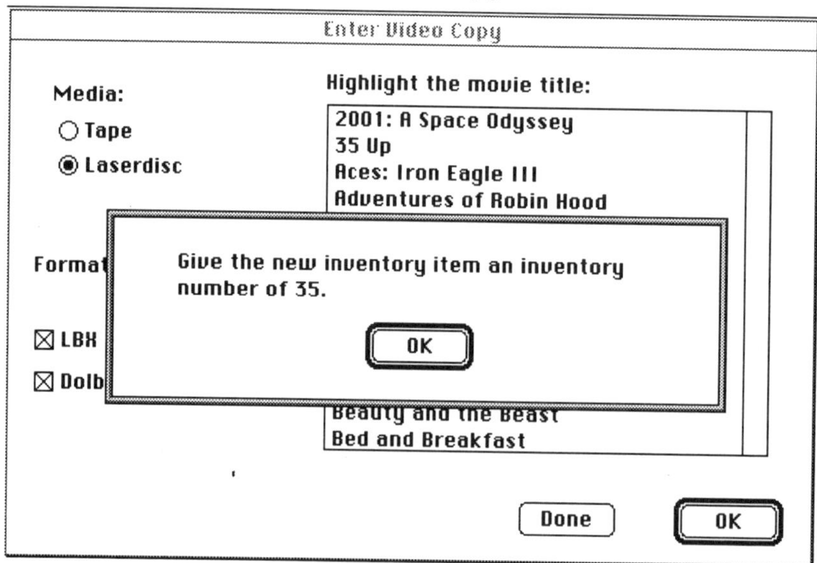

The Find Item menu ultimately displays information about a merchandise item. Choosing the menu item (or pressing the associated command-key equivalent) displays a scrolling list of all titles in inventory (Figure 2.6). The user then double-clicks on the title to display an information window such as that in Figure 2.7. Notice that the Title Information window also provides access to QuickTime. If there happens to be a QuickTime clip available, the user can choose and play it by clicking the View Movie Clip button.

Figure 2.6 A scrolling list of all titles in inventory

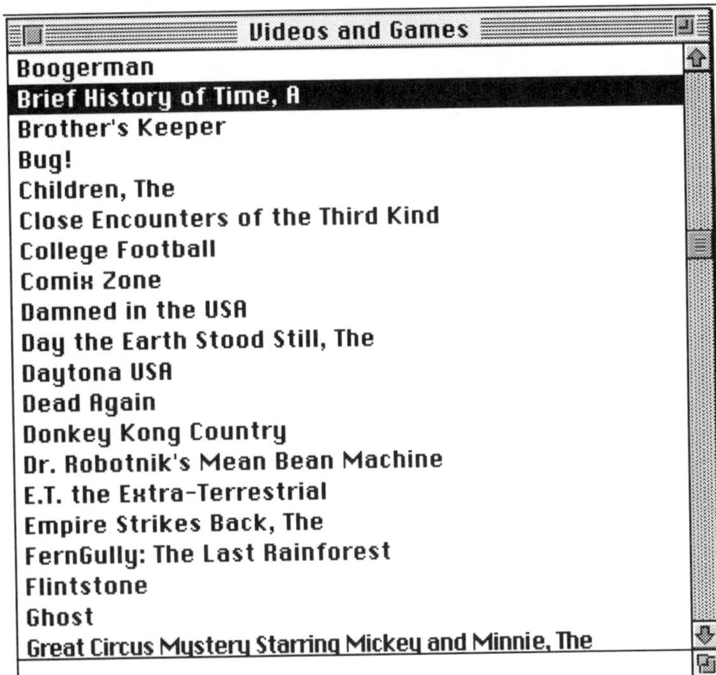

NOTE

The Penultimate Videos program does not store the names of movie clip files. Clicking the View Movie Clip button brings up a GetFile dialog box that the user can use to select the clip.

The Inventory Graph menu item is a demonstration of drawing within the PowerPlant framework. It displays a graph of the number of titles of each type (movie,

Figure 2.7 Displaying inventory information

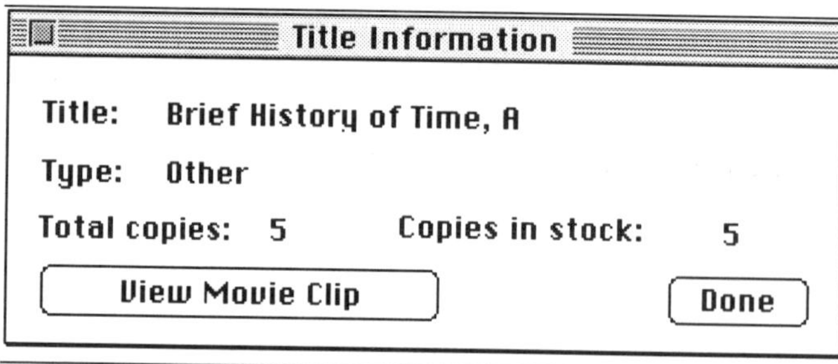

miscellaneous video, and game) currently carried by the video store. You will see this graph and how it is constructed in Chapter 5.

HANDLING CUSTOMERS

The Customers menu (Figure 2.8) provides access to program functions dealing with customer activities, including maintaining customer data, viewing items rented by a customer, and writing a note to a customer using the text editing window you saw in Chapter 1.

Figure 2.8 The Customers menu

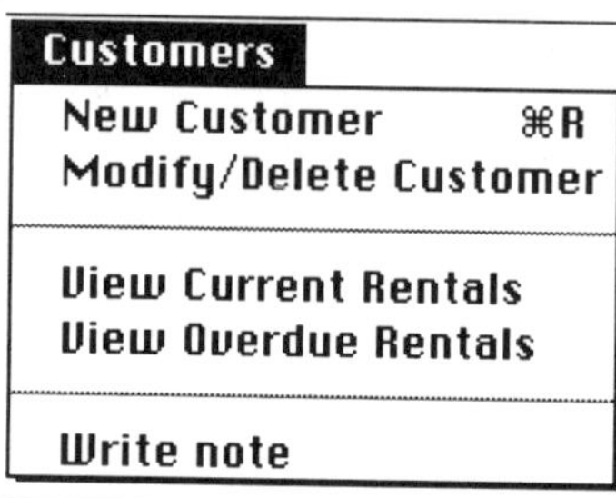

Data about Penultimate Video customers are entered and maintained using a dialog box similar to those used for managing inventory items (Figure 2.9). Because the user reaches the modify/delete dialog box by double-clicking on the customer's name in a scrolling list of names, this dialog box can also be used to find the customer number should the customer's membership card not be available when he or she is trying to rent merchandise.

Figure 2.9 **Modifying customer data**

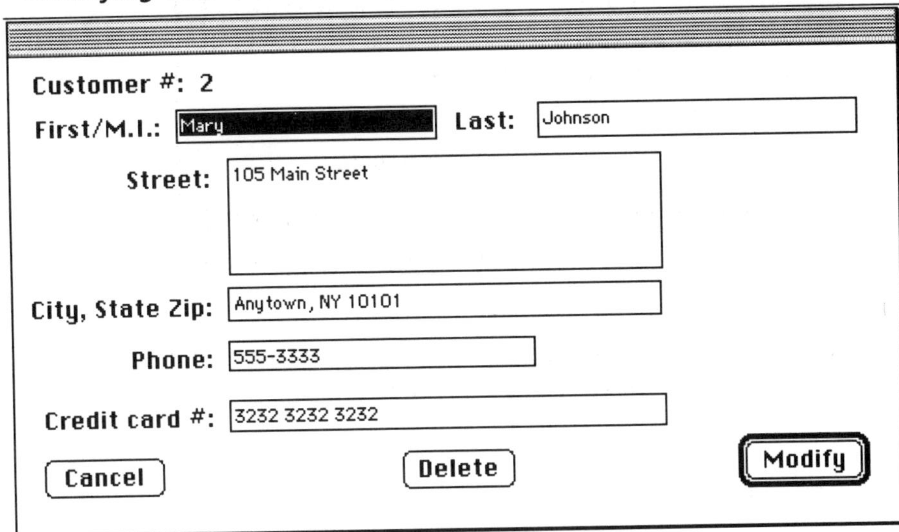

The View Current Rentals and View Overdue Rentals provide lists of inventory numbers of the items currently rented by a customer or currently rented and overdue. (Overdue is defined as having a date due prior to the current day.)

NOTE

As mentioned in the Preface, the Penultimate Videos program is a demonstration program that isn't intended to be equivalent to a commercial application that could actually be used to manage a video store. A more complete version of the program would certainly include a way to enter an inventory number and view data about that copy, such as its title and who, if anyone, has rented it.

HANDLING TRANSACTIONS

In its current state, the Penultimate Videos program handles two types of transactions with its Transactions menu: renting and returning copies of merchandise items (Figure 2.10). Renting is the more complex transaction because it involves printing a receipt that the user can take with the rented items.

When renting an item, the program first displays a window for the receipt. This is a screen image of what will be printed. The program then overlays the receipt with a dialog box used to collect data for a rental (Figure 2.11). As data are entered for

Figure 2.10 The Transactions menu

individual items, the items appear on the receipt. Both the customer number and the inventory number can be scanned from a bar code or typed at the keyboard.

Figure 2.11 Renting an item

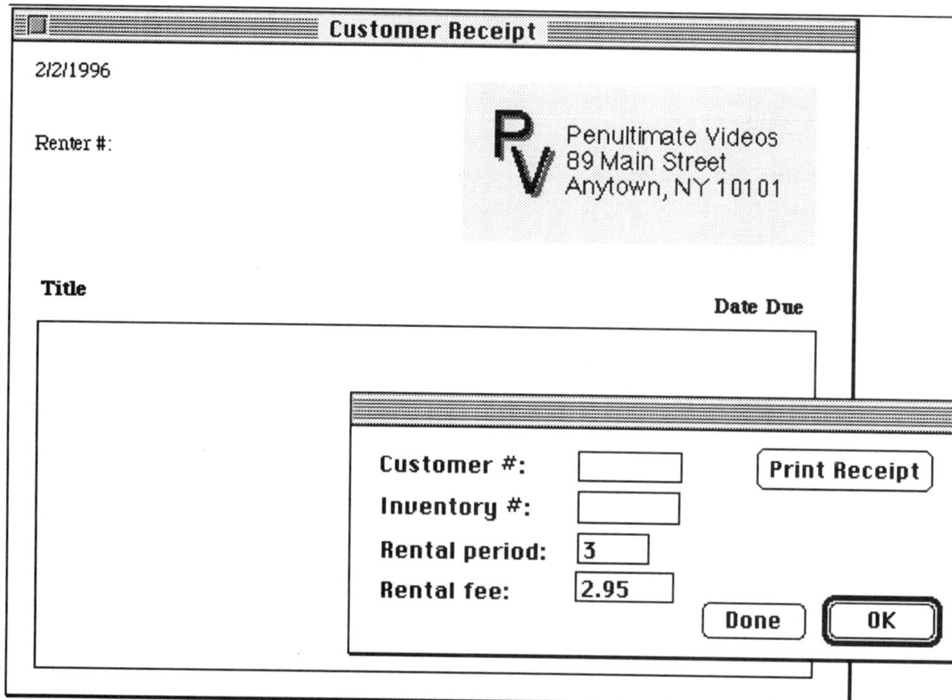

When the receipt is complete (all items recorded), the user clicks the Print Receipt button to generate the receipt. The Print dialog box appears, letting the user choose the number of copies to print (in this case, usually two, one for the customer and one for the store).

Recording the return of an item is straightforward: The user opens the dialog box for recording the inventory number of the returned item (Figure 2.12) and then either scans the item's bar code or types the inventory number on the keyboard. Assuming the store is using a bar-code system, recording returns will proceed very quickly.

Figure 2.12 Recording the return of an item

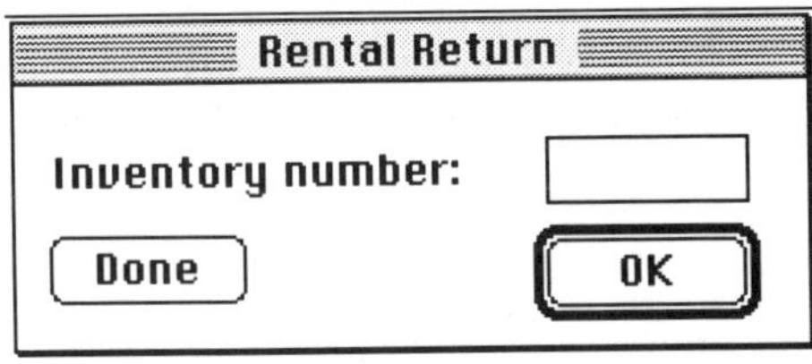

The Programmer's View

At its heart, Penultimate Videos is a data management application. In addition to the PowerPlant classes that manage the program's user interface, the program requires a group of classes to handle the data and the data structures in which they are stored. As with most object-oriented programs, these classes that manage data are purposely kept separate from the classes that manage the user interface.

The basic class hierarchies can be found in Figure 2.13. The hierarchy at the top of the figure represents data about types of merchandise stocked by the store. This middle hierarchy represents data about copies of merchandise that are rented. Although the Customer class interacts with the other classes, it isn't part of any inheritance hierarchy.

As you will see as you look at the classes throughout this section, the data modification functions for each class are complete. Users can enter data for new objects, modify object data (including the title), and delete objects. The classes also provide functions for returning data that can be used in a variety of on-screen and printed displays. In addition, they maintain a collection of pointers used by binary trees and linked lists.

The Merchandise_Item Hierarchy

Data about merchandise items are stored in objects created from one of three classes: Game, Film, and Other. (The Film class was originally called Movie, but using that

Figure 2.13 The Penultimate Videos data class hierarchies

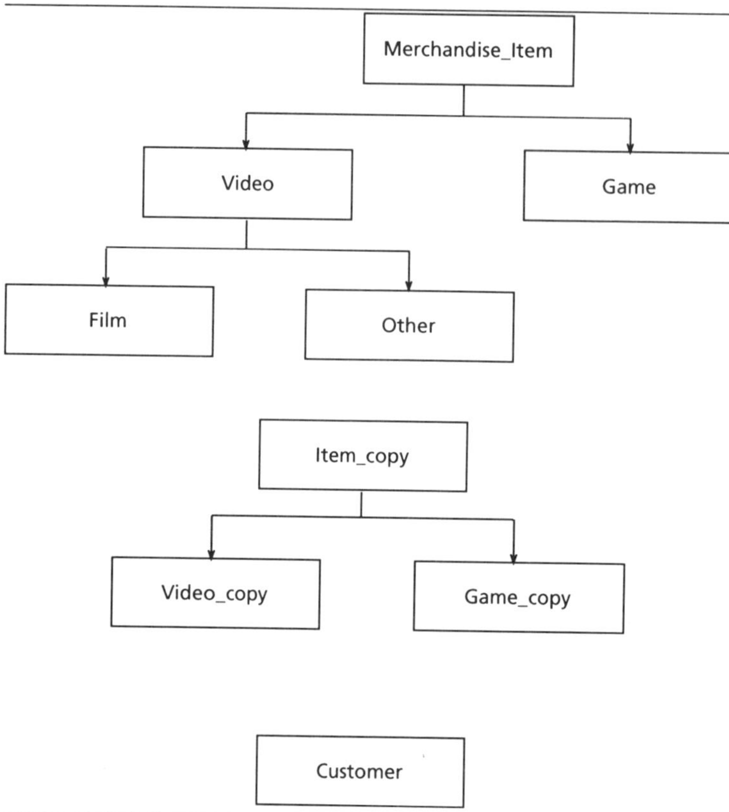

term conflicted with the QuickTime data structure by the same name!) The base class for the entire hierarchy in which the preceding classes participate is Merchandise_Item (Listing 2.1). This abstract base class stores data common to all types of merchandise carried by the store, along with pointers for the data structures in which objects of this class participate. These include two binary search trees (one ordered by item name, the other by title number) and a linked list of objects for the copies of this item in the store's inventory. The linked list provides the only physical relationship between the Merchandise_Item hierarchy and the Item_copy hierarchy, although, as you will see, each Item_copy does contain the title number its Merchandise_Item to provide a logical one-to-many relationship between titles and copies of those titles.

The Game class (Listing 2.2) adds two item-specific variables to its base class. It is derived directly from Merchandise_Item and is used to create objects. However,

Listing 2.1 The Merchandise_Item class

```
class Merchandise_Item
{
    protected:
        int Title_numb, Copy_count, Item_type;
        ANSIstring Title;
        ANSIstring Distributor;
        // binary search tree of titles by name
        Merchandise_Item * LeftName, * RightName;
        // binary search tree of titles by number
        Merchandise_Item * LeftNumb, * RightNumb;
        Item_copy * First, * Last;// linked list of items
    public:
        Merchandise_Item (int, ANSIstring, ANSIstring);
        Merchandise_Item (ifstream &, int);
        char * getTitle();
        char * getDistributor();
        void incCopy_count();
        int getCopy_count(); // return number of copies
        Merchandise_Item * getLeftName();
        Merchandise_Item * getRightName();
        Merchandise_Item * getLeftNumb();
        Merchandise_Item * getRightNumb();
        Item_copy * getFirst();
        void setLeftName (Merchandise_Item *);
        void setRightName (Merchandise_Item *);
        void setLeftNumb (Merchandise_Item *);
        void setRightNumb (Merchandise_Item *);
        void Insert (Item_copy *);
        Item_copy * getLast ();
        int getItem_type ();
        int getTitle_numb();
        Item_copy * available (); // check to see if any copies are available
        void setTitle (ANSIstring);
        void setDistributor (ANSIstring);
        virtual void write (ofstream &) = 0;

};
```

classes for movies and other videos can't be derived direclty from Merchandise_Item because the data to be stored about videos vary depending on whether the item is a movie. A movie has stars and a rating, where other videos such as how-to films and documentaries don't. (You can argue the point if you wish, but the preceding represents the world as seen by Penultimate Videos.)

Listing 2.2 The Game class

```
class Game : public Merchandise_Item
{
     private:
         ANSIstring System;
         rate_string Rating;
     public:
         Game (int, ANSIstring, ANSIstring, ANSIstring, rate_string, MerchTree *,
MerchNumbTree *);
         Game (ifstream &, MerchTree *, MerchNumbTree *, int);
         void write (ofstream &);
         char * getSystem();
         char * getRating();
         void setSystem (ANSIstring);
         void setRating (rate_string);
};
```

The class hierarchy therefore includes an abstract base class (Video) that is derived from Merchandise_Item and adds variables for data common to all types of videos (see Listing 2.3). The two classes from which objects are actually created (Film, in Listing 2.4 and Other in Listing 2.5) are then derived from the Video class.

Listing 2.3 The Video class

```
class Video : public Merchandise_Item
{
     protected:
         ANSIstring Director;
         ANSIstring Producer;
         ANSIstring Classification;
         int Length;
     public:
         Video (int, ANSIstring, ANSIstring, ANSIstring, ANSIstring, ANSIstring, int);
         Video (ifstream &, int);
         char * getDirector();
         char * getProducer();
         char * getClass();
         int getLength ();
         void setDirector (ANSIstring);
         void setProducer (ANSIstring);
         void setClass (ANSIstring);
         void setLength (int);
         virtual void write (ofstream &) = 0;
};
```

Listing 2.4 The Film class

```
class Film : public Video
{
    private:
        ANSIstring Stars[MAX_STARS]; // array of strings for stars
        int numbStars;
        rate_string Rating;
    public:
        Film (int, ANSIstring, ANSIstring, ANSIstring, ANSIstring, ANSIstring,
            int, int, ANSIstring [], rate_string, MerchTree *, MerchNumbTree *);
        Film (ifstream &, MerchTree *, MerchNumbTree *, int);
        char * getRating();
        ANSIstring * getStars (int &);
        void setRating (rate_string);
        void setStars (ANSIstring [], int);
        void write (ofstream &);
};
```

Listing 2.5 The Other class

```
class Other : public Video
{
    public:
        Other (int, ANSIstring, ANSIstring, ANSIstring, ANSIstring, ANSIstring, int,
            MerchTree *, MerchNumbTree *);
        Other (ifstream &, MerchTree *, MerchNumbTree *, int);
        void write (ofstream &);
};
```

THE ITEM_COPY HIERARCHY

The actual physical inventory that Penultimate Videos rents is described by objects in the Item_copy hierarchy. The Item_copy class (Listing 2.6) is an abstract base class that contains variables for data common to all types of merchandise item copies. It also provides support for the data structures in which copies of merchandise participate (a binary search tree ordered by inventory number and the linked list of copies of the same merchandise item).

Objects are actually created from the two derived classes Video_copy (Listing 2.7) and Game_copy (Listing 2.8). The only difference between the two is the additional variables found in Video_copy.

Listing 2.6 The Item_copy class

```
class Item_copy
{
    protected:
        int Inventory_numb, Title_numb, Renter_numb;
        int In_stock; // boolean
        date * Date_due; // pointer to object of class date
        Item_copy * Next, * Right, * Left;
    public:
        Item_copy (int, int);
        Item_copy (ifstream &, CustNumbTree *);
        date * Rent (Customer *, int); // returns the date due
        void Return (CustNumbTree *);
        int getStatus();
        int getInventory_numb();
        int getTitle_numb();
        Item_copy * getNext();
        void setNext (Item_copy *);
        void setRight (Item_copy *);
        void setLeft (Item_copy *);
        Item_copy * getRight ();
        Item_copy * getLeft ();
        date * getDate_due();
        virtual void write (ofstream &) = 0;
};
```

Listing 2.7 The Video_copy class

```
class Video_copy : public Item_copy
{
    private:
        ANSIstring Media, Format;
        int Dolby, LBX; // these are booleans
    public:
        Video_copy (int, int, ANSIstring, ANSIstring, int, int, Merchandise_Item *,
CopyTree *);
        Video_copy (ifstream &, Merchandise_Item *, CopyTree *, CustNumbTree *);
        char * getMedia();
        char * getFormat ();
        int getDolby ();
        int getLBX ();
        void setMedia (ANSIstring);
        void setFormat (ANSIstring);
        void setDolby (int);
        void setLBX (int);
        void write (ofstream &);
};
```

Listing 2.8 The Game_copy class

```
class Game_copy : public Item_copy
{
    public:
        Game_copy (int, int, Merchandise_Item *, CopyTree *);
        Game_copy (ifstream &, Merchandise_Item *, CopyTree *, CustNumbTree *);
        void write (ofstream &);
};
```

THE CUSTOMER CLASS

The Customer class can be found in Listing 2.9. This class participates in two binary search trees, one organized by customer name and the other by customer number. In addition, the Customer class manages a linked list of items that the customer has rented. This list, an object of the PowerPlant class LList, serves to illustrate the use of the PowerPlant list class and a PowerPlant list iterator.

NOTE
The preceding class declarations can be found in video.h. The implementations of the Merchandise_Item and Video classes are in base.cpp. The remaining classes in the hierarchy are in movie.cpp (Film class), other.cpp (Other class), and game.cpp (Game class). The implementation of the Item_Copy class is in itembase.cpp. The remaining copy implementations (Video_copy and Game_copy) are in copies.cpp. Customer class functions can be found in customers.cpp.

THE BINARY SEARCH TREES

The Penultimate Videos program manages most of its data using binary search trees. All merchandise items, regardless of type, are stored in the same tree. The MerchTree class (Listing 2.10) organizes the merchandise items by title. A similar class (MerchNumbTree) organizes merchandise items by item number.

NOTE
If you are unfamiliar with binary search trees or with how binary search trees are implemented in object-oriented C++, see the Appendix , which provides an explanation of binary search tree algorithms and iterators.

The MerchTree class is accompanied by two iterators. The in-order traversal for MerchTree (MerchItr in Listing 2.11) provides a listing in alphabetical order by title

Listing 2.9 The Customer class

```
class Customer
{
    private:
        int Renter_numb;
        ANSIstring fname, lname, street, CSZ, phone;
        ANSIstring credit_card_numb;
        Customer * RightName, * LeftName, * RightNumb, * LeftNumb;
        LList * Items_rented; // list of items currently rented
    public:
        Customer (int, ANSIstring, ANSIstring, ANSIstring, ANSIstring, ANSIstring,
           ANSIstring, CustTree *, CustNumbTree *);
        Customer (ifstream &, CustTree *, CustNumbTree *);
        int getRenter_numb();
        void setRightName (Customer *);
        void setLeftName (Customer *);
        void setRightNumb (Customer *);
        void setLeftNumb (Customer *);
        Customer * getRightName();
        Customer * getLeftName();
        Customer * getRightNumb();
        Customer * getLeftNumb();
        char * getLongname(); // note: lname + fname
        char * getDisplayName (); // Note lname, fname
        int getRenterNumb();
        char * getFname();
        char * getLname();
        char * getStreet();
        char * getCSZ();
        char * getPhone();
        char * getCCN();
        void setFname (ANSIstring);
        void setLname (ANSIstring);
        void setStreet (ANSIstring);
        void setCSZ (ANSIstring);
        void setPhone (ANSIstring);
        void setCCN (ANSIstring);
        void InsertRentedItem (Item_copy *);
        void RemoveRentedItem (Item_copy *);
        void BuildRentalsList (ListHandle, int, MerchNumbTree *, Item_copy *);
        void write (ofstream &);
};
```

and is therefore used for searching by title and building scrolling lists of titles. However, if an in-order traversal is used to write data to a file, the next time the file is read and the tree recreated, the tree will end up the equivalent of a linked list. On the other hand, a pre-order traversal will result in a recreated tree that is structured

Listing 2.10 The MerchTree class

```
class MerchTree
{
    private:
        Merchandise_Item * root;
        int Item_count, lastTitle_numb;

    public:
        MerchTree (int, int); // base constructor
        void Insert (Merchandise_Item *, ANSIstring, Boolean);
        Merchandise_Item * find (ANSIstring); // find
        // used just for games (based on title and system)
        Game * find (ANSIstring, ANSIstring);
        // Flag indicates whether copies should be deleted along with the title
        Boolean Delete (Boolean, Merchandise_Item *, CopyTree *);
        // for videos
        void find (ANSIstring, Merchandise_Item * &, Merchandise_Item * &);
        // for games
        void find (ANSIstring, ANSIstring, Merchandise_Item * &, Merchandise_Item * &);
        int getItem_count();
        void setItem_count (int);
        int getlastTitle_numb ();
        int inclastTitle_numb ();
        Merchandise_Item * getRoot();
};
```

exactly like the tree that was in memory the last time the program was run. (Assuming a relatively random pattern of data entry, the alphabetical title tree will remain more or less balanced without resorting to tree balancing algorithms.) MerchTree is therefore also supported by a pre-order traversal iterator class (MerchItrPre in Listing 2.12). Because MerchNumbTree is used only for searching, and not for listings, it has no iterators.

The remaining tree classes are very similar to the merchandise item tree. Item copies of both types are organized into a single binary tree (CopyTree). This tree, which is ordered by inventory number, is used only for searching and therefore has no iterators.

Like merchandise items, the Customer class participates in two binary tree classes. The CustTree class orders customers by last name and first name; CustNumbTree orders customers by customer number. The CustItr class provides an in-order traversal used for searching and listing by name. The CustItrPre class delivers a pre-order traversal used to write customer data to a file.

Listing 2.11 The MerchItr class

```
class MerchItr
{
    private:
        Merchandise_Item * stack[25], * root;
        int stackPtr;
        void push (Merchandise_Item *); // push onto stack
        Merchandise_Item * pop (); // pop from stack
        void goLeft (Merchandise_Item *);

    public:
        MerchItr ();
        int Init (MerchTree *);
        int operator++ (); // find node
        int operator! (); // check for end of traversal
        Merchandise_Item * operator() (); // return pointer to current object
};
```

Listing 2.12 The MerchItrPre class

```
class MerchItrPre
{
    private:
        Merchandise_Item * stack[25], * root;
        int stackPtr;
        void push (Merchandise_Item *); // push onto stack
        Merchandise_Item * pop (); // pop from stack
    public:
        MerchItrPre ();
        int Init (MerchTree *);
        int operator++ (); // find node
        int operator! (); // check for end of traversal
        Merchandise_Item * operator() (); // return pointer to current object
};
```

NOTE

The declarations of the tree classes can be found in tree.h. The implementations are in tree.cpp.

The Date Class

Penultimate Videos, like many programs, makes extensive use of dates. It therefore includes a date class that makes it easy for a programmer to handle dates. The class, which can be found in Listing 2.13, includes two constructors. The first accepts a date entered as a C string; the second accepts a Macintosh `DateTimeRec`, the data structure that is returned by the ToolBox call `GetTime`.

Listing 2.13 The Date class

```
class date
{
    friend date operator+ (int, date);
    friend date operator+ (date, int);

    typedef char date_string[11];

    private:
        int month, day, year;
        void itoa (int, char *); // convert integer back to ASCII
    public:
        date (char *);
        date (DateTimeRec); // constructor that works off the result of ::GetTime
        int getMonth ();
        int getDay ();
        int getYear ();
        char * showDate (date_string);
        // overloaded operators
        int operator== (date);
        int operator!= (date);
        int operator> (date);
        int operator>= (date);
        int operator< (date);
        int operator<= (date);
        void operator= (date *); // assignment--lets you copy one date to another
};
```

Dates are stored as three integers (`month`, `day`, and `year`). Overloaded operators handle date comparisons, adding fixed values to dates, and assigning one date to another. The Date class also includes a function that returns the date as a C string (`showDate`). This function is used to display a date and when writing a date to a text file. To support `showDate`, the Date class also includes its own function to convert an integer back to ASCII (`itoa`).

Penultimate Videos stores the date on which a rented item is due in an object of class Date. To compute the return date, a rented item—an object of class Video_copy or class Game_copy, both of which are derived from Item_copy—retrieves the current date with `GetTime` (see Listing 2.14). It then creates a Date object, initializing the object with the `DateTimeRec` returned by the ToolBox call. Finally, it adds the rental period, which is expressed as a whole number of days (an integer), to the current date.

Listing 2.14 Computing the return date

```
DateTimeRec todayRec;
date * today;

::GetTime (&todayRec); // call ToolBox routine to get current date and time
today = new date (todayRec);
*Date_due = (*today) + rentalPeriod; // uses overloaded operators
```

Utility Functions

In addition to the classes about which you have been reading, Penultimate Videos includes the following global utility functions:

- `convertPascalStr`: Converts a Str63 into a C string.
- `convertPascal255`: Converts a Str255 into a C string.
- `convertC2Pascal255`: Converts a C string into a Str255.
- `convertC2Pascal63`: Converts a C string into a Str63.
- `itoaP`: Converts an integer into a Str255.

The functions that convert between Str255 and a C string are not widely used. As you will see in Chapter 10, Penultimate Videos provides Pascal and C string classes to handle manipulation of 255-character strings. However, the remaining three functions are used extensively.

NOTE

It's very true that the Macintosh ToolBox contains NumToString and StringToNum functions. However, those functions modify the source string, something which Penultimate Videos needs to avoid in many cases, hence these specialized utility classes.

CHAPTER

3

PowerPlant Projects

Like any other CodeWarrior project, a PowerPlant project usually begins its life as Project Stationery. However, because PowerPlant programs require the source code for the PowerPlant libraries as well as the source code you write, a starter PowerPlant project contains much more than a standard C++ project.

In this chapter you will be introduced to the contents of PowerPlant starter projects. You will learn what they contain, and perhaps more importantly, what they are missing. You will also learn how to customize PowerPlant projects for your particular environment.

The Starter Projects

The Project Stationery folder contains stationery documents for both PowerPC and 69K PowerPlant projects. Because the libraries used by these projects are slightly different, we'll look first at the individual default projects, and then turn to the libraries you'll need to add to both.

The Starter Projects

In Figure 3.1 you will find a project created from PowerPlant 68K Project Stationery. Notice that the project contains three libraries, one starter source code file, and three starter resource files. In addition, most (but not all) of the source code for the PowerPlant libraries is included in the sections labeled Commanders, Features, Panes, File & Stream, Apple Events, Lists, Support, and Utilities.

Figure 3.1 A 68K PowerPlant starter project

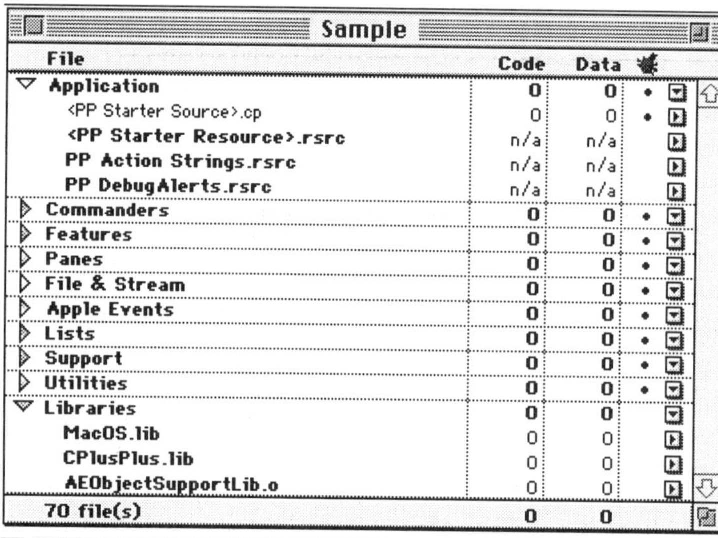

A PPC starter project, created from the PPC Project Stationery, can be found in Figure 3.2. Like the 68K starter project, it contains three libraries, a starter source code file, and three resource files.

Figure 3.2 A PPC PowerPlant starter project

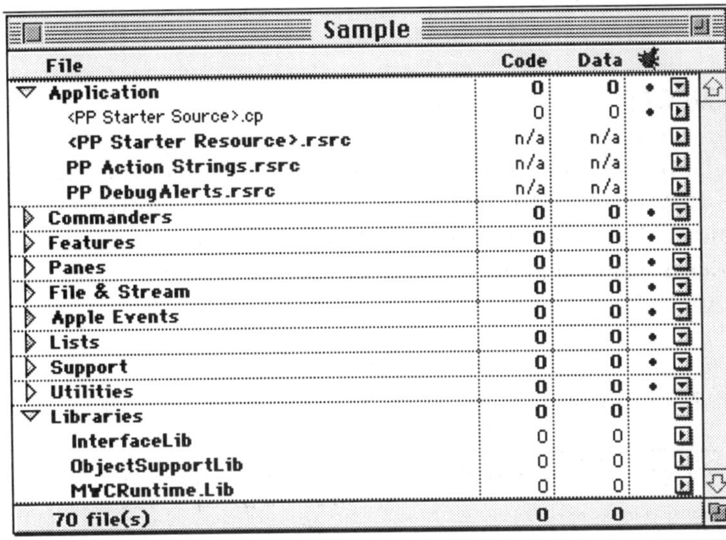

The Starter Source Code File

Each PowerPlant starter project comes equipped with one source code file and an associated header file. In Figure 3.1 and Figure 3.2, the source code file is named *<PP Starter Source>.cp*; its header file is *<PP Starter Header>.h*.

The first thing you should do is copy these two files from the Stationery Support Files folder into the folder that will be holding the source code for your program. Then, rename them something meaningful. For example, the Penultimate Videos program calls them *PPVideoStoreApp.cpp* and *PPVideoStoreApp.h*. Then, remove *<PP Starter Source.cp>* from the project and add your renamed file.

The starter source code file contains a `main` function and member functions for an application class. The program will actually run, but won't do any useful work: All it does is display the menu bar and trap for events related to active menu options, such as anything in the menu and the File menu's Quit option. You therefore begin the development of your PowerPlant program by customizing the starter source code file.

CUSTOMIZING THE APPLICATION CLASS HEADER

The class from which an application is created is always a derived class. The default starter application class is derived from LApplication (Listing 3.1). It contains prototypes for a constructor, a destructor, an `ObeyCommand` function, and a `FindCommandStatus` function. The class also includes a `StartUp` function, which is discussed later in this chapter.

Listing 3.1 The starter application class

```
// ===========================================================================
//  <PP Starter Header>.h 1994-1995 Metrowerks Inc. All rights reserved.
// ===========================================================================

#pragma once

#include <LApplication.h>


class CPPStarterApp : public LApplication {
public:
                        CPPStarterApp(); // constructor registers all PPobs
    virtual     ~CPPStarterApp();// stub destructor

        // this overriding function performs application functions

    virtual Boolean ObeyCommand(CommandT inCommand, void* ioParam);

        // this overriding function returns the status of menu items

    virtual void FindCommandStatus(CommandT inCommand,
                        Boolean &outEnabled, Boolean &outUsesMark,
                        Char16 &outMark, Str255 outName);
protected:

    virtual void StartUp(); // overriding startup functions
};
```

If your program's class will be a subclass of LApplication, all you need to do immediately to the starter header file is change the name of the class from CPPStarterApp to something meaningful. However, if you want to derive your application class from LDocument, LDocApplication, or LSingleDoc, you need to do two things:

- Replace the name of the base class (LApplication) in the class header with the name of the class from which your application class should be derived (LDocument, LDocApplication, or LSingleDoc).
- Replace the name of the base class header file (LApplication.h) with the name of the header file for the appropriate base class (LDocument.h, LDocApplication.h, or LSingleDoc.h).

Because the application class is a derived class, you can add attributes and functions to it as needed. In fact, the Penultimate Videos application class (Listing 3.2) contains a number of program-specific functions. It also includes declarations for the container classes used to manage the program's data structures, and variables that might otherwise be considered "globals."

PROGRAM STRUCTURE: TO SUBCLASS OR NOT TO SUBCLASS

The structure of the Penultimate Videos program is in large measure determined by all of those functions that have been added to the application class. They are the result of the choice not to create subclasses unless absolutely necessary, but instead to create objects directly from PowerPlant classes wherever possible. The alternative is to always create subclasses, even if it is possible to use PowerPlant classes without modification. (This is the strategy used by the sample PowerPlant applications that accompany the PowerPlant class libraries.)

As you would expect, there are pros and cons to each strategy. If you always create subclasses, you end up with a large number of short files. Shorter files are easier to work with and can cut down on compile time when only a few have been modified and need to be recompiled. In addition, creating subclasses makes it easier to reuse code because the classes are stand-alone.

However, because there are so many files, it can be difficult to keep track of which source files trap and handle which commands: Event dispatching and menu activation/deactivation is split among many `ObeyCommand` and `FindCommandStatus` functions. Multiple files can also increase compile time when many files need to be recompiled.

On the other hand, if you subclass only when absolutely necessary, you have fewer source code files. It is much easier to keep track of where commands are handled, which for some programmers makes the program logic clearer and therefore easier to maintain. However, the application class becomes lengthy, including a long `ObeyCommand` function, and graphic elements, such as dialog boxes, are unavailable for reuse.

Listing 3.2 The Penultimate Videos application class

```
// ===========================================================================
// PPVideoStore.h ©1996 Black Gryphon Ltd.
// ===========================================================================
// PPVideoStore.cpp (press Command-Tab to open the associated source file)
//

#pragma once

#include <LApplication.h>
#include <Dialogs.h>

const Str255 null  = "\p"; // null string for cleaning out edit fields

class LDialogBox;
struct SDialogResponse;

class MerchTree;
class MerchNumbTree;
class CopyTree;
class CustTree;
class Film;
class Other;
class Game;
class Video_copy;
class Game_copy;
class Customer;
class CustNumbTree;

class CPPVideoStoreApp : public LApplication
{
    typedef char string[81];

    public:
                        CPPVideoStoreApp();// constructor registers all PPobs
        virtual ~CPPVideoStoreApp();// stub destructor

        // this overriding function performs application functions

        virtual Boolean ObeyCommand(CommandT inCommand, void* ioParam);

        // this overriding function returns the status of menu items

        virtual void FindCommandStatus(CommandT inCommand,
                        Boolean &outEnabled, Boolean &outUsesMark,
                        Char16 &outMark, Str255 outName);

    // This overridden function allows the quit action to save data
        virtual void SendAEQuit();
```

Continued next page

Listing 3.2 (Continued) The Penultimate Videos application class

```
// begin functions added for this program
       int Load ();
       void Unload ();
       void SaveAs();
       void New();
       void Open();
       void MakePathName (FSSpec, CString &); // construct full path name
       void SetUpNewMovie ();
       void SetUpNewCust ();
       void SetUpModCust(SDialogResponse *);
       void SetUpNewMisc ();
       void SetUpNewGame ();
       void ItemList (int);
       void SetUpItemModify (SDialogResponse *);
       void DisplayStarModify (LDialogBox *, ResIDT, ANSIstring);
       void ModifyMovie (SDialogResponse *);
       int LoadStarsArrayModify (LDialogBox *, ANSIstring [], ResIDT, int);
       void ModifyMisc (SDialogResponse *);
       void ModifyGame (SDialogResponse *);
       void DeleteItem (SDialogResponse *);
       void SetUpNewVideoCopy ();
       void SetUpNewGameCopy ();
       void ChooseCopy2Modify ();
       void SetUpCopyModify (SDialogResponse *);
       void ModifyVideoCopy (SDialogResponse *);
       // note: game copies contain no modifiable data
       void DeleteCopy (SDialogResponse *);
       void SetUpFindItem ();
       void SetUpRent ();
       void SetUpReturn ();
       void ProcessNewMovie (SDialogResponse *);
       void ProcessNewCust (SDialogResponse *);
       void DisplayCustList();
       void BuildCustList (LListBox *);
       void ProcessModifyCust (SDialogResponse *);
       void ProcessDeleteCust (SDialogResponse *);
       void ViewCurrentCustList ();
       void ViewOverdueCustList();
       void ShowCurrentRentals (SDialogResponse *, int); // ALL or OVERDUE
       void ProcessNewMisc (SDialogResponse *);
       void ProcessNewGame (SDialogResponse *);
       void ProcessNewVideoCopy (SDialogResponse *);
       void ProcessNewGameCopy (SDialogResponse *);
       void DisplayTitleInfo (SDialogResponse *);
       void ViewQuickTime(SDialogResponse *);
       void ProcessRent (SDialogResponse *);
       void PrintReceipt (SDialogResponse *);
       void CloseRentWindow (SDialogResponse *);
       void ProcessReturn (SDialogResponse *);
```

Continued next page

Listing 3.2 (Continued) The Penultimate Videos application class

```
        void WriteNote ();
        void DisplayGraph ();
        void CloseDialogBox (SDialogResponse *);
        // pass in number of objects handled & thermometer window
        void ManageThermometer (int, LWindow *);
    // end functions added for this program

    protected:
        virtual void StartUp(); // overriding startup function

        // File management stuff
        string FileName;
        FSSpec FileSpec;

        // Data structures
        MerchTree * Items; // alphabetical list of all titles
        MerchNumbTree * ItemsByNumb; // titles by title number
        CopyTree * Copies;
        CustTree * Customers; // customers by name
        CustNumbTree * CustByNumb; // customers by customer number

        // flags
        Boolean save_flag; // used to determine whether to warn user about saving changes

        // Pointers for new objects; used all over the place
        Film * newMovie;
        Other * newOther;
        Game * newGame;
        Video_copy * newVideo;
        Game_copy * newGC;
        Customer * newCust;

        // "save" variables (used to hold values that can't be captured or passed
        // in any other reasonable way)
        Customer * currentCustomer;
        LDialogBox * receiptDialog;
        int row;
        LListBox * receiptList;
};
```

Which should you choose? In most cases, it's a matter of personal preference. However, if you are planning to create classes that you intend to reuse, then you should subclass wherever possible. On the other hand, if reusability isn't an issue—for example, if the screen displays in your program are too program-specific to be reused—then the choice can be based on whatever makes the program clearer to you (and perhaps your programming team members) in the long run.

MODIFYING STARTER APPLICATION FUNCTIONS

Regardless of the overall strategy you use in your PowerPlant program, you will probably need to add code to the application object's overriding member functions. For example, the destructor in the starter source code file is empty. You should therefore add to it any code that should be executed before the application terminates. The Penultimate Videos program, for example, uses the destructor to close QuickTime (Listing 3.3).

Listing 3.3 The Penultimate Videos application destructor function

```
// ---------------------------------------------------------------------------
//      • ~CPPVideoStoreApp
// ---------------------------------------------------------------------------
//  Destructor
//

CPPVideoStoreApp::~CPPVideoStoreApp()
{
   UQuickTime::Finalize();
}
```

PowerPlant Starter Resource Files

As you saw in Figure 3.1 and Figure 3.2, a starter project comes with three resource files. *PP Action Strings.rsrc* contains four STR# resources for undoing and redoing edit and drag actions. *PP DebugAlerts.rsrc* contains two alerts that are used by the debugger to display exception and signal information.

The third resource file—*<PP Starter Resource>.rsrc*—contains resources that are used by the starter source code file (Figure 3.3). This is where you will find the default menu bar (a combination of the MBAR, Mcmd, and MENU resources), along with an ALRT for a default about box that you can customize, and some default icon resources.

You may also have noticed that there is a PPob resource. (The WIND resource accompanies the PPob resource.) Its name is "replace me," and it is only intended as a placeholder for other PowerPlant objects that you will be adding. If you are going

Figure 3.3 Resources in the starter resource file

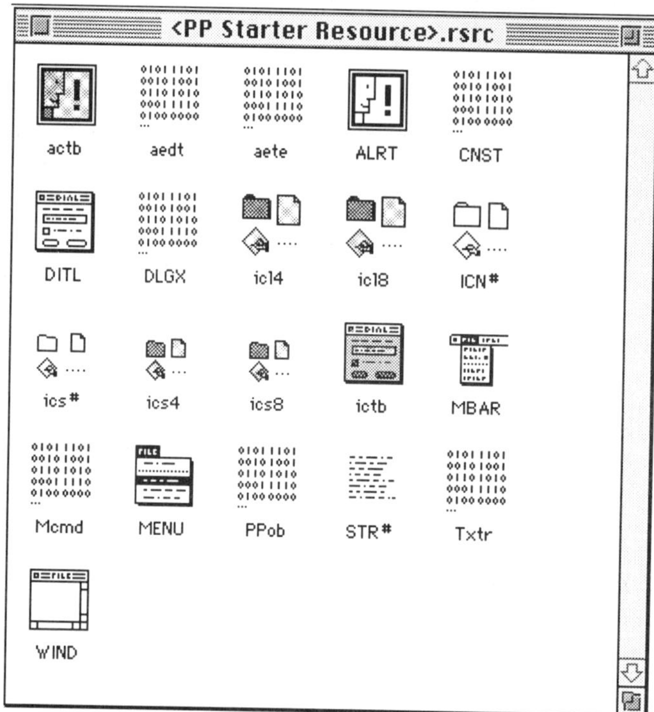

to keep two resource files (one for PowerPlant objects and one for all other resources), then you can either ignore this PPob resource or delete it.

The *<PP Starter Resource>.rsrc* file is physically located in the Stationery Support Files folder. Copy it from that folder into the folder containing your application and rename it. (The Penultimate Videos resource file is called *PPVideoStore.rsrc*.) Then, remove *<PP Starter Resource>.rsrc* from the project and add the newly renamed file.

NOTE

If you are using two separate resource files for application-specific resources, then you'll add the file for PowerPlant objects after you create the first PPob resource using Constructor.

Adding Support for Apple Events

PowerPlant makes extensive use of Apple Events, even if you don't specifically add support for them to your program. For example, Apple Events are used to trigger a startup event (and a subsequent call to an application object's `Startup` function) and to exit the program. In Listing 3.4, for example, you can see the `StartUp` function for the Penultimate Videos program. This function, which is supplied as part of the application object starter file, is triggered by a startup event whenever the program is launched. In this particular case, the program calls a function added to the application object (`Load`) to read data from disk. If the user cancels the load and asks to quit the program, the function calls `SendAEQuit`, an application object function that uses an Apple Event to quit the program and return to the Finder. (This is the same function that is called when the user chooses Quit from the File menu.)

Listing 3.4 The Penultimate Videos Startup function

```
void CPPVideoStoreApp::StartUp()
{
    // Load initial data structures
    int keep_going = Load();
    if (!keep_going)
        SendAEQuit();  // quit program if no master file
}
```

However, a vital file is missing from the default projects to support Apple Events. If you don't add the missing piece, the `Startup` function won't be called and `SendAEQuit` won't work. The missing file is a resource file: You should always add *PP AppleEvents.rsrc* to your PowerPlant projects.

Adding Support for ANSI Functions

It is theoretically possible to write a PowerPlant program without ever using an ANSI C or C++ function. Practically, however, you will probably want access to at least some of the standard libraries. For example, you might want the C math or string functions or some C++ file stream I/O. In that case, you need to add some libraries and perhaps a source file to your project. The needed files are summarized in Table 3.1.

Table 3.1 Additional files needed for C and C++ library support

Project Type	Support Provided	File Name
68K	ANSI C	*MathLIb68KFa(2a).Lib*[a]
		ANSIFa(2i)C.68K.Lib
	ANSI C++	*ANSIFa(2i)C++.68K.Lib*
	ANSI stream I/O	*console.stubs.c*[b]
PPC	ANSI C	*MathLib*
		ANSI C.PPC.Lib
	ANSI C++	*ANSI C++.PPC.Lib*
	ANSI stream I/O	*console.stubs.c*

a. There are several groups of 68K ANSI libraries that vary based on the amount of space to be allocated for number storage and the code model (for example, near or far). The Penultimate Videos program uses a far code model with 2-byte integers. Pick which group is appropriate to your program. Just be sure that all 68K libraries come from the same model and that the project Preferences are set for that model.

b. ANSI stream file I/O requires the ANSI C++ library as well as the console.stubs.c file.

The Penultimate Videos Projects

The Penultimate Videos program uses all of the libraries and resources about which you have been reading, although the specific libraries do differ between the PowerPC and 68K platforms.

The complete PPC project appears in Figure 3.4. Notice that there are five resource files (the three PowerPlant resource files [*PP Action Strings.rsrc, PPDebugAlerts.rsrc, PP AppleEvents.rsrc*], a file for PPob resources [*PPob.rsrc*], and a file for other resources specific to the program [*PP VideoStore.rsrc*]). The libraries include the standard PPC libraries, the ANSI libraries, and the QuickTime library.

The 68K project can be found in Figure 3.5. This project includes the standard 68K libraries and a set of ANSI libraries. Notice that there is no QuickTime library because that library is required only for PowerPC programs.

PowerPlant and Precompiled Headers

You can significantly speed up the compilation of a Macintosh program by using a file containing precompiled headers as a prefix to your source. The precompiled headers mean that CodeWarrior doesn't need to translate header files into binary each time a source code file is compiled; the translation has already been done.

By default, a PowerPlant project uses a precompiled header that contains most of the PowerPlant and Macintosh OS headers, along with additional support for debugging (*PP_DebugHeadersPPC* or *PP_DebugHeaders68K*, whichever is appropriate). The default precompiled headers, along with the source code from which they are generated, are stored in the *PP Precompiled Headers* folder.

Sometime during the program development process you will want to create your own precompiled header. At the very least, you will want to remove the debugging headers before generating shipping code. In addition, because PP DebugHeaders doesn't include all PowerPlant classes and all Macintosh OS headers, you may want to create your own precompiled header file during the program development process.

The Penultimate Videos program, for example, uses QuickTime. None of the QuickTime headers (PowerPlant or Macintosh OS) are included in the default *PP_DebugHeaders*. Therefore, the program has its own precompiled header file.

To create a custom precompiled header file, do the following:

1. Open the project for which the precompiled header file will be generated.
2. If you are adding a PowerPlant header file, open *PP_ClassHeaders.cp* and add a `#include` for each additional header you want to include.

Figure 3.4 The PPC version of the Penultimate Videos project

video π

File	Code	Data	
▽ **Application**	**82K**	**26K**	•
base.cpp	1336	432	•
console.stubs.c	60	56	•
copies.cpp	2376	293	•
customer.cpp	2564	726	•
dates.cpp	2412	313	•
game.cpp	1168	185	•
graph.cpp	1888	1348	•
itembase.cpp	904	285	•
LTextEditM.cp	6428	1742	•
memorymonitor.cpp	1136	1194	•
movie.cpp	1904	186	•
note.cpp	3572	1146	•
other.cpp	1144	129	•
PPVideoStore.cpp	33836	12813	•
receipttable.cpp	1228	697	•
statstable.cpp	1824	764	•
statswindow.cpp	1368	1178	•
stringobjects.cpp	4252	1101	•
Ther.cpp	888	576	•
tree.cpp	9068	1008	•
UTextMenus.cp	4192	841	•
utilities.cpp	844	396	•
PPob.rsrc	n/a	n/a	
PPVideoStore.rsrc	n/a	n/a	
PP Action Strings.rsrc	n/a	n/a	
PP DebugAlerts.rsrc	n/a	n/a	
PP AppleEvents.rsrc	n/a	n/a	
▷ **Commanders**	**8K**	**2K**	•
▷ **Features**	**7K**	**1K**	•
▷ **Panes**	**98K**	**29K**	•
▷ **File & Stream**	**9K**	**1K**	•
▷ **Apple Events**	**47K**	**8K**	•
▷ **Lists**	**6K**	**1K**	•
▷ **Support**	**31K**	**5K**	•
▷ **Utilities**	**19K**	**3K**	•
▽ **Libraries**	**118K**	**27K**	
MathLib	0	0	
ANSI C.PPC.Lib	54456	13679	
ANSI C++.PPC.Lib	57564	11888	
InterfaceLib	0	0	
ObjectSupportLib	0	0	
MWCRuntime.Lib	9352	2472	
QuickTimeLib	0	0	
100 file(s)	**429K**	**108K**	

Figure 3.5 The 68K version of the Penultimate Videos project

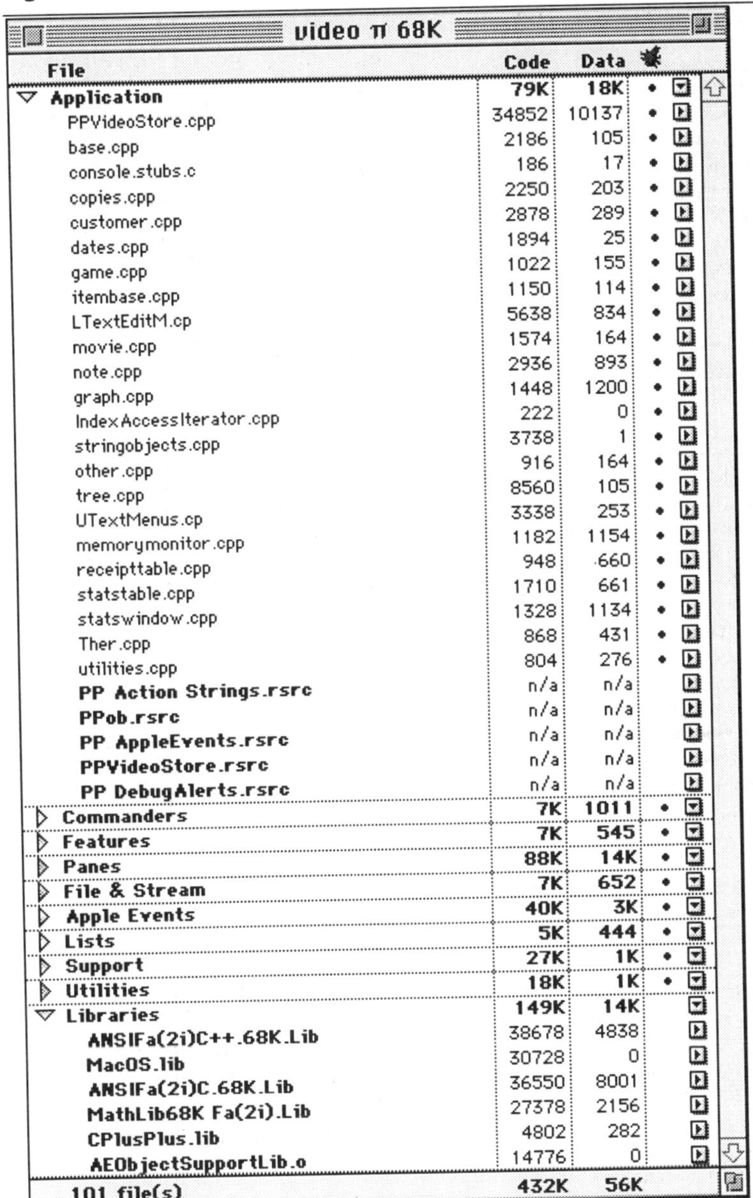

video π 68K

File	Code	Data	Debug
▽ **Application**	**79K**	**18K**	•
PPVideoStore.cpp	34852	10137	•
base.cpp	2186	105	•
console.stubs.c	186	17	•
copies.cpp	2250	203	•
customer.cpp	2878	289	•
dates.cpp	1894	25	•
game.cpp	1022	155	•
itembase.cpp	1150	114	•
LTextEditM.cp	5638	834	•
movie.cpp	1574	164	•
note.cpp	2936	893	•
graph.cpp	1448	1200	•
IndexAccessIterator.cpp	222	0	•
stringobjects.cpp	3738	1	•
other.cpp	916	164	•
tree.cpp	8560	105	•
UTextMenus.cp	3338	253	•
memorymonitor.cpp	1182	1154	•
receipttable.cpp	948	660	•
statstable.cpp	1710	661	•
statswindow.cpp	1328	1134	•
Ther.cpp	868	431	•
utilities.cpp	804	276	•
PP Action Strings.rsrc	n/a	n/a	
PPob.rsrc	n/a	n/a	
PP AppleEvents.rsrc	n/a	n/a	
PPVideoStore.rsrc	n/a	n/a	
PP DebugAlerts.rsrc	n/a	n/a	
▷ **Commanders**	**7K**	**1011**	•
▷ **Features**	**7K**	**545**	•
▷ **Panes**	**88K**	**14K**	•
▷ **File & Stream**	**7K**	**652**	•
▷ **Apple Events**	**40K**	**3K**	•
▷ **Lists**	**5K**	**444**	•
▷ **Support**	**27K**	**1K**	•
▷ **Utilities**	**18K**	**1K**	•
▽ **Libraries**	**149K**	**14K**	
ANSIFa(2i)C++.68K.Lib	38678	4838	
MacOS.lib	30728	0	
ANSIFa(2i)C.68K.Lib	36550	8001	
MathLib68K Fa(2i).Lib	27378	2156	
CPlusPlus.lib	4802	282	
AEObjectSupportLib.o	14776	0	
101 file(s)	**432K**	**56K**	

3. If you are adding support for additional Macintosh OS headers, open *PP_MacHeaders.c* and uncomment the lines for the new headers. For example, the following lines were uncommented in the Penultimate Videos precompiled headers:

```
#include <Movies.h>
#include <MoviesFormat.h>
#include <QuickTimeComponents.h>
```

4. If necessary, save and close *PP_ClassHeaders.cp* and *PP_MacHeaders.c.*
5. Open *PP_DebugHeaders.cp.*
6. Choose Precompile from the Project menu. CodeWarrior will precompile all the included headers. Even on a PowerMac, this will take some time. Eventually, a Save File dialog box appears.
7. Enter a name for the new precompiled header file and save the file. Although you can put it anywhere, the most convenient location is the PP Precompiled Headers folder where the default precompiled header files can be found.
8. Open the Preferences dialog box and select the C/C++ Language panel.
9. Enter the name of new precompiled header file at the bottom of the dialog box as the Prefix File (Figure 3.6).

NOTE

Precompiled header files are different for PPC and 68K projects. If you are going to be generating both types of code, you must repeat the precompilation for each project, giving each precompiled header file a unique name. This is why the CD-ROM that accompanies book has two precompiled header files (PPVidSHeaders and PPVidSHeaders (68K)).

NOTE

Changing a project's Prefix File forces a recompilation of all source code in the program. To avoid unnecessary long compiles, consider creating your custom precompiled header file early in the development process.

NOTE

Depending on your CodeWarrior installation, you may need to enlarge your memory allocation before you can precompile headers.

Figure 3.6 Installing a custom precompiled header file

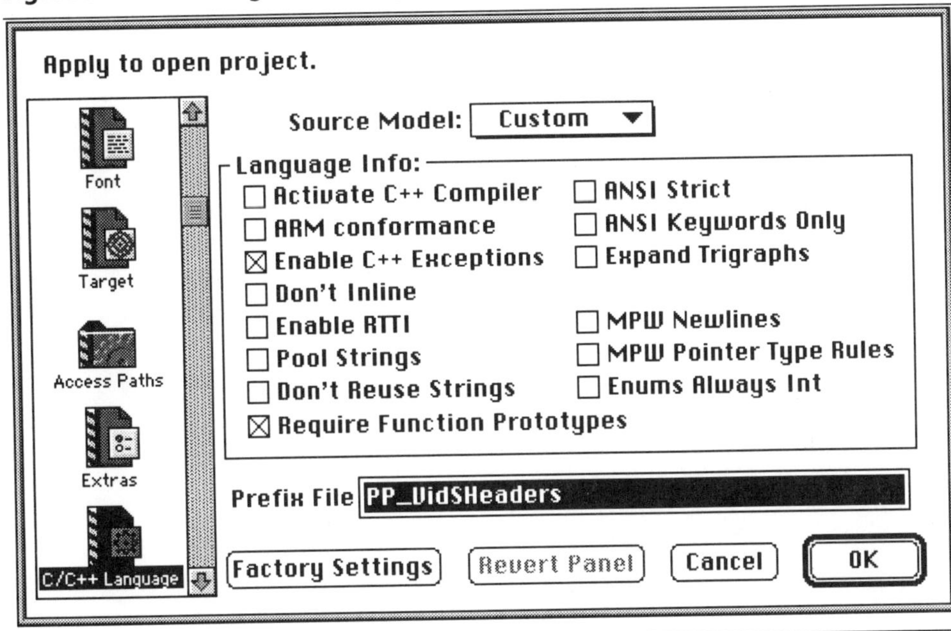

CHAPTER

PowerPlant Menus

4

PowerPlant menus are managed by two classes: LMenuBar, which handles the menu bar, and LMenu, which handles individual menus. If you begin a PowerPlant program with the starter source file, then you will rarely have to deal with either LMenuBar or LMenu objects directly. However, you will have to create menu resources as well as to write code to activate menu items and to trap menu selections. In this chapter you will learn how to do those three things. (We'll leave the special cases of handling the Font, Size, and Style menus for later, when we talk about windows for editing text.)

NOTE
Because LMenuBar and LMenu are stand-alone classes—not part of the PowerPlant class hierarchy—they can be used in non-PowerPlant C++ programs.

Creating Menu Resources with a Standard Resource Editor

Assuming that you have started your PowerPlant project from the starter files supplied with project stationery, your resource file will contain the MBAR resource in Figure 4.1, which corresponds to the MENU resources in Figure 4.2. (Both Figure 4.1 and Figure 4.2 are screen shots taken from ResEdit.)

Figure 4.1 The starter MBAR resource

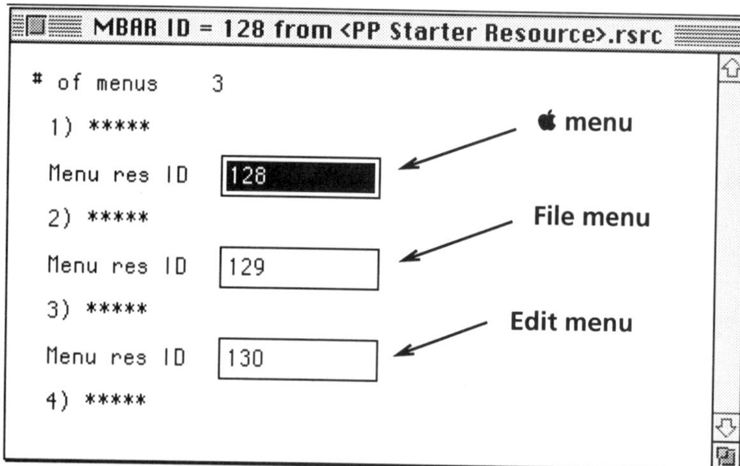

In a typical Macintosh program, these four resources would be enough to support the menu bar and the menus. However, PowerPlant uses an additional resource—Mcmd—to associate integers with each menu option. In Figure 4.3 you can see the ResEdit version of the Mcmd resource for the default File menu. Notice that there is one integer for each item in the File menu, including the separator lines. Items such as the separator lines that should not respond to menu selections are given a menu command value of zero. However, every other item is given a unique integer.

Some menus—for example, the and Font menus—don't have fixed menu items. Such menus have *synthetic commands* and must be handled differently from most other menus. If you look again at Figure 4.2, for example, you'll notice that the menu contains only one command for the About box. The rest of the items are added

Figure 4.2 The starter MENU resources

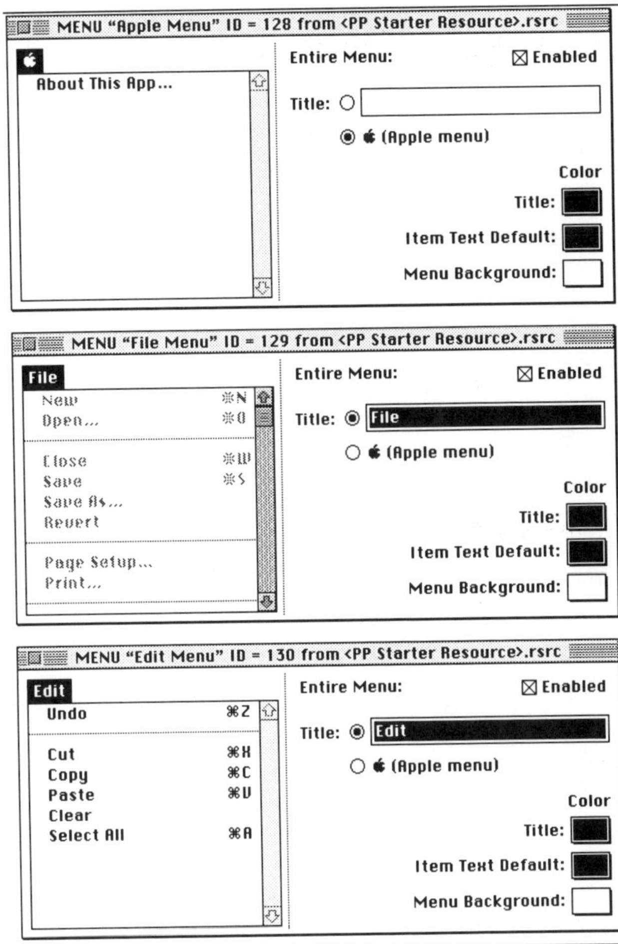

when the program is launched. For that reason, the menu's Mcmd resource has only one item (see Figure 4.4). A Font menu doesn't need a Mcmd resource at all.

There are two important things to keep in mind when assigning menu command numbers:

- The integer values assigned to menu options (with the exception of those such as the separator lines) must be unique throughout the entire program.
- There is no data value in a Mcmd resource to associate it with the MENU resource to which it applies. If you are creating Mcmd resources using a resource editor other than Constructor, you must be careful to give a Mcmd resource the same

Figure 4.3 The Mcmd resource for the default File menu

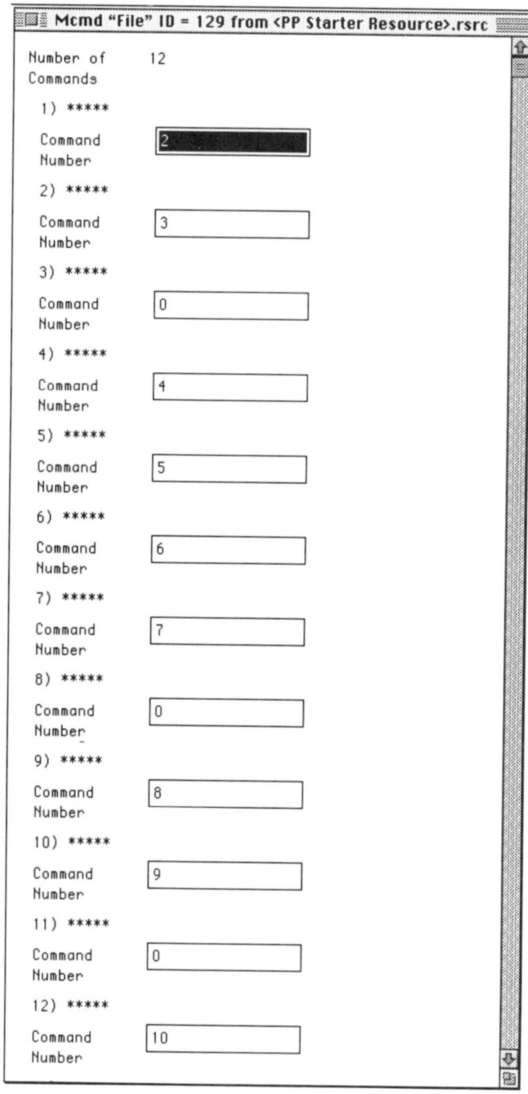

resource ID as its MENU resource. This is the only way that PowerPlant has to associate the two.

To customize the starter menu resources for your program, you can add to the default resources using your favorite resource editor or compiler. There is just one

Figure 4.4 The Mcmd resource for the menu

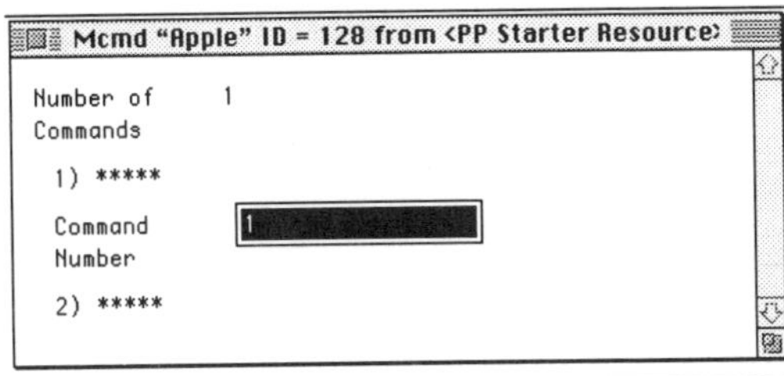

small detail to keep in mind: PowerPlant reserves resource IDs up to 999 for its own use. To avoid conflicts, your resource IDs should therefore be greater than 999.

Menu Resources for the Penultimate Videos Program

The Penultimate Videos program adds six menus to the default menu bar (Figure 4.5). The Inventory, Customers, and Transactions menus to which you were introduced in Chapter 2 are standard application menus and have IDs greater than 999. The Font, Size, and Style menus use the IDs they are typically given in Macintosh programs. (The remaining five MENU resources are used for popup menus and therefore aren't related to the current discussion.) The Inventory, Customers, Transactions, Size, and Style menus also have accompanying Mcmd resources. The Font menu, whose contents are built based on the current fonts installed in the Fonts folder, has no fixed menu items and therefore no Mcmd resource.

Constants for Menu Commands

A PowerPlant program identifies menu commands by the integers assigned in Mcmd resources. (The exception, of course, is menus with synthetic commands). To make working with the commands easier, you should declare constants for them.

By convention, a menu command has a data type of `MessageT`, a 16-bit integer. The constants for PowerPlant-supplied menus can be found in the file *PP_Messages.h*. As you can see in Listing 4.1, the constants correspond directly to the Mcmd resources. Menu command constants for the Penultimate Videos program (Listing 4.1) are stored in a file named *MenuConstants.h*.

Figure 4.5 MENU resources in the Penultimate Videos program

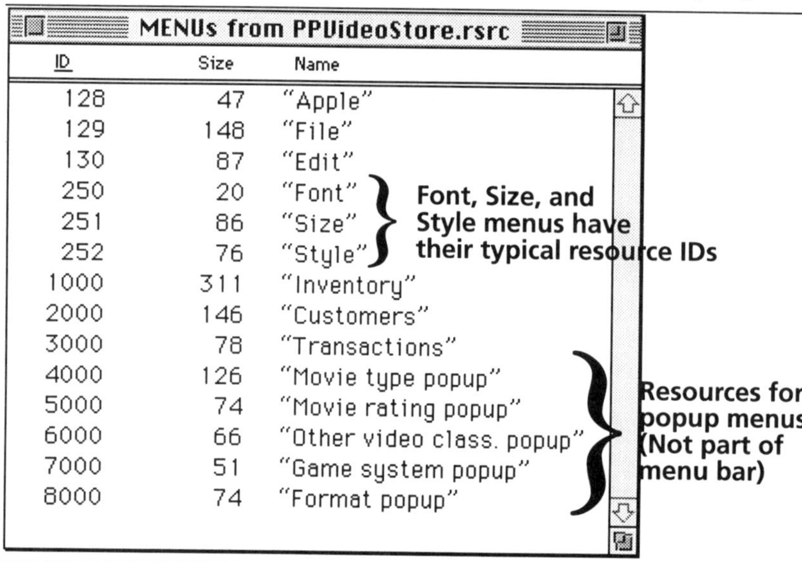

Notice that four items have been added to the default File menu, producing the menu in Figure 4.6. These commands duplicate the standard Open, Save, SaveAs, and Revert commands for the Note window. (The standard file management commands manage the video store's data.) Because these are custom menu items, they have resource IDs greater than 1000.

NOTE

Penultimate Videos resource IDs are usually constructed from a four-digit integer. The first two digits represent the resource number. For example, a MENU with ID 1000 is menu 10 (not necessarily the 10th menu, however). The second two digits represent a part of the resource. Therefore, a Mcmd containing 1010 is the 10th item in menu 10. There are a few exceptions to this convention, such as the items added to the File menu, which are associated with a default resource with a resource ID of less than 1000.

Listing 4.1 Menu command constants for Penultimate Videos menus

```
// Items added to File menu
const MessageT cmd_open_note = 4001;
const MessageT cmd_save_note = 4002;
const MessageT cmd_save_note_as = 4003;
const MessageT cmd_revert_note = 4004;

// Inventory menu
const MessageT cmd_new_movie = 1001;
const MessageT cmd_mod_movie = 1002;
const MessageT cmd_new_misc = 1003;
const MessageT cmd_mod_misc = 1004;
const MessageT cmd_new_video_copy = 1006;
const MessageT cmd_mod_video_copy = 1007;
const MessageT cmd_new_game = 1009;
const MessageT cmd_mod_game = 1010;
const MessageT cmd_new_game_copy = 1011;
const MessageT cmd_mod_game_copy = 1012;
const MessageT cmd_find_item = 1014;
const MessageT cmd_graph = 1015;

// Customers menu
const MessageT cmd_new_customer = 2001;
const MessageT cmd_mod_customer = 2002;
const MessageT cmd_view_current = 2005;
const MessageT cmd_view_overdue = 2006;
const MessageT cmd_write_note = 2008;

// Transactions menu
const MessageT cmd_rent = 3001;
const MessageT cmd_return = 3002;
const MessageT cmd_sell = 3004;
```

Creating Menu Resources with Constructor

Unlike earlier versions of the program, Constructor 2.1 can be used to define MENU and Mcmd resources. However, Constructor can't handle the MBAR resource. This means that even if you take advantage of Constructor's ease of use for MENU and Mcmd resources, you will still need to use a standard resource editor or compiler to attach menus to the MBAR resource.

Figure 4.6 The Penultimate Videos File menu

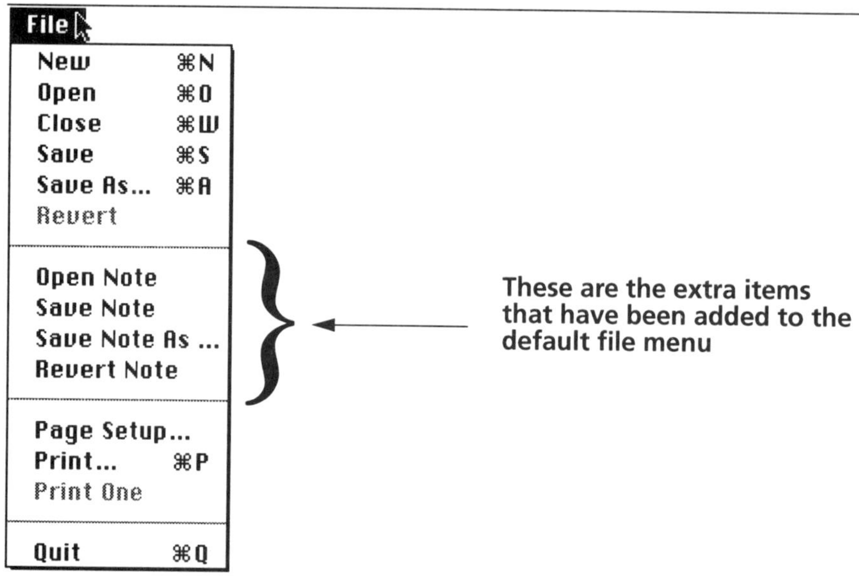

NOTE

Be sure you are using at least version 2.1.1 of Constructor. There are some bugs in version 2.1 that can cause the program (and maybe your Mac) to crash. If you have version 2.1, you can find the update patches on major information services and on Metrowerks's WWW site (http://www.metrowerks.com/).

If you are working with two resource files and decide to use Constructor for MENU and Mcmd resources, you begin by launching constructor and opening the starter resource file. As you can see in Figure 4.7, the interface provides information similar to that of a traditional resource editor, include the resources by type, along with their names and resource IDs.

To see the details of a MENU resource, double-click on the resource. Figure 4.8, for example, contains the starter File menu. Notice that all menu options except Quit are disabled.

The characteristics of each menu option are contained in a properties window. To display it, double-click on the menu option. In Figure 4.9, for example, you can see the properties for the starter File menu's Quit option. The Mcmd number appears in the box labeled Command Number. Notice that the check box directly below it determines the menu item's initial state (enabled or disabled).

Figure 4.7 The starter MENU resources, viewed with Constructor

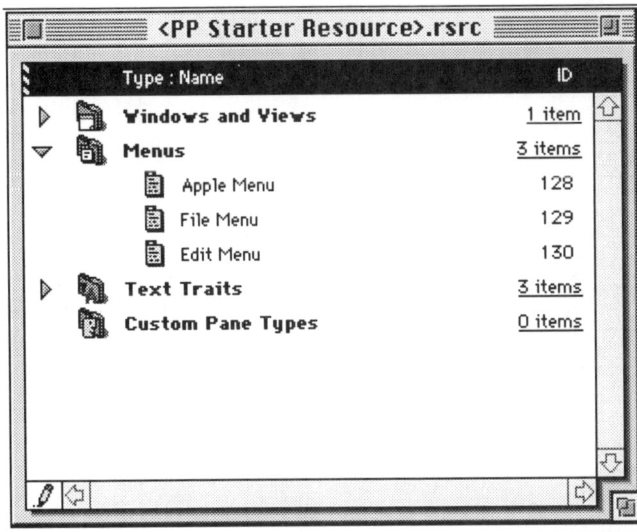

Figure 4.8 The starter File MENU resource

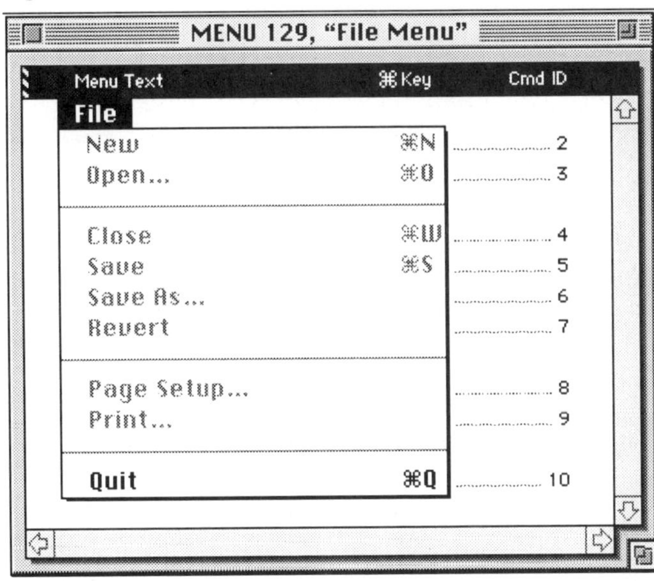

Figure 4.9 Menu item properties

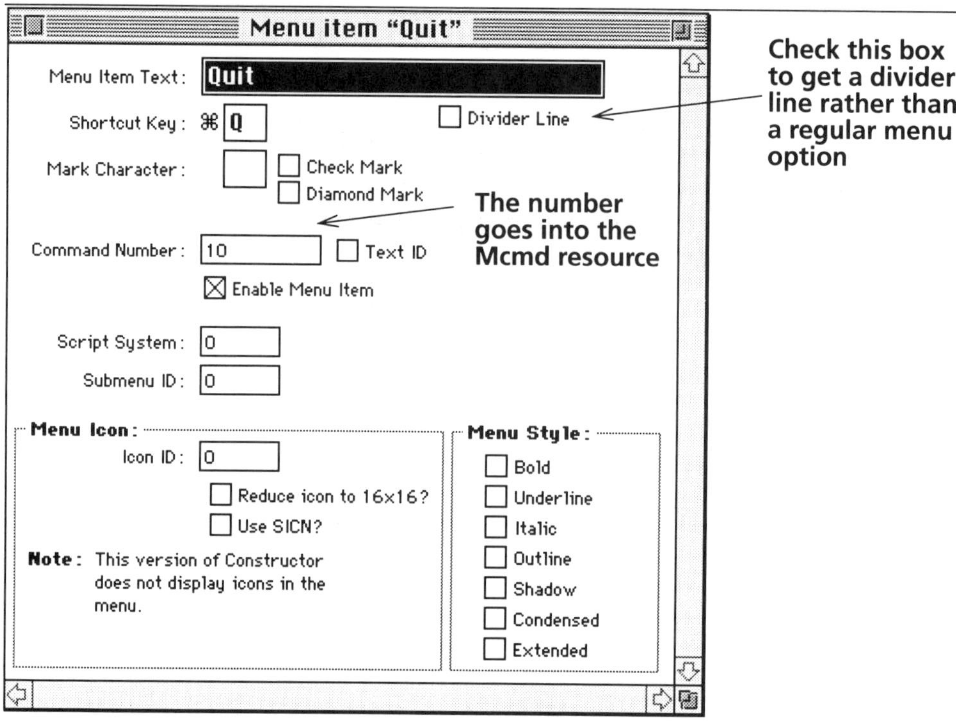

CREATING A NEW MENU RESOURCE

Most programs, including the Penultimate Videos program, need menus other than those provided in the starter resource file. To add a new MENU resource, do the following:

1. Press ⌘-K or choose New Resource from the Edit menu. The Create New Resource dialog box appears.
2. Choose MENU from the Resource Type popup (Figure 4.10).
3. Enter a name for the resource.
4. Enter the resource ID.
5. Click the Create button or press Enter. Constructor creates the resource and places it in the resource file's window.

Figure 4.10 Creating a new menu resource

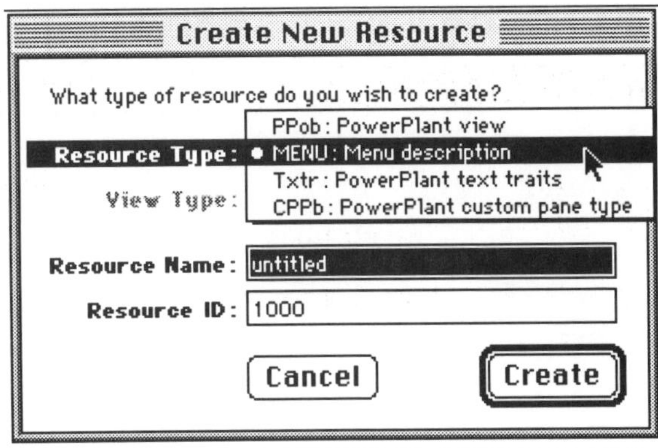

> **NOTE**
>
> *Although you can add the new menus using Constructor, don't forget that you will need to use one of the standard resource editors to attach those menus to a menu bar.*

ADDING A NEW MENU ITEM

As you would expect, creating a new MENU resource generates an empty menu. To customize the menu's title and add items, you do the following:

1. Double-click on the MENU resource to open it. Notice that at this point the menu has the default name of Menu (Figure 4.11).

Figure 4.11 A menu with its default menu name

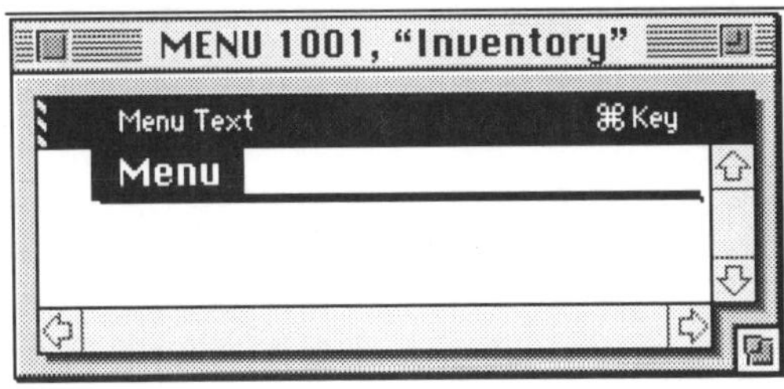

2. Double-click on the menu title to display the menu title's property dialog box.
3. Change the menu name, as in Figure 4.12, and close the window to save the changes.

Figure 4.12 Changing a menu's name

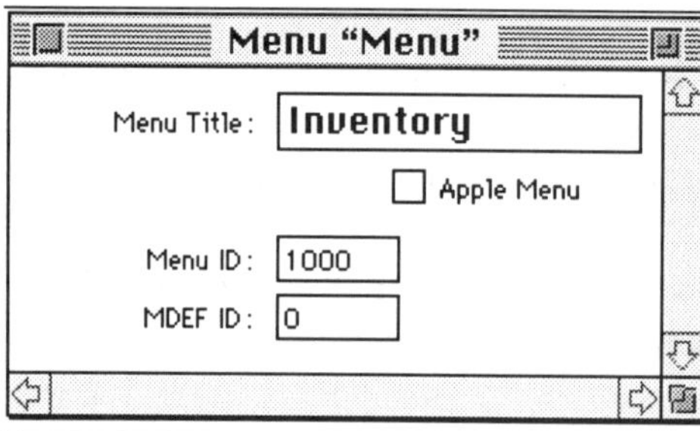

NOTE

Constructor has one interface quirk: Many windows don't have an "Apply" button. To apply changes, you close the window with which you have been working. The drawback to this is, of course, that the only way to cancel changes is to restore the window to its original state before you close it.

4. Press ⌘-K or choose New Menu Item from the Edit menu. A new item appears in the menu window (Figure 4.13)l

Figure 4.13 A new menu item

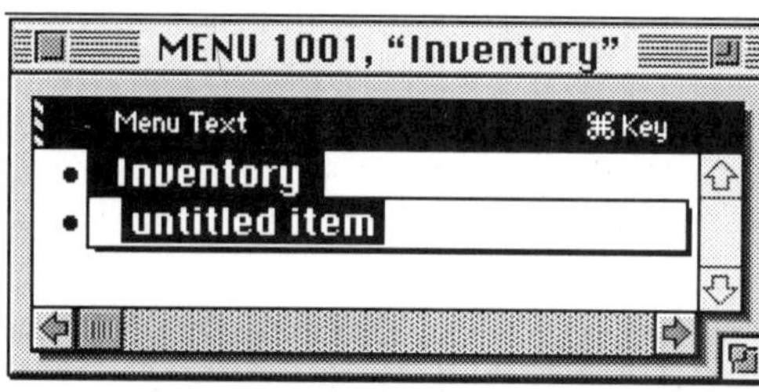

5. Double-click on the new item to open its properties window (for example, Figure 4.9) and configure the menu item as needed. Closing the properties window saves the changes.

MAINTAINING MENU ITEMS

One of the biggest advantages of using Constructor to create MENU resources is that you don't have to worry about Mcmd resources. This is particularly handy when you rearrange or delete menu items because Constructor automatically adjusts the Mcmd resource for you.

To rearrange menu items, open the MENU resource's window. Then, drag menu items to their new locations. To delete a menu item, select it to highlight it and press Delete.

Creating the Menu Bar

An application object creates its menu bar by creating an object of class LMenuBar:

```
new LMenuBar (MBAR_Initial);
```

The constant `MBAR_Initial` contains the resource ID of the program's MBAR resource. This statement appears in the LApplication class constructor. If your application object is derived from that class, you needn't add code to create the menu bar object.

The LMenuBar constructor calls its own routine `InstallMenu` to add each menu to the menu bar. As you can see in Listing 4.2, the call to `InstallMenu` takes a pointer to a new LMenu object as its first parameter. The second parameter is a Boolean that indicates whether the new menu should be placed at the end of the list of menus in the menu bar.

Once the menus are installed, the LMenuBar constructor adds items to the menu. The process is the same as that used in a non-PowerPlant program: Get the menu handle and then use the ToolBox routine `AppendResMenu` to add the menu items.

Listing 4.2 The LMenuBar constructor

```
LMenuBar::LMenuBar(
    ResIDT inMBARid)
{
    StResourcetheMBAR('MBAR', inMBARid);
    ::HLockHi(theMBAR.mResourceH);

    sMenuBar = this;
    mMenuListHead = nil;
                    // Install each menu in the MBAR resource
    Int16 *menuIDP = (Int16 *) *theMBAR.mResourceH;
    Int16 numMenus = *menuIDP++;
    for (Int16 i = 1; i <= numMenus; ++i) {
        InstallMenu(new LMenu(*menuIDP++), InstallMenu_AtEnd);
    }

                    // Populate the Apple Menu
    MenuHandlemacAppleMenuH = ::GetMenuHandle(MENU_Apple);
    if (macAppleMenuH != nil) {
        ::AppendResMenu(macAppleMenuH, 'DRVR');
    }

    ::InvalMenuBar();
}
```

This call installs a single menu in the menu bar

Activating and Deactivating Menus

Although a MENU resource typically indicates that the menu it defines is enabled, when you run a PowerPlant program for the first time, you will discover that the menus you have added to the program are disabled. This is the result of the way PowerPlant is structured to handle menu bar update events.

PowerPlant first disables all menu items, which in turn disables the menus. Then, when a menu bar update event occurs, the program passes that event to the commander that is lowest in the chain of command. (Remember that if there are multiple objects at the same level in the chain of command, PowerPlant selects whichever object is the current target.) PowerPlant then executes the `FindCommandStatus` function for that commander to see which menu items should be enabled. Any menu that has at least one enabled item will be enabled.

The `FindCommandStatus` function for the PowerPlant starter application appears in Listing 4.3. Notice that the function is designed to handle one menu command at a time; the input parameter inCommand identifies which menu command the function call is to handle. The function returns three Booleans: outEnabled, which indicates whether the menu item should be enabled; outUsesMark, which indicates whether the item uses a check mark when selected; and outMark, which indicates whether the item actually has a check mark. (Check marks appear, for example, in the Font menu to indicate the current font.)

Listing 4.3 A FindCommandStatus function

```
void
CPPStarterApp::FindCommandStatus(
    CommandT inCommand,
    Boolean &outEnabled,
    Boolean &outUsesMark,
    Char16 &outMark,
    Str255 outName)
{

    switch (inCommand) {

        // Return menu item status according to command messages.
        // Any that you don't handle will be passed to LApplication

        case cmd_New:  // EXAMPLE
            outEnabled = true; // enable the New command
            break;

        default:
            LApplication::FindCommandStatus(inCommand, outEnabled,
                        outUsesMark, outMark, outName);
            break;
    }
}
```

By default, all three Booleans are false. To enable a menu item, you add a case for it to the function's switch and then change the value in the appropriate Boolean. For example, in Listing 4.3, the function enables the New option in the File menu by trapping for cmd_New and then setting outEnabled to true.

If the chosen command isn't part of the FindCommandStatus function being executed, the switch passes control to its default option, which calls the FindCommandStatus function of the current class's base class. As you can see in Listing 4.4, the base class function (in this example, LApplication) handles events appropriate for the base class (for example, the menu). However, if the event is one not handled by the base class, then the base class function calls LCommander's FindCommandStatus function (Listing 4.5), which calls `FindCommandStatus` for the supercommander. In this way, menu update events are passed up the chain of command.

Listing 4.4 LApplication's FindCommandStatus function

```
void
LApplication::FindCommandStatus(
    CommandT inCommand,
    Boolean &outEnabled,
    Boolean &outUsesMark,
    Char16  &outMark,
    Str255  outName)
{
    switch (inCommand) {

        case cmd_About:
        case cmd_Quit:
            outEnabled = true;
            break;

        case cmd_Undo:
            outEnabled = false;
            ::GetIndString(outName, STRx_UndoEdit, str_CantRedoUndo);
            break;

        default:
            LCommander::FindCommandStatus(inCommand, outEnabled,
                        outUsesMark, outMark, outName);
            break;
    }
}
```

NOTE

For more extensive examples of the FindCommandStatus function, see PPVideoStore.cpp and note.cpp, as well as the source files for all PowerPlant classes derived from LCommander.

Trapping Menu Selections

Once menu items are enabled, users can make choices from those menus. A PowerPlant program traps those menu selections with an `ObeyCommand` function. When a

Listing 4.5 LCommander's FindCommandStatus function

```
void
LCommander::FindCommandStatus(
    CommandTinCommand,
    Boolean &outEnabled,
    Boolean &outUsesMark,
    Char16  &outMark,
    Str255  outName)
{
    if (mSuperCommander != nil) {
        mSuperCommander->ProcessCommandStatus(inCommand, outEnabled,
                        outUsesMark, outMark, outName);
    } else {
        outEnabled = false;// Query has reached the top of a command
        outUsesMark = false;//   chain without any object dealing with
                        //   it, so command is disabled and unmarked
    }
}
```

menu selection event occurs, PowerPlant executes the `ObeyCommand` function of the lowest object in the chain of command (the current target).

NOTE

The ObeyCommand function also traps other messages sent by objects, such as messages sent when a user clicks on a button in a dialog box or when a user double-clicks on an item in a list. You will read more about handling these events later in this book.

Like `FindCommandStatus`, `ObeyCommand` contains a `switch` that identifies which menu option has been chosen. If the command can't be handled by the current object, it is passed up the chain of command. For example, the `ObeyCommand` function for the starter application appears in Listing 4.6. If the command isn't one trapped by the function, the `default` option in the `switch` calls the `ObeyCommand` function of the current object's base class, which, as you saw in Chapter 1, ultimately calls LCommander's `ObeyCommand` function to pass the event up the chain of command.

You have two choices for handling `ObeyCommand` functions. If the action to be performed is short—no more than a half-dozen or so lines of code—you may choose to include that code directly in the `ObeyCommand` function's `switch`. (This is the choice made in Listing 4.6.) Alternatively, you may decide to call a function that performs the required action. This latter solution helps keep `ObeyCommand` functions to a reasonable length.

Listing 4.6 An ObeyCommand function

```
Boolean
CPPStarterApp::ObeyCommand(
    CommandT inCommand,
    void    *ioParam)
{
    Boolean cmdHandled = true;

    switch (inCommand) {

        // Deal with command messages (defined in PP_Messages.h).
        // Any that you don't handle will be passed to LApplication

        case cmd_New:
                        // EXAMPLE, create a new window
            LWindow *theWindow;
            theWindow = LWindow::CreateWindow(window_Sample, this);
            theWindow->Show();
            break;
        default:
            cmdHandled = LApplication::ObeyCommand(inCommand, ioParam);
            break;
    }

    return cmdHandled;
}
```

NOTE

For more extensive examples of the ObeyCommand function, see PPVideoStore.cpp and note.cpp, as well as the source files for all PowerPlant classes derived from LCommander.

CHAPTER 5

Panes and Views

As you have read, a pane is where PowerPlant drawing takes place. Understanding panes (and ultimately how they relate to views) is fundamental to understanding the operation of a PowerPlant program. This chapter therefore provides a first look at working directly with panes and views. Along the way, you will see your first PowerPlant subclass. In addition, you will be introduced to using Constructor for creating PowerPlant objects that contain simple panes for drawing, how PowerPlant objects are created, and how to write functions for pane classes.

The major example that we'll be using in this chapter is the Penultimate Videos inventory graph window (Figure 5.1). This simple window is built from one LWindow object that contains a single pane of a class that is a subclass of LPane. The LWindow object is therefore a view that contains one pane.

As a second, smaller example, at the end of this chapter we'll look at creating a pane in which you can play a QuickTime movie. Not only will you learn to use PowerPlant's QuickTime classes, but you'll see a method for creating a pane that doesn't involve a PowerPlant object.

Figure 5.1 The inventory graph

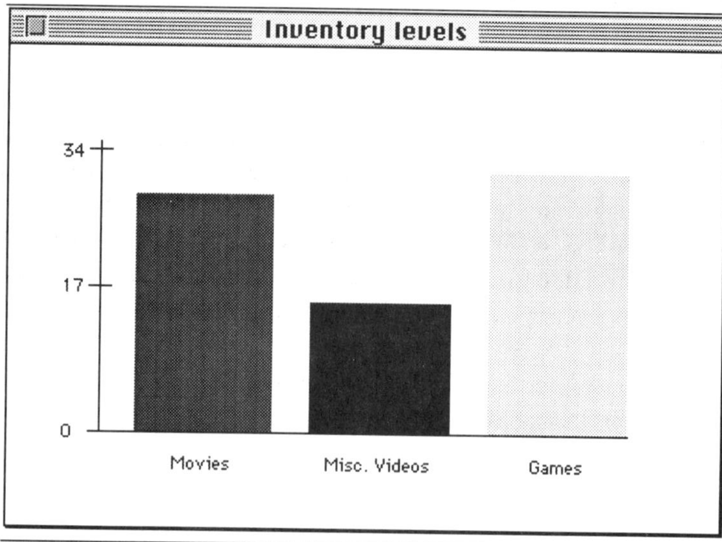

The final example looks at creating a custom pane—one which is derived from LPane but adds attributes of its own—whose objects can be defined using Constructor. The custom pane is a thermometer that will be displayed in a window to show the progress of saving Penultimate Videos data to a text file.

Pane Geography

Every PowerPlant pane keeps information that identifies itself, indicates where it is located, and records its size. These values are held in three variables:

- `mPaneID`: A 16-bit integer that should uniquely identify the pane. As you will see, this pane ID acts as the pane's resource ID and is most easily assigned when you are using Constructor to create a pane object.
- `mFrameSize`: A data structure consisting of two 16-bit integers that records the height and width of a pane's *frame*, the rectangle that forms the border of the pane.
- `mFrameLocation`: A data structure consisting of two 32-bit integers that records the coordinates of the pane's frame's top left corner.

Declaring a Subclass for a Pane

There are several reasons to subclass a PowerPlant class, one of the most common of which is to provide a vehicle for overriding functions to customize class behavior. The graph window, for example, requires a subclass of LPane so that it can override the `DrawSelf` function, which actually draws the contents of the pane. You will create a subclass and override `DrawSelf` whenever you need to draw directly in a pane.

For this particular example, the subclass is called Graph. As you can see in Listing 5.1, Graph is derived directly from LPane. The subclass must of course include its own constructors and destructor. It also overrides the `FinishCreateSelf` function (which does nothing in this class) and the `DrawSelf` function (which does all the work).

Listing 5.1 The Graph class

```
// The Graph class
// A display window that uses QuickDraw routines to draw something
const NUMB_BARS = 3;
const MARGIN = 50;
const SPACE_BETWEEN = 20;
const TEXT_SIZE = 9;

#include <LPane.h>

class Graph : public LPane
{
    public:
        static Graph * CreateGraphStream (LStream * inStream);
        Graph();
        Graph(LStream *inStream);
        virtual ~Graph();

    protected:
        virtual void FinishCreateSelf();
        virtual void DrawSelf();
};
```

Creating a Pane Resource for Drawing

The easiest way to declare the objects that underlie the graph window (an object of class LWindow and an object of class Graph) is to use Constructor, which provides a graphic environment in which you can "draw" panes and views. In this section we will look at using Constructor to do just that.

Starting a Constructor Resource File

Assuming that you are going to work with two program-specific resource files (one for PowerPlant resources and one for all other resources), you begin by launching Constructor. Like many well-behaved Macintosh programs, it automatically creates a new document for you (Figure 5.2).

Figure 5.2 A new Constructor file

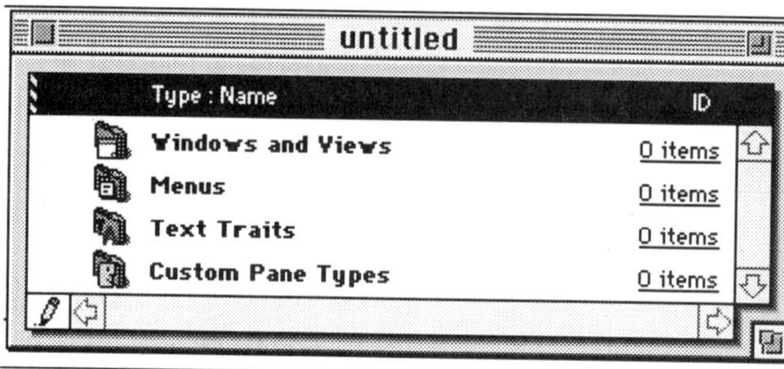

The four icons in the body of the window represent the four major types of resources that Constructor can manage for you:

- Windows and Views: PowerPlant objects created from LWindow, LView, LPrintout, LDialogBox, or LGraphPortView. In addition, Window and View resources can be used for subclasses that have one (and generally only one) of the types in the preceding sentence in their inheritance hierarchy.
- Menus: MENU and Mcmd resources.

- Text Traits: Text characteristics (font, size, style, alignment, and so on) that you can associate with objects that display text, including objects created from LCaption, LEditField, and LTextEdit.
- Custom Types: Programmer-defined classes whose objects can be represented as PowerPlant objects.

Creating a Resource

To create a new window or view resource, do the following:

1. Type ⌘-K or choose New Resource from the Edit menu. Constructor displays the Create New Resource dialog box so you can choose the type of resource you need.
2. Enter a name for the resource, choose its type from the View Type popup menu, and enter the resource ID. For this example, the new view is an LWIndow (Figure 5.3).

Figure 5.3 Creating a new View resource

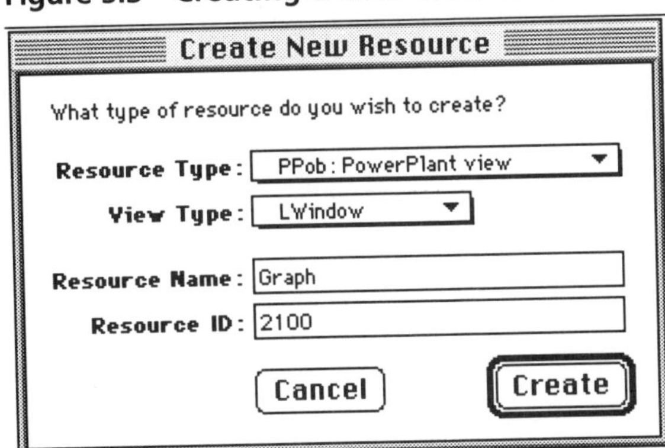

3. Click the Create button. Constructor adds the resource to its list (Figure 5.4).

> **NOTE**
>
> *To change the name or resource ID of an existing resource, highlight the resource in the Constructor window's resource list and press ⌘-I. The resource's properties box appears, in which you can make the necessary changes.*

Figure 5.4 A new resource in the resource list

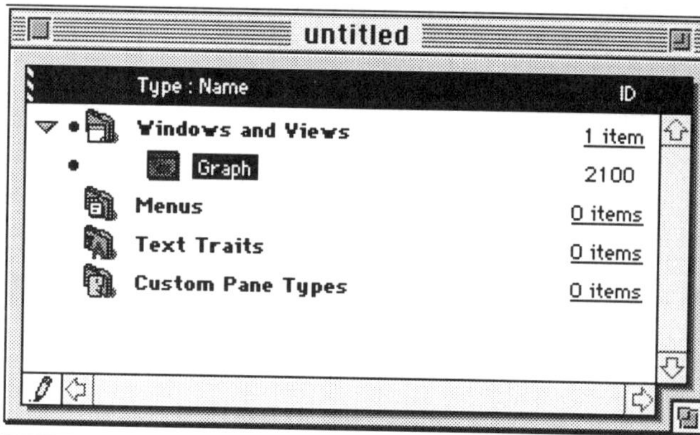

CUSTOMIZING RESOURCE CONTENTS

To add to or modify the contents of a PowerPlant object, you first open the resource window by double-clicking on its name or icon in the Constructor file window. As you can see in Figure 5.5, the window is a standard document window with a title of "untitled." There are two major tasks that should be completed at this point: configuring the LWindow object, and adding the objects that the LWindow object will contain.

Configuring the LWindow Object

Each object that makes up a PowerPlant object has its own set of properties. To access those properties, double-click anywhere on the object. The properties for an object of class LWindow (Figure 5.6) include the window title, its type, a WDEF ID, its PowerPlant class ID, and whether it has characteristics such as a zoom, close, or size box.

Two of the properties in the Clicking/Drawing section are of particular interest. The "Targetable" check box determines whether an object can become the target. Even if the object's class is derived from LCommander, the object won't be able to respond to commands if the Targetable box is unchecked. Items designed for display only (for example, lines of text declared as LCaption objects) shouldn't be targetable. However, items with which the user should interact, such as LEditField or LStdButton objects, must be targetable. Windows must also be targetable if they are to respond to events such as clicks in close boxes and window manipulation key presses.

Figure 5.5 A default LWindow object

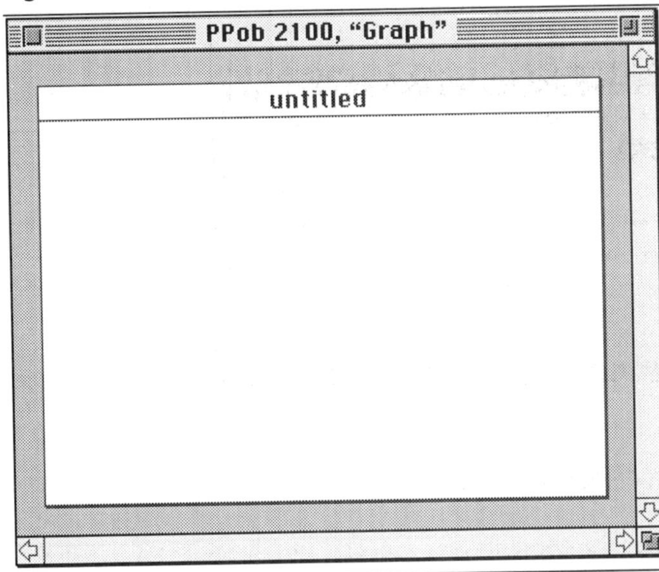

The Erase on Update box determines whether the contents of the object are completely erased and then redrawn whenever an update event occurs. Removing the check from this box can result in some interesting ghosts appearing on the screen!

NOTE

Like many other Constructor windows, closing the LWindow Info window saves any changes you've made. If you don't want to save changes, restore the window to its original state before closing.

Adding a Pane

The types of objects that can be added to a PowerPlant resource are collected in a Tools palette (Figure 5.7). Notice that there are icons for all classes that represent visible, graphic objects that might appear in a window, dialog box, or printout.To add an object of a given class to a view, drag it from the Tools palette into an open view window. For this particular example, you would drag an object of class LPane (the base class for the Graph class).

Figure 5.6 LWindow object properties

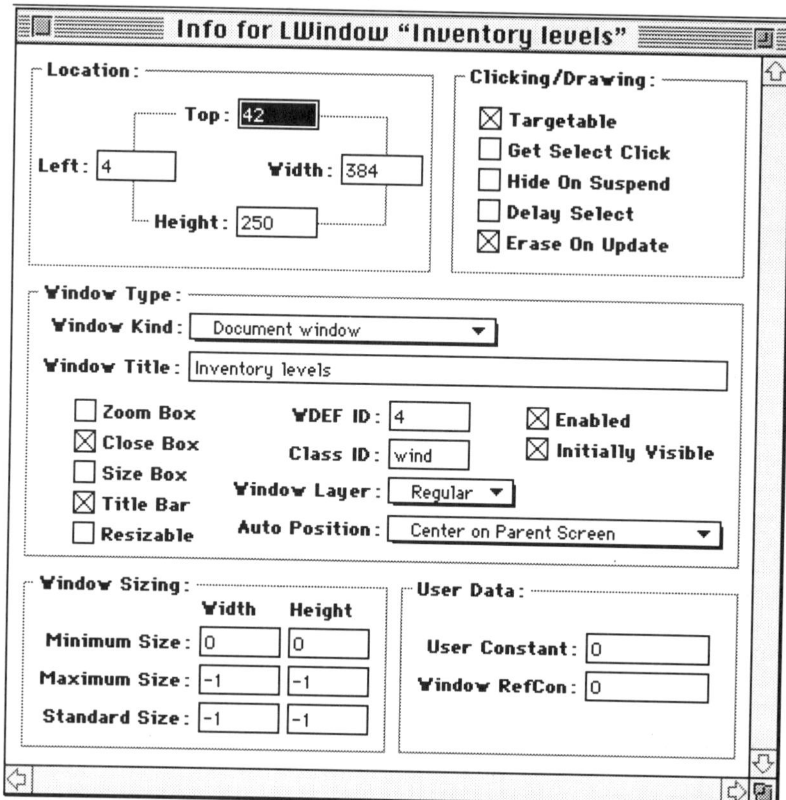

NOTE

If the Tools palette was visible the last time you used Constructor, it will open automatically whenever you open a view. However, if the Tools palette isn't visible when a view is open, choose Show Tool Palette from the Display menu to make it appear.

In this case, the new pane appears as a small square (Figure 5.8). However, the initial state and size of a given type of object depends on the class from which the object has been created.

Notice in Figure 5.9 that the new pane has been given a resource ID of 0. You will need to change this, along with any other properties of the pane that must be modified to fit your program's needs. If resource IDs aren't visible, display them by choosing ShowPane IDs from the Display menu; if you no longer want to see the pane IDs, choose Hide Pane IDs from the Display menu.

Figure 5.7 The Constructor Tools palette

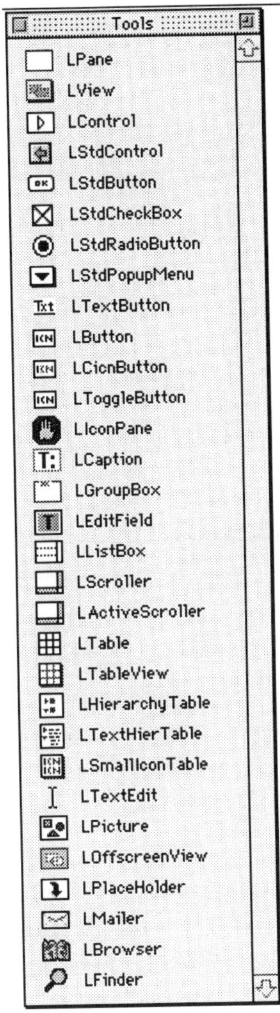

NOTE

One of the most frustrating deficiencies of Constructor 2.1 is that it doesn't provide tools for aligning objects within a view. However, you can nudge objects one pixel at a time using the arrow keys. You can also force objects to align to a grid by choosing Snap to Grid from the Arrange menu. The Arrange menu's Edit Grid option lets you set the number of pixels between grid points.

Figure 5.8 A new LPane object in a view

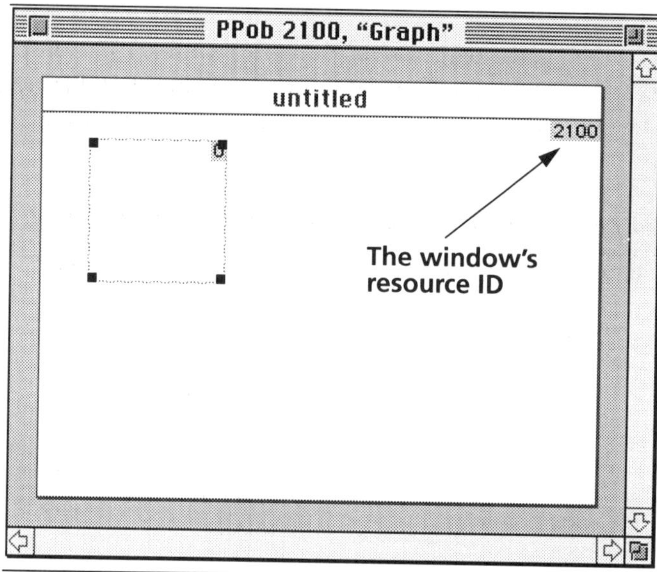

When an object is highlighted, you can use the mouse to drag it around a view and use the object's handles to resize it. In this case, the view's single object should fill the entire view (with the exception of the title bar).

Setting Basic Object Properties

There are some basic properties that must be set for every object you add to a view, regardless of what else you do to the way in which the view appears. First, each new object must be given its own unique resource ID. Duplicate resource IDs may cause a running program to use the wrong object, producing bugs that may cause program crashes because of memory allocation problems.

In addition, a pane that represents an object from a derived class won't function correctly unless the pane is somehow linked to its class. For the example we are following, this means that the pane that will display the graph must be identified as a definition for the Graph class. To make this change, you must replace the LPane object's default four-character ID with the ID that has been chosen for the Graph class. The choice of an ID for a subclass is arbitrary, but it must be unique within the entire program. In other words, it must be different from the IDs used by all other PowerPlant classes.

To set an object's two basic properties, do the following:

1. Double-click on the object to display its properties window. The properties for an object of class LPane (or a class derived from LPane) appear in Figure 5.9. As you can see, the default resource ID is 0 and the default class ID is *pane*.

Figure 5.9 Configuration options for an object of class LPane

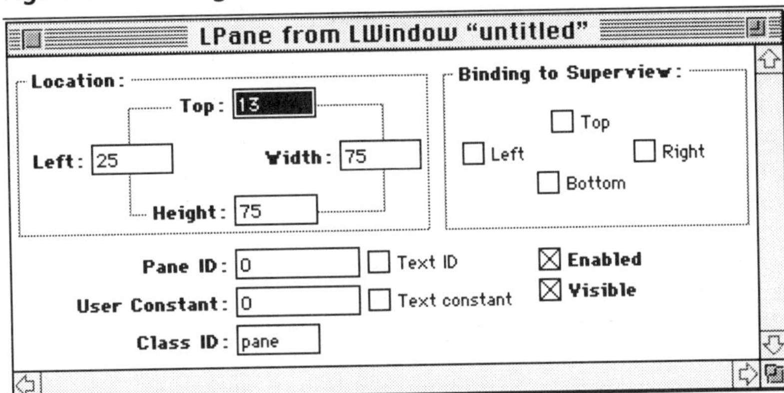

2. Replace the default resource ID with the resource ID you've chosen for the object. Note that in a properties window, the resource ID box is labeled "Pane ID." For this example, the ID is 2101.

> **NOTE**
>
> *Because resource IDs are arbitrary, it helps to have some scheme for numbering resources that makes sense to you. The Penultimate Videos program uses the first two digits of the ID to represent the PowerPlant object (for example, the 21 in 2100). The last two digits are a sequential number within the PowerPlant object. The graph view's single pane is therefore numbered 2101.*

3. Replace the default class ID with the ID you've chosen for the subclass, which in this case is *grph*.
4. If necessary, use the Location boxes to set the size of the object. In this case, using –1 for the top and left edges makes sure that the pane that will hold the graph is anchored at the top left corner of the LWindow object. The height and width are expressed in pixels.

5. The pane is also bound to its superview (the LWindow object) on all four corners. This means that as the superview is resized, the pane is resized as well. You will read more about binding in the next section of this chapter.
6. The completed properties window appears as in Figure 5.10. Close the properties window to save the changes.

Figure 5.10 The completed properties for an object of class Graph

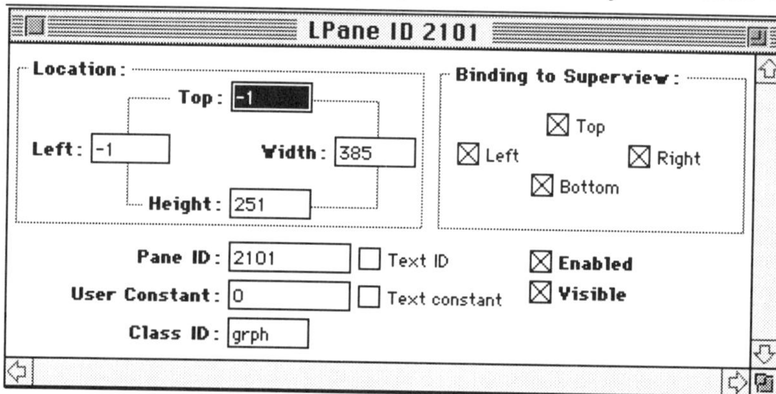

At this point, the PowerPlant object is ready to use. Don't forget, however, that the program that uses this object must register the class from which the object is created by calling `URegistrar::RegisterClass`:

```
URegistrar::RegisterClass('grph',Graph::CreateGraphStream);
```

The function call specifies the class's ID, as well as the name of the function that should be called to create an object of this class from an input stream. By convention, such functions have the name `Create`*X*`Stream`, where *X* is the name of the class.

PANE BINDING

Binding attaches one or more sides of a pane to its superview such that when the superview is resized, the side of the pane remains the same distance from the side of the superview. If a pane is bound on all four sides, then resizing the pane's superview stretches or shrinks the pane to fit within the superview's new size. However, if a pane is bound on only two sides, such as the top and left, then resizing the superview keeps the pane in the same position relative to the superview's top and left but allows the pane's right and bottom edges to move. The result is that the pane doesn't change size. By the same token, a pane that is not bound to its superview will remain in the same location and stay the same size when the superview is resized.

The type of binding you use therefore depends on the type of pane you are creating and the way in which you want the pane to move or change size when the superview is resized:

- A control—such as a standard button, push button, or check box—is usually bound to its superview on two sides (either top and left or bottom and right).
- A pane used for display (such as the Graph pane) or a pane used for entering the contents of a document (such as a pane of class LTextEdit) is usually bound on all four sides.

The Graph Subclass and Its Constructors

At a minimum, a subclass needs to include its own constructors and, optionally, a destructor. Most PowerPlant classes have at least two constructors, one that creates an object using data supplied in the function's parameter list and another that creates an object using data from an input stream defined in a resource file. In Listing 5.2, for example, you can see both types of constructors.

In the case of the Graph class, the default constructor, which could be used to accept data in its parameter list, is empty. Because objects of the Graph class will always be created as PowerPlant objects using data from a resource file, there is no need to complete the first type of constructor.

The second constructor expects an object of class LStream as input. Its sole action is to call the base class constructor. Although in some cases you may need to add additional functionality to a stream input constructor, keep in mind that in this particular example the reason for creating the Graph class was to allow the program to override the DrawSelf function. All other class actions are the same as the base class, and therefore a call to the base class constructor will suffice.

Listing 5.2 Constructors and destructor for the Graph class

```
#include <LStream.h>
#include <UTextTraits.h>
#include <UDrawingState.h>

#include "graph.h"
// converts an integer to a pascal string
extern void itoaP (int, Str255);

Graph * Graph::CreateGraphStream (LStream * inStream)
    { return (new Graph(inStream)); }

Graph::Graph()
{
    // default constructor does nothing
}

Graph::Graph (LStream * inStream)
    : LPane (inStream)
{
    // call the base class constructor
}

Graph::~Graph()
{
    // default destructor deletes object but does nothing else
}

void Graph::FinishCreateSelf()
{
    // no work here either
}
```

NOTE

As with many PowerPlant classes, there are no actions that need to be taken when an object of class Graph is destroyed. Therefore, although the member functions include a destructor, the body of the destructor is empty.

The Create*X*Stream Function and How PowerPlant Objects Are Created

In addition to one or more constructors and a destructor, a class whose objects are defined as PowerPlant objects includes a function whose name takes the form `CreateXStream`, where *X* is the name of the class. This function initiates actions that take care of reading the resource data and creating the object.

A `CreateXStream` function is usually very simple: It uses the `new` operator to create an object of class *X*, returning a pointer to that object. Because you can't call a constructor directly (except when calling a base class constructor in a derived class's constructor, of course), this function provides the necessary mechanism for creating an object whose characteristics are provided to the program as an input stream.

Where does the actual resource read occur? It is triggered by a series of functions that are executed when the graph window is created. The process begins with a call to the Penultimate Video's `DisplayGraph` function, which can be found in Listing 5.3. Notice that the function contains only one line: a call to the `CreateWindow` function.

Listing 5.3 Creating the graph window

```
// ******************************************************************
//      • DisplayGraph
// ******************************************************************
// Display a graph of items in inventory to demonstrate using
// QuickDraw commands in a pane.

void CPPVideoStoreApp::DisplayGraph()
{
    LWindow * theWindow = LWindow::CreateWindow (WINDOW_GRAPH, this);
}
```

`CreateWindow` takes two parameters: the resource ID of the window being created, and a pointer to the object that should become the new window's supercommander. In many cases, new windows—whether they are document windows or dialog boxes—use the object whose member function creates the window as their supercommander. (In this example, an application object function is creating the window.) Therefore, the second parameter is often `this`.

The sequence of actions initiated by the call to CreateWindow appears in Listing 5.4. As you can see, CreateWindow begins by setting the new object's supercommander. It then calls UReanimator::ReadObjects (the second function in Listing 5.4), passing the resource ID and resource type as input parameters.

ReadObjects does the following:

- Creates an object of class StResource to store the resource identification data that was passed in as function parameters. Notice that because this class's name begins with "St," we know that it is a stack-based class that restores parameters when it terminates.
- Moves the resource identification data upward in memory and places it in a non-relocatable block of memory, in a locked relocatable block, or at the top of the heap using the ToolBox routine HLockHi. HLockHi finishes by locking the block of memory now occupied by the resource.
- Creates an object of class LDataStream that will hold the resource read from the file. The two input parameters are a pointer to the resource identification data's handle and the size of the block of memory occupied by that data.
- Calls the ReadData function of the LDataStream object to retrieve the resource from the file. (This function is inherited from LStream and is implemented as an inline function in *LStream.h*). As you can see in Listing 5.4, ReadData calls the LDataStream function GetBytes, which actually performs the read.

Once the data describing the new object have been read from the file, ReadObjects creates the object with a call to the UReanimator function ObjectsFromStream (Listing 5.5), passing in the stream containing the data. The main structure in ObjectsFromStream is a do while loop that continues as long as the stream contains tags that identify parts of a resource. The tags are recognized in a switch using the enum values in Listing 5.6.

If the tag indicates that data about an object follows (tag of tag_ObjectData), ObjectsFromStream extracts the object data from the stream, and then calls the URegistrar function CreateObject (Listing 5.7). This function finds the class ID of the object being created in the table of classes built when PowerPlant object classes were registered at the beginning of the program. It then calls the Create*X*Stream function for the class from which the object is being created, which finally gets around to actually creating the object and drawing it on the screen.

If the tag indicates the beginning of a subpane (tag_BeginSub), ObjectsFromStream calls itself to create the subpane(s). Given the way PowerPlant objects are stored in a resource file, the pane is created first, followed by all of its subpanes.

The order in which panes are created can sometimes be important. For example, if you plan to store subpane IDs as part of an object, you can't extract those IDs until the subpanes have been created. The code to store the subpane IDs therefore can't be

Listing 5.4 Using a PowerPlant resource to generate a visible screen object

```
LWindow* LWindow::CreateWindow(ResIDT inWindowID,LCommander *inSuperCommander)
{
    SetDefaultCommander(inSuperCommander);
    LWindow *theWindow = (LWindow*) UReanimator::ReadObjects('PPob', inWindowID);
    theWindow->FinishCreate();
    if (theWindow->HasAttribute(windAttr_ShowNew))
        theWindow->Show();
    return theWindow;
}

void * UReanimator::ReadObjects(OSType inResType,ResIDT inResID)
{
    StResource objectRes(inResType, inResID);
    ::HLockHi(objectRes.mResourceH);
    LDataStream objectStream(*objectRes.mResourceH,
        ::GetHandleSize(objectRes.mResourceH));
    Int16 ppobVersion;
    objectStream.ReadData(&ppobVersion, sizeof(Int16));
    SignalIf_(ppobVersion != 2);
    void *theObject = ObjectsFromStream(&objectStream);
    return theObject;
}

// This inline function is found in LStream.h
virtual Int32 ReadData(void *outBuffer, Int32 inByteCount)
                    {
                        GetBytes(outBuffer, inByteCount);
                        return inByteCount;
                    }
}

ExceptionCode LDataStream::GetBytes(void *outBuffer, Int32 &ioByteCount)
{
    ExceptionCodeerr = noErr;
                        // Upper bound is number of bytes from
                        //   marker to end
    if (GetMarker() + ioByteCount > GetLength()) {
        ioByteCount = GetLength() - GetMarker();
        err = readErr;
    }
    ::BlockMoveData((Int8*) mBuffer + GetMarker(), outBuffer, ioByteCount);
    SetMarker(ioByteCount, streamFrom_Marker);
    return err;
}
```

part of a constructor. However, you *can* put code that needs to execute after all panes are created in a `FinishCreateSelf` function. If you look back at Listing 5.4, you'll notice that after calling `ReadObjects`, the `CreateWindow` function calls its own `FinishCreate` function, which is actually inherited from the LView class. As you

Listing 5.5 UReanimator::ObjectsFromStream

```
void* UReanimator::ObjectsFromStream(LStream *inStream)
{
    void    *firstObject = nil;
    ClassIDT aliasClassID = 'null';

                        // Save current defaults
    LCommander *defaultCommander = LCommander::GetDefaultCommander();
    LView   *defaultView = LPane::GetDefaultView();
    Boolean readingTags = true;

    do {
        void *currentObject = nil;// Object created by current tag
        TagID theTag = tag_End;
        // read the next tag to figure out what type of data follow
        inStream->ReadData(&theTag, sizeof(TagID));

        switch (theTag) {
            case tag_ObjectData: {
                    // Restore default Commander and View
                LCommander::SetDefaultCommander(defaultCommander);
                LPane::SetDefaultView(defaultView);

                    // Object data consists of a byte length, class ID,
                    // and then the data for the object. We use the
                    // byte length to manually set the stream marker
                    // after creating the object just in case the
                    // object constructor doesn't read all the data.

                Int32 dataLength;
                inStream->ReadData(&dataLength, sizeof(Int32));
                Int32  dataStart = inStream->GetMarker();

                ClassIDT classID;
                inStream->ReadData(&classID, sizeof(ClassIDT));

                if (aliasClassID != 'null') {
                        // The previous tag specified an Alias for
                        // the ID of this Class
                    classID = aliasClassID;
                }

                currentObject = URegistrar::CreateObject(classID, inStream);
                inStream->SetMarker(dataStart + dataLength, streamFrom_Start);

                aliasClassID = 'null'; // Alias is no longer in effect
```

Continued next page

Listing 5.5 UReanimator::ObjectsFromStream

```
        if (currentObject == nil  &&  classID != 'null') {
            SignalPStr_("\pnil object created from tag");
        }
        break;

    case tag_BeginSubs:
        currentObject = ObjectsFromStream(inStream);
        break;

    case tag_EndSubs:
    case tag_End:
        readingTags = false;
        break;

    case tag_UserObject: {

            // The UserObject tag is only needed for the Constructor
            // view editing program. It tells Constructor to treat
            // the following object as if it were an object of the
            // specified superclass (which must be a PowerPlant
            // class that Constructor knows about). We don't need
            // this information here, so we just read and ignore
            // the superclass ID.

        ClassIDT superClassID;
        inStream->ReadData(&superClassID, sizeof(ClassIDT));
        break;

    case tag_ClassAlias:

            // The ClassAlias tag defines the ClassID the for
            // the next object in the Stream. This allows you
            // to define an object which belongs to a subclass
            // of another class, but has the same data as that
            // other class.

        inStream->ReadData(&aliasClassID, sizeof(ClassIDT));
        break;

    default:
        SignalPStr_("\pUnrecognized Tag");
        readingTags = false;
        break;
```

Continued next page

Listing 5.5 UReanimator::ObjectsFromStream

```
        }

        if (firstObject == nil) {
            firstObject = currentObject;
        }

    } while (readingTags);

    return firstObject;
}
```

Listing 5.6 An enum for resource tags

```
enum {
    tag_ObjectData = 'objd',
    tag_BeginSubs = 'begs',
    tag_EndSubs = 'ends',
    tag_Include = 'incl',
    tag_UserObject = 'user',
    tag_ClassAlias = 'dopl',
    tag_End = 'end.',

    object_Null = 'null'
};
```

Listing 5.7 URegistrar::CreateObject

```
void* URegistrar::CreateObject (ClassIDT inClassID, LStream *inStream)
{
    void*theObject = nil;
    Int16 index = FetchClassIndex(inClassID);
    if (index != 0) {
        theObject = (*(*sTableH)[index - 1].creatorFunc)(inStream);
    }

    return theObject;
}
```

can see in Listing 5.8, `FinishCreate` sets up an iterator (an object of class LListIterator) to handle the object's linked list of subpanes. It then performs `FinishCreate` for each subpane, and finally calls `FinishCreateSelf` for the object itself. By default, LWindow inherits an empty `FinishCreateSelf` from LPane. However, if you need to add something to that function, you should create a subclass for your pane or view and override the default.

Listing 5.8 Functions to finish creating an object

```
void LView::FinishCreate()
{
    LListIterator iterator(mSubPanes, iterate_FromStart);
    LPane *theSub;
    while (iterator.Next(&theSub)) {
        theSub->FinishCreate();
    }

    if (mSuperView != nil) {
        mSuperView->OrientSubPane(this);
    }
    FinishCreateSelf();
}

voidLPane::FinishCreateSelf()
{
    // default function is empty
}
```

Drawing in a Pane

When you draw in a window created as a WIND resource, you use a QuickDraw coordinate system to indicate where elements of the window should appear. However, PowerPlant uses its own coordinate systems for panes and views. You therefore need to understand something about coordinate systems before you can draw directly in a pane. Once you know where you will put the contents of a pane, you can start drawing using QuickDraw commands. In this section, you will first be introduced to PowerPlant coordinates systems and then see how drawing in a pane takes place.

Coordinate Systems

The QuickDraw drawing coordinate system, limited as it is to 16-bit coordinate values, provides coordinates in the range –32,768 to 32,767. Calculations in the first PowerPlant manual suggest that this holds about 100 pages of text.

The PowerPlant drawing area, however, uses 32-bit coordinate values in the range 0 to 2,147,483,647. According that same manual, going to 32 bits provides storage for over 3.3 million pages of text. In addition to the PowerPlant coordinate system, each view and grafport has its own coordinate system. To keep this all straight, PowerPlant actually works with four separate coordinate systems, which are summarized in Table 5.1. To make your life easier, PowerPlant also supplies several functions that convert among these four coordinate systems (see Table 5.2).

Table 5.1 PowerPlant coordinate systems

Coordinate System	Size	Top Left	Use
Global	16-bit	Top left corner of main screen	Used primarily by QuickDraw. Used in PowerPlant programs only when ToolBox calls require global coordinates.
Port	16-bit	Top left corner of current grafport	Normal QuickDraw coordinate system used when not working with PowerPlant objects.
Image	32-bit	Top left corner of image	Coordinates used in drawing spaces defined by classes descended from LView. Coordinates are typically mapped to local coordinates for drawing.
Local	16- or 32-bit	Maps top left corner of image to top left corner of grafport	Used most frequently for drawing in a PowerPlant pane or view.

The way in which you use these coordinate systems depends to some extent on whether what you are drawing fits within the QuickDraw coordinate system. If this is the case, then image and local coordinates are the same. PowerPlant routines use `::SetOrigin` to make the top left corner of the port the same as the top left corner

Table 5.2 Coordinate conversion functions

Function	From	To
`GlobalToPortPoint`	Global	Port
`PortToGlobalPoint`	Port	Global
`PortToLocalPoint`	Port	Local
`LocalToPortPoint`	Local	Port
`LocalToImagePoint`	Local	Image
`ImageToLocalPoint`	Image	Local

of the image. At that point, you can use QuickDraw routines for drawing, just as you would if your program wasn't using PowerPlant.

However, if your drawing is larger than the QuickDraw drawing space, then you will have to map your coordinates into a QuickDraw space before you can draw anything. The first step is to determine whether your image fits within the QuickDraw space, using one of the following two functions, both of which are member functions of LView:

- `ImageRectIntersectsFrame`: Takes the image coordinates of a rectangle as input parameters and returns a Boolean that indicates whether any part of that rectangle intersects the frame of the view calling the function.
- `ImagePointIsInFrame`: Takes image coordinates of a point as input parameters, converts them to port coordinates, and returns a Boolean that indicates whether the point falls within the frame of the pane or view calling the function.

If the call to `ImageRectIntersectsFrame` or `ImagePointIsInFrame` returns FALSE, you will then need to convert the image coordinates to local coordinates, using `ImageToLocalPoint`, before you can draw.

DOING THE DRAWING

Often, as with the inventory graph that you saw in Figure 5.1, a drawing easily fits within the QuickDraw drawing space. That being the case, a program can immediately begin drawing without any coordinate conversions. However, you still need to figure out the local coordinates of the frame within which drawing will occur.

Listing 5.9 contains the `DrawSelf` function from the Graph class. The bulk of the function is taken up with QuickDraw calls that produce the graph (along with some simple math that determines the intervals on the *y*-axis and the height of the bars). Nonetheless, there are two PowerPlant tasks that must be performed before drawing can begin:

Listing 5.9 The Graph class's DrawSelf function

```
// ************************************************************
// • DrawSelf
// ************************************************************
// This is where all the work takes place

void Graph::DrawSelf()
{
    extern int Movie_count, Other_count, Game_count;  // gain access to the globals

    StColorPenState theState; // used to save current pen state; restored on destruction
    Rect frame; // "frame" is superview's local coordinates; used for all drawing
    int xAxis, yAxis; // length of axes
    int usableArea, barWidth, maxCount, intervalSize, barTop, barLeft, axisPoint;
    Rect bar;
    Str255 axisLabel;

    // get superview's local coordinates
    CalcLocalFrameRect (frame);
    ::PenNormal();
    ::PenMode (patCopy);

    // draw the graph axes
    ::MoveTo (frame.left + MARGIN, frame.top + MARGIN);
    ::LineTo (frame.left + MARGIN, frame.bottom - MARGIN);
    ::LineTo (frame.right - MARGIN, frame.bottom - MARGIN);

    // figure out the sizes and positions of the three bars
    xAxis = frame.right - frame.left - (MARGIN * 2);
    yAxis = frame.bottom - frame.top - (MARGIN * 2);
    usableArea = xAxis - (SPACE_BETWEEN * NUMB_BARS);
    barWidth = usableArea / NUMB_BARS;

    // figure out maximum of the three counts; this becomes number of intervals on y axis
    maxCount = Movie_count;
    if (Other_count > maxCount)
        maxCount = Other_count;
    if (Game_count > maxCount)
        maxCount = Game_count;

    // compute interval size
    intervalSize = yAxis / maxCount;

    // Label the y axis
    ::TextFont (geneva);
    ::TextSize (TEXT_SIZE);
    ::ForeColor (blueColor);
```

Continued next page

Listing 5.9 (Continued) The Graph class's DrawSelf function

```
// Top
::MoveTo (frame.left + MARGIN - SPACE_BETWEEN, frame.top + MARGIN + TEXT_SIZE);
itoaP (maxCount, axisLabel);
::DrawString (axisLabel);
::ForeColor (blackColor);
::MoveTo (frame.left + MARGIN - 6, frame.top + MARGIN + (TEXT_SIZE/2));
::LineTo (frame.left + MARGIN + 6, frame.top + MARGIN + (TEXT_SIZE/2));

// Middle
::ForeColor (blueColor);
axisPoint = yAxis / 2; // find middle of y axis
::MoveTo (frame.left + MARGIN - SPACE_BETWEEN, frame.top + MARGIN + axisPoint +
    (TEXT_SIZE/2));
itoaP (maxCount / 2, axisLabel);
::DrawString (axisLabel);
::ForeColor (blackColor);
::MoveTo (frame.left + MARGIN - 6, frame.top + MARGIN + axisPoint);

::LineTo (frame.left + MARGIN + 6, frame.top + MARGIN + axisPoint);

// Bottom
::ForeColor (blueColor);
::MoveTo (frame.left + MARGIN - SPACE_BETWEEN, frame.top + MARGIN + yAxis +
    (TEXT_SIZE/2));
itoaP (0,axisLabel);
::DrawString (axisLabel);
::ForeColor (blackColor);
::MoveTo (frame.left + MARGIN - 6, frame.top + MARGIN + yAxis);
::LineTo (frame.left + MARGIN, frame.top + MARGIN + yAxis);

// first bar
// Note: SetRect uses "left, top, right, bottom" -- go figure ...
barTop = (yAxis - (intervalSize * Movie_count)) + frame.top + MARGIN;
::SetRect (&bar, frame.left + MARGIN + SPACE_BETWEEN, barTop, frame.left + MARGIN +
    SPACE_BETWEEN + barWidth, frame.bottom - MARGIN);
::ForeColor (redColor);
::PaintRect (&bar);

// second bar
barTop = (yAxis - (intervalSize * Other_count)) + frame.top + MARGIN;
barLeft = frame.left + MARGIN + (SPACE_BETWEEN * 2) + barWidth;
::SetRect (&bar, barLeft, barTop, barLeft + barWidth, frame.bottom - MARGIN);
::ForeColor (blueColor);
::PaintRect (&bar);
```

Continued next page

Listing 5.9 (Continued) The Graph class's DrawSelf function

```
    width = ::TextWidth (otherLabel, 1, 12);
    indent = (barWidth/2) - (width/2);
    ::MoveTo (frame.left + MARGIN + (SPACE_BETWEEN * 2) + barWidth + indent,
        frame.bottom - 30);
    ::DrawString (otherLabel);

    width = ::TextWidth (gameLabel, 1, 5);
    indent = (barWidth/2) - (width/2);
    ::MoveTo (frame.left + MARGIN + (SPACE_BETWEEN * 3) + (barWidth * 2) + indent,
        frame.bottom - 30);
    ::DrawString (gameLabel);
}
    // third bar
    barTop = (yAxis - (intervalSize * Game_count)) + frame.top + MARGIN;
    barLeft = frame.left + MARGIN + (SPACE_BETWEEN * 3) + (barWidth * 2);
    ::SetRect (&bar, barLeft, barTop, barLeft + barWidth, frame.bottom - MARGIN);
    ::ForeColor (yellowColor);
    ::PaintRect (&bar);

    // Label x axis
    Str255 movieLabel = "\pMovies";
    Str255 otherLabel = "\pMisc. Videos";
    Str255 gameLabel = "\pGames";

    ::ForeColor (blueColor);

    int width = ::TextWidth (movieLabel, 1, 6);
    int indent = (barWidth/2) - (width/2);
    ::MoveTo (frame.left + MARGIN + SPACE_BETWEEN + indent, frame.bottom - 30);
    ::DrawString (movieLabel);

    int width = ::TextWidth (movieLabel, 1, 6);
    int indent = (barWidth/2) - (width/2);
    ::MoveTo (frame.left + MARGIN + SPACE_BETWEEN + indent, frame.bottom - 30);
    ::DrawString (movieLabel);

    width = ::TextWidth (otherLabel, 1, 12);
    indent = (barWidth/2) - (width/2);
    ::MoveTo (frame.left + MARGIN + (SPACE_BETWEEN * 2) + barWidth + indent,
        frame.bottom - 30);
    ::DrawString (otherLabel);

    width = ::TextWidth (gameLabel, 1, 5);
    indent = (barWidth/2) - (width/2);
    ::MoveTo (frame.left + MARGIN + (SPACE_BETWEEN * 3) + (barWidth * 2) + indent,
        frame.bottom - 30);
    ::DrawString (gameLabel);
}
```

- `Graph::DrawSelf` first saves the current state of the pen using one of PowerPlant's stack-based classes: StColorPenState. The constructor for this class pushes the current pen state onto the stack. When the function terminates and the object is destroyed, the destructor restores the pen state. Saving and restoring the pen state makes sure that windows drawn after the graph window don't appear in strange colors.
- `Graph::DrawSelf` then gets the superview's local coordinates with a call to `CalcLocalFrameRect`. As you will remember, the Graph class is a pane whose superview is a window. The call to `CalcLocalFrameRect` therefore returns the coordinates of the window, with 0,0 at the top left corner, not including the title bar. Since the Graph pane fills the entire area of its superview and since image and local coordinates are the same in this case, finding the superview's local coordinates provides coordinates that can be used for drawing in the Graph pane.

Once the frame coordinates are known, the function gets down to business by drawing the axes, doing the math necessary to determine the height of the bars, drawing the bars, and labeling the axes. Although you can't see the color in Figure 5.1, the bars will appear on your screen in red, blue, and yellow. The axes are black and the axis labels are blue.

Playing a QuickTime Movie: Panes without PPobs

A pane does not necessarily have to be defined as a PowerPlant object. There are some circumstances under which you might want to create a pane by filling the fields in the data structure that defines a pane and then passing that structure to the appropriate constructor. As an example of why and how you might do this, we'll be taking a look at playing a QuickTime movie in a pane.

The movie pane appears in a window that is a defined as a WIND resource (Figure 5.11). The pane will therefore be defined to fill the entire body of the window.

PowerPlant provides two classes for interacting with QuickTime—UQuickTime and LMovieController—both of which can be found in *UQuickTime.cpp*. The UQuickTime class supports the QuickTime environment, including initializing QuickTime and retrieving a movie from a file. LMovieController defines a QuickDraw movie controller and handles actually playing the movie.

Figure 5.11 The WIND resource (ResEdit format) in which the pane for a QuickTime movie will appear

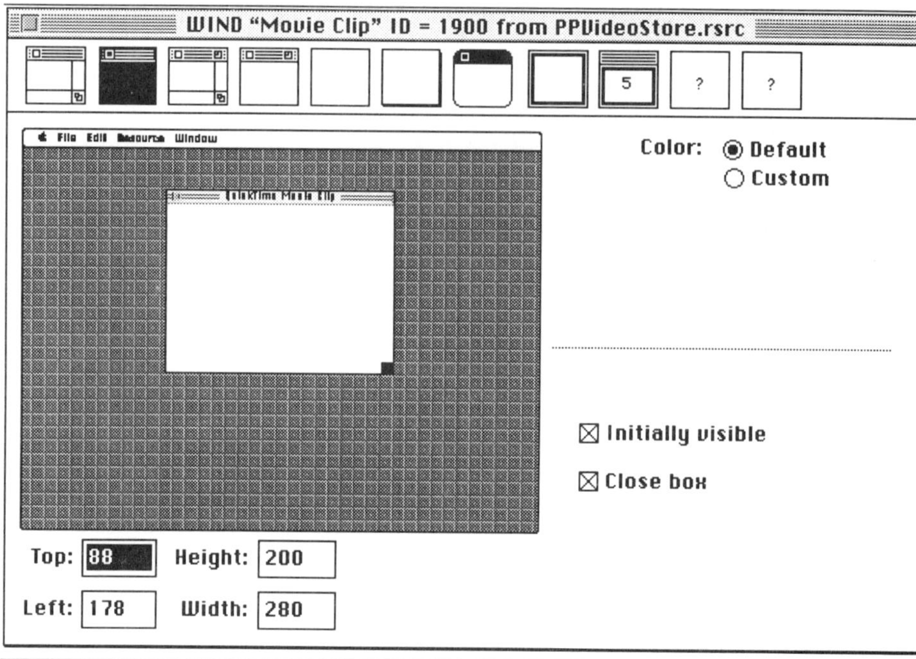

Using these two classes, playing a QuickTime movie requires the following steps:

- Initialize QuickTime. This is usually handled in the application object's constructor by calling `UQuickTime::Initialize`. You only need to do it once at the beginning of the program rather than each time you want to play a movie.
- Retrieve the movie from its file using `UQuickTime::GetMovieFromFile`. The function displays a QuickTime Get File dialog box (Figure 5.12), retrieves the selected movie, stores it in memory, and returns a movie identifier to the calling function.
- Create a window object that will serve as the superview of the pane in which the movie will play.
- Initialize the pane.
- Create the movie controller by creating a new object of class LMovieController.
- Display the window (for example, Figure 5.13). At this point, the PowerPlant application takes over and processes the events generated when the user plays the movie.
- Close QuickTime. This can be done in the application object's `SendAEQuit` function or in the application object's destructor.

Figure 5.12 Retrieving a QuickTime movie from a file

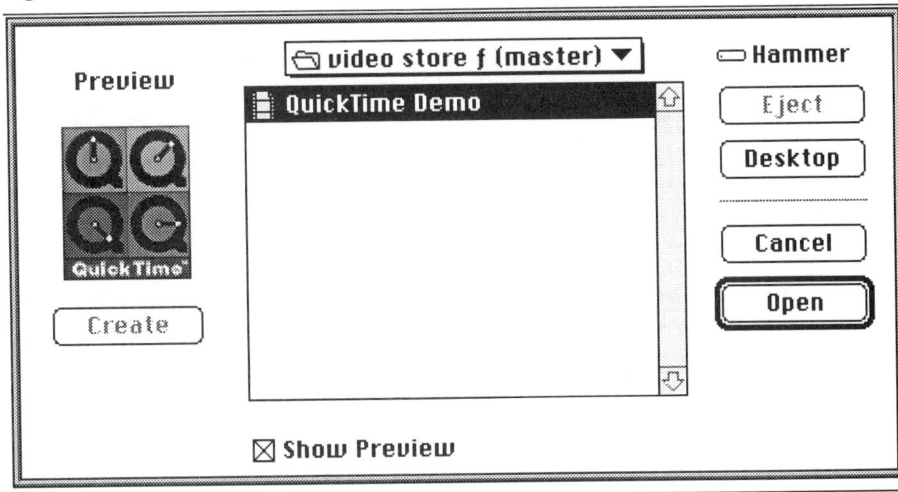

Figure 5.13 The QuickTime movie in a pane in a window

The Penultimate Videos application sets up its QuickTime movie player in its `ViewQuickTime` function (Listing 5.10). The code first uses `GetMovieFromFile` to load the movie into memory and provide a movie identifier for the remaining QuickTime-related function calls to use. It then creates the window, passing the parameters directly to the LWindow constructor rather than using a PowerPlant object. Once the window object has been created, the function initializes an SPane-Info structure that contains all the data needed to define a pane. Notice that the fields in the structure correspond directly to the pane characteristics you specify when you define a pane as a PowerPlant resource.

> **NOTE**
> *Documentation for the structures used by PowerPlant can be found in the PP Core Reference manual. See the "PowerPlant Reference Glossary and Notes" at the end of the book.*

The next step is to create an LMovieController object, passing the SPaneInfo structure and the movie identifier as parameters to the constructor. Then, the function only needs to show the window. As mentioned earlier, PowerPlant responds to events generated by the movie controller and plays the movie.

Custom Panes

A custom pane is a derived class whose objects can be defined as PowerPlant objects. You might decide, for example, to create a custom control that is derived from LControl or LStdControl. In the example we'll be considering, the custom pane is derived directly from LPane.

Many Macintosh programs use thermometers to show the user the progress of an action that takes a bit of time. To demonstrate a custom pane, Penultimate Videos displays the little window in Figure 5.14. As you would expect, the thermometer begins with an empty box that is filled with a progressively longer bar as saving data proceeds.

Defining the Custom Pane

The easiest way to create a custom pane is to work with Constructor. Once you've decided on the custom pane's base class and know what attributes you want to add to your pane, you're ready to begin the following process:

1. Highlight Custom Pane Types in the Constructor window and create a new item. A new untitled custom pane appears.
2. Highlight the new custom pane and press ⌘-I to display its Info window (for example, Figure 5.15). Give the custom pane a resource ID and a name. Leave its re-

Listing 5.10 Setting up a QuickTime movie

```
void CPPVideoStoreApp::ViewQuickTime (SDialogResponse * dialogResponse)
{
    Movie theMovie = UQuickTime::GetMovieFromFile();

    if (theMovie == nil)
        return;

    // Create a window by passing parameters directly to constructor rather than
    // as a PowerPlant object.
    // Parameters: (1) resource ID; (2) window attributes; (3) pointer to superview
    LWindow * theWindow = new LWindow (WINDOW_MOVIE_CLIP,windAttr_Regular +
        windAttr_Enabled + windAttr_Targetable, this);

    // Initialize the structure that defines the pane
    SPaneInfo thePaneInfo;
    thePaneInfo.paneID = CLIP_PANE;
    thePaneInfo.width = 280;
    thePaneInfo.height = 200;
    thePaneInfo.left = 10;
    thePaneInfo.top = 15;
    thePaneInfo.visibile = true;
    thePaneInfo.enabled = true;
    thePaneInfo.bindings.left = false;
    thePaneInfo.bindings.right = false;
    thePaneInfo.bindings.top = false;
    thePaneInfo.bindings.bottom = false;
    thePaneInfo.userCon = 0;
    thePaneInfo.superView = theWindow;

    LMovieController * theMovieController = new LMovieController (thePaneInfo,
        theMovie);

    theWindow->Show();
}
```

Figure 5.14 Showing the progress of saving data

source type as CPPb, which identifies it as a custom PowerPlant resource. Close the Info window to save the changes.

Figure 5.15 The custom pane Info window

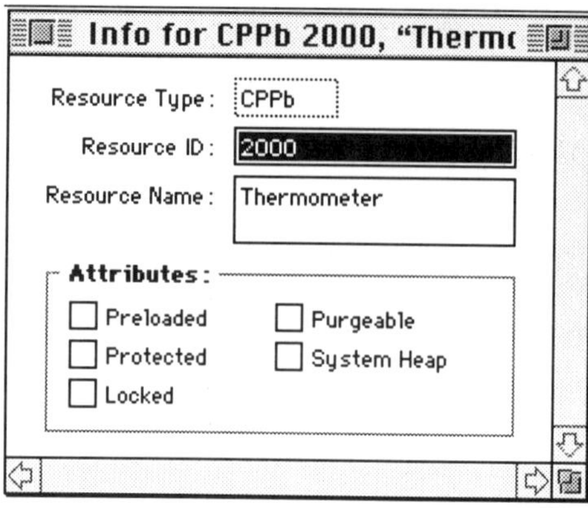

3. Double-click on the custom pane resource to open its window. You will see only the name of the class. A Tools palette displaying data types of attributes you can add to the class also appears (see Figure 5.16).

Figure 5.16 The custom pane Tools palette

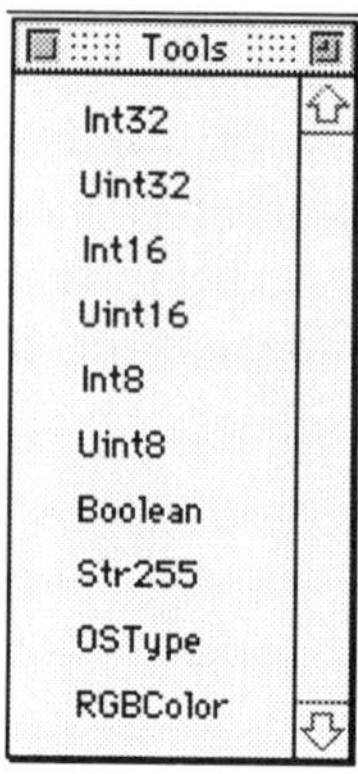

4. Double-click on the name of the class to display its properties window. As you can see in Figure 5.17, you use this window to set the class ID, to specify the size of the pane, and to indicate the ID of the base class from which it is derived (the superclass ID).
5. If necessary, add attributes to the class. To do so, drag a data type from the Tools palette into the resource's window. In Figure 5.18, for example, you can see the

Figure 5.17 A custom pane properties window

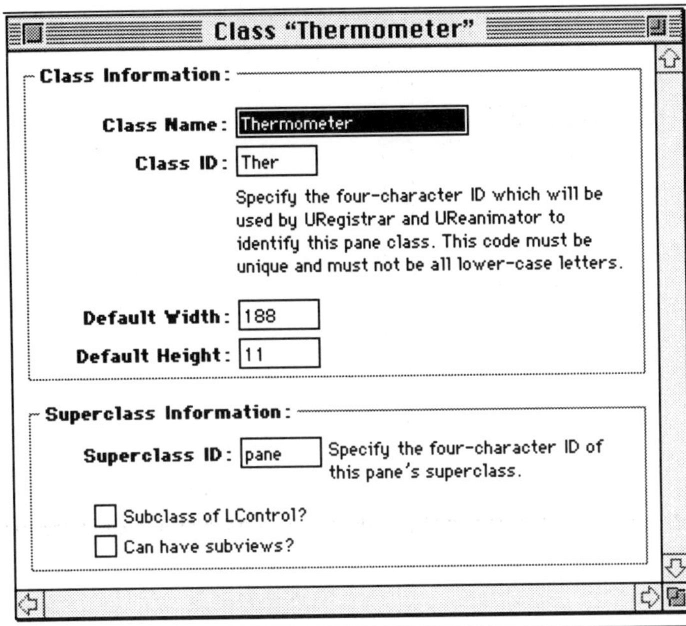

name of the class and the two attributes that have been added to it. In this particular example, the attributes contain the resource IDs of the first and last PICT resources used to display the thermometer. A thermometer is made up of a sequence of still images, just like any other animation (for example, Figure 5.19). As you will see later in this section, the Ther class uses the first and last resource IDs when figuring out which PICT to display at any given time.

Figure 5.18 The content of a custom pane

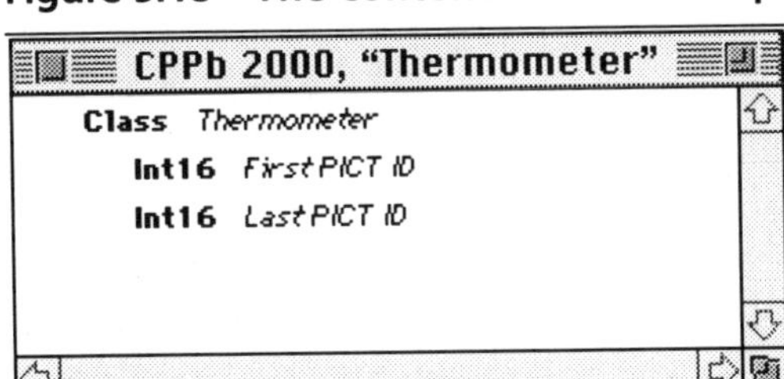

Figure 5.19 PICT resources for a thermometer

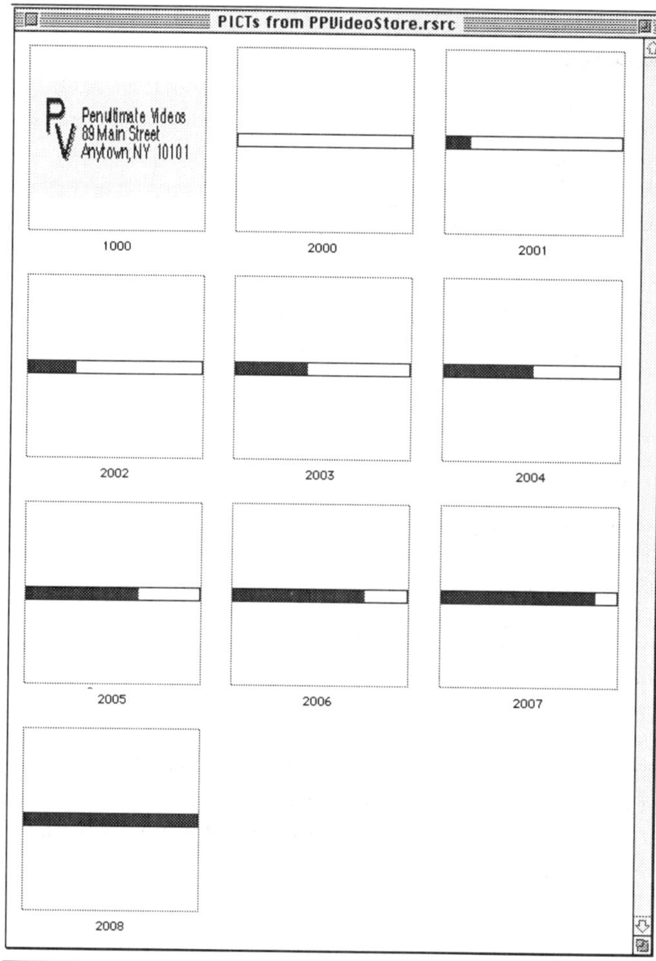

6. Double-click on an attribute to display the attribute's properties window (for example, Figure 5.20). Give the attribute a name and, optionally, a default value. If you want to prevent this attribute from showing up in the pane's properties window, place a check in the Hide Value check box.
7. Repeat Step 6 for each attribute you've added to the custom pane.

At this point, you can use the custom pane in a view. The Penultimate Videos thermometer window (Figure 5.21), for example, is an object of class LWindow. It contains only one pane: an object of class Ther. To add a custom pane object to a view,

Figure 5.20 Custom pane attribute properties

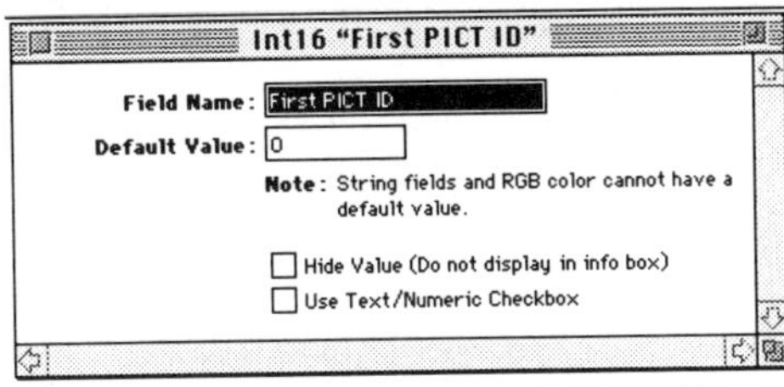

you drag it onto the view, just as you would an object of any other class. As you can see in Figure 5.22, the name of the custom pane type has been added to the bottom of the Tools palette.

Figure 5.21 Using a custom pane

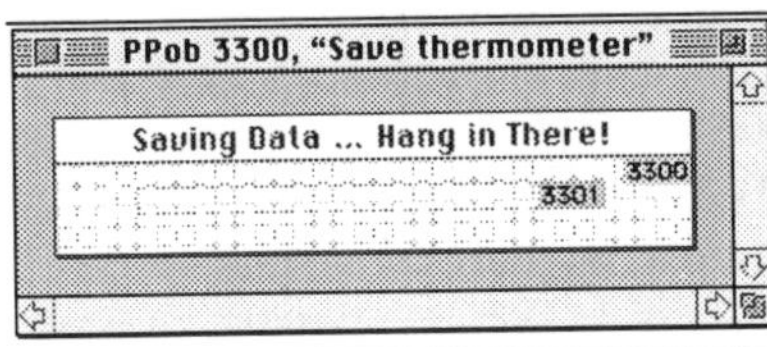

Assuming that the Hide Value check box is empty, the attributes that were added to the custom pane when it was defined appear in the pane's properties box (for example, Figure 5.23). In the case of the thermometer window, this makes it easy to attach the PICT resource IDs.

CREATING THE PANE SUBCLASS

A custom pane class needs a subclass to manage it. At the minimum, it will need constructors, a destructor, and a `DrawSelf` function. As you can see in Listing 5.11, the Ther class contains variables for the first and last PICT ID, along with a variable for the current PICT ID (the PICT to be displayed at any given time). In addition to the `DrawSelf` function, the class includes a function to determine which PICT resource should be displayed, based on the percentage of objects written to the data file.

The implementation of the Ther class is relatively simple, primarily because it inherits most of its behavior from LPane. In Listing 5.12, you can see that the stream input constructor is a bit different from those you have seen previously. The first

Figure 5.22 A custom pane at the bottom of the Tools palette

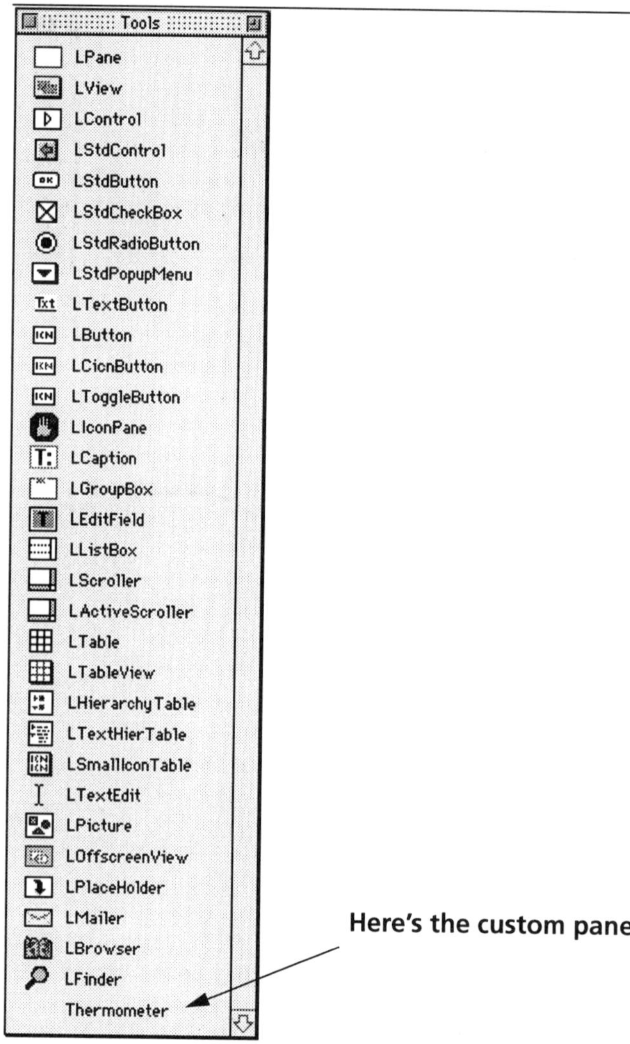

thing it does is to call LPane's constructor. Doing so reads from the file the portion of the resource that has been inherited from LPane. The constructor must then execute code to explicitly read the custom attributes that were added to the derived class using `LStream::ReadData`. The constructor passes `ReadData` a reference to where the attribute's value should be placed and the size of that value.

Figure 5.23 A custom pane object's properties

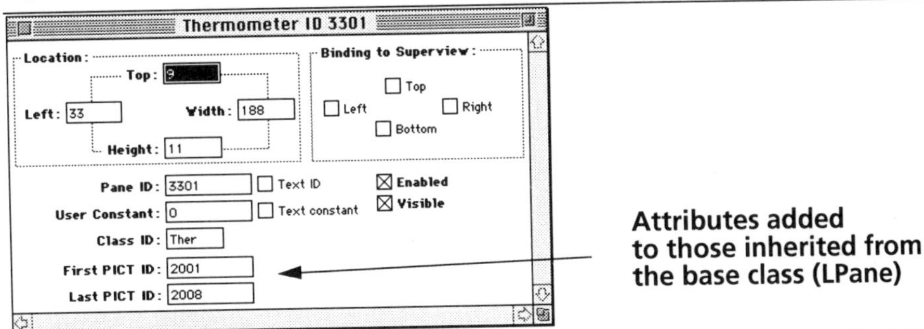

Listing 5.11 The Ther class

```
#include <LPane.h>

class Ther : public LPane
{
    protected:
        ResIDT FirstPictID;
        ResIDT LastPictID;
        ResIDT CurrentPictID;

    public:
        enum { class_ID = 'Ther' };

        static Ther * CreateTherStream (LStream * inStream);
                Ther ();
                Ther (LStream * inStream);
                ~Ther ();

        void DrawSelf();
        void SetCurrentPict (float); // pass in percent complete
};
```

NOTE

The order in which the attributes were declared in Constructor determines the order in which their values are written to a resource file. You must therefore be sure to read the attributes in exactly the same order.

As you would expect, much of the work in this class takes place in its `DrawSelf` function. To actually draw an image in the custom pane, the function does the following:

Listing 5.12 Member functions for the Ther class

```
Ther * Ther::CreateTherStream (LStream * inStream)
{
    return new Ther (inStream);
}

Ther::Ther ()
{
    FirstPictID = FIRST_PICT;
    LastPictID = LAST_PICT;
    CurrentPictID = FIRST_PICT;
}

Ther::Ther (LStream * inStream)
    : LPane (inStream)
{
// Need to read the custom attributes

    inStream->ReadData (&FirstPictID, sizeof (ResIDT));
    inStream->ReadData (&LastPictID, sizeof (ResIDT));
    CurrentPictID = FirstPictID;
}

Ther::~Ther()
{
    // destructor does nothing right now
}


void Ther::DrawSelf ()
{
    // First get a handle to the PICT to be drawn
    PicHandle PictH = ::GetPicture (CurrentPictID);

    Rect theFrame;
    CalcLocalFrameRect (theFrame);

    ::DrawPicture (PictH, &theFrame);
}

void Ther::SetCurrentPict (float PercentComplete)
{
    // The math below works because the PICT IDs are numerically sequentially
    // and begin with a number that ends in zero (2000)
    CurrentPictID = (PercentComplete * (LastPictID - FirstPictID)) + FirstPictID;
    if (CurrentPictID > LastPictID)
        CurrentPictID = LastPictID;
}
```

1. Obtains a handle to the PICT resource to be displayed with the ToolBox routine `GetPicture`.
2. Finds local coordinates of the pane's frame using `CalcLocalFrameRect`, a function inherited from LPane.
3. Uses the ToolBox routine `DrawPicture` to draw the PICT image within the pane's frame.

The image that is displayed in a Ther pane is determined by the percentage of objects that have been written to the data file. To set the ID of the current PICT resource, the `SetCurrentPict` function takes the percent of objects written and does a bit of math. When you examine the function, keep in mind that the math only works if the PICT resources are numbered sequentially and if the first one in the sequence ends with a zero.

Programming for a Window with a Custom Pane

The window containing the thermometer pane is a part of the Penultimate Videos application object's `Unload` function (Listing 5.13). The way in which the thermometer window has been integrated into the data saving process is as follows:

1. Compute the total number of objects to be written to the data file. This will be used to compute the percentage of objects written.
2. Use `LWindow::CreateWindow` to create a thermometer window object.
3. Display the window with the window object's `Show` function.
4. Open the data file for writing.
5. Write object counts to the file.
6. Enter a loop to write customer data to the file. After writing a single customer, compute the precentage of objects written to the file. Call the `ManageThermometer` function (found at the end of Listing 5.13) to update the current PICT ID, redraw the thermometer window, and make it the active window.
7. Write an additional object count to the file.
8. Enter a loop to write merchandise items and their copies to the file. After writing data about a merchandise item and all its copies, compute the percentage of objects written to the file and call `ManageThermometer`.
9. Close the data file.
10. If necessary, set the file type and creator.
11. Close the thermometer window by deleting its object.

Listing 5.13 The Penultimate Videos application object's Unload function

```
void CPPVideoStoreApp::Unload ()
{
    float totalObjects = Cust_count + Movie_count + Game_count + Other_count
        + Item_count;
    int ObjectsWritten = 0;
    float percentWritten;

    // Create thermometer window
    LWindow * theThermometerWindow = LWindow::CreateWindow (WINDOW_SAVE_THER, this);
    theThermometerWindow->Show();

    ofstream fout (FileName);

    if (!fout.is_open())
    {
        // need an alert here
        return;
    }
    fout << Items->getlastTitle_numb() << ' ' << Copies->getlastCopy_numb() << ' ';

    // write the customer data
    fout << Cust_count << ' ';
    CustItrPre writer;
    Customer * currentCust;
    for (writer.Init (Customers); !writer; ++writer)
    {
        currentCust = writer();
        currentCust->write (fout);
        ObjectsWritten++;
        percentWritten = (float) ObjectsWritten / totalObjects;
        ManageThermometer (percentWritten, theThermometerWindow);
    }

    fout << Items->getItem_count() << ' ';

    // traverse merchandise tree and write
    MerchItrPre traversal;
    for (traversal.Init (Items); !traversal; ++traversal)
    {
        Merchandise_Item * currentOne;
        currentOne = traversal();
        currentOne->write (fout);
        ObjectsWritten += currentOne->getCopy_count() + 1;
        percentWritten = (float) ObjectsWritten / totalObjects;
        ManageThermometer (percentWritten, theThermometerWindow);
    }
    fout.close();
```

Continued next page

Listing 5.13 (Continued) The Penultimate Videos application object's Unload function

```
// if necessary, set file type and creator
    FInfo fndrInfo;

    ::FSpGetFInfo (&FileSpec, &fndrInfo);

    if (fndrInfo.fdType != MASTER_TYPE)
    {
        fndrInfo.fdType = MASTER_TYPE;
        fndrInfo.fdCreator = CREATOR;
        ::FSpSetFInfo (&FileSpec, &fndrInfo);
    }

    save_flag = TRUE; // switch flag to indicate save has occurred

    // remove thermometer window
    delete theThermometerWindow;
}

void CPPVideoStoreApp::ManageThermometer (float percentComplete, LWindow * theWindow)
{
    Ther * theThermometer = (Ther *) theWindow->FindPaneByID (THER_PANE);
    theThermometer->SetCurrentPict (percentComplete);
    theThermometer->DrawSelf();
    theWindow->Activate();
}
```

CHAPTER 6

Editing Text

TextEdit, the group of ToolBox routines that handles editing text, has been a part of the Macintosh since 1984, so it comes as no surprise that PowerPlant provides support for text manipulation. Its class LTextEdit provides a monostyled text edit record that supports the basic text editing operations of cut, copy, paste, and clear.

In this chapter you will learn how to create windows with scroll bars for text editing. You will also learn how to modify the PowerPlant class LTextEdit so that it supports multistyled rather than monostyled text. In addition, you'll be introduced to managing the Font, Size, and Style menus. Finally, you'll see how to implement Undo actions in a text edit window.

The example we'll be examining in this chapter is the Penultimate Video program's facility for writing a note to a customer. (Perhaps it's a note to some customer who hasn't returned videos or who has returned videos that haven't been rewound?) The chapter therefore begins with a look at the Note class and then continues with the underlying features of LTextEdit that make it work.

NOTE

We will look at printing the contents of an LTextEdit object in Chapter 12, when we discuss printing in general. File operations (opening and saving a note) are covered in Chapter 10.

The Note Class

The window in which a note appears is a combination of three objects:

- The window (created directly from LWindow)
- The scroller (created directly from LScroller)
- The note (created from a class named Note that is derived from a clone of LTextEdit—LTextEditM)

As you can see in Figure 6.1, the LWindow object is at the top of the view hierarchy. It has one subview, the LScroller object, which in turn contains the LTextEdit object. The LScroller object is a subview of the LWindow object *and* the superview of the LTextEdit object.

Figure 6.1 The hierarchy of elements in the note window

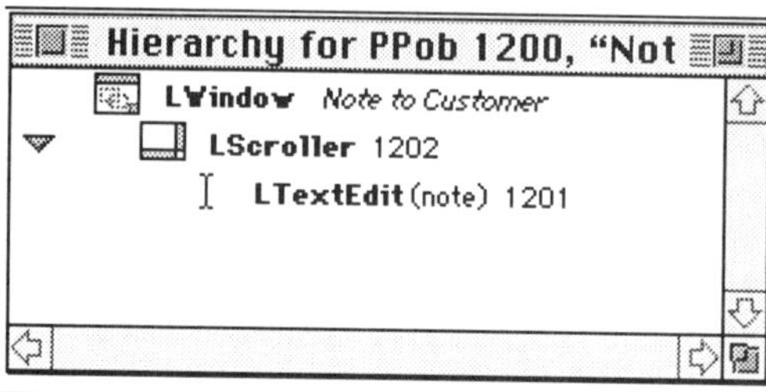

Notice in Figure 6.1 that the Note object appears as if it were created directly from LTextEdit, but that the class name is followed by "(note)." This indicates that the pane was indeed created as an LTextEdit object, but that its class ID was changed from the default *text*. This works because an LTextEditM object is virtually identical to an LTextEdit object, containing all the same attributes. The difference lies in the type of text edit record that is set up when an object is created from the class: LTextEdit creates a monostyled text edit record; LTextEditM creates a multistyled one.

The declaration of the Note class can be found in Listing 6.1. Because this class inherits from a cloned class—LTextEditM—that inherits from LCommander, Note is a commander. It therefore has `FindCommandStatus` and `ObeyCommand` functions. It also uses its `FinishCreateSelf` function to store some data about the object and to name the window in which the note appears. In addition, the class adds functions to its base class's editing support to handle opening, saving, and printing the note.

PowerPlant Objects for Editing Text

The PowerPlant object that supports writing a note to a Penultimate Video customer appears in Figure 6.2. Because the LScroller object covers the entire body of the window, all that appears of the LWindow object is its title bar. The default title ("Note to Customer") should never appear to the user because the Note class's `FinishCreateSelf` function sets the title of a new note window to "untitled note" plus a sequence number (for example, "untitled note 1," for the second unsaved note window).

ADDING THE SCROLL BAR

PowerPlant implements scrolling through the class LScroller. Assuming that you are working with Constructor and taking advantage of the LScroller class, you will rarely need to write code for scrolling.

NOTE
Scrolling lists of items on which a user can double-click are not defined using an LScroller object. If you need such a list, use an LListBox, which provides its own scroll bars along with other functions that support double-clickable lists. LListBox and scrolling lists are discussed in Chapter 9.

An LScroller object is a view that is designed to contain a pane or view whose contents will be scrolled. In other words, just as in the note window, the scroller must be the superview of the scrolled object.

The LScroller class handles the following scrolling tasks:

Listing 6.1 The Note class

```
// ******************************************************************
//      Note.h
// ******************************************************************
//   This is a subclass of LTextEditM that allows the program to
//   add its own code to handle the Font, Style, and Size menus
//   and to manage the text in a TextEdit pane. In this program,
//   the Note pane is used to write the customer a short note.
//

#include "LTextEditM.h"
#include <LCommander.h>

class Note : public LTextEditM
{
    public:
        static Note * CreateNoteStream (LStream * inStream);
                Note ();
                ~Note();
                Note (LStream * inStream);
        virtual Boolean ObeyCommand (CommandT inCommand, void * ioParam);
        virtual void FindCommandStatus (CommandT inCommand,
                        Boolean &outEnabled, Boolean &outUsesMark,
                        Char16 &outMark, Str255 outName);
        void PrintNote ();
        void NameNote (); // name the note window
        void OpenNote (); // load note from file
        void SaveNote (); // save note to file
        void SaveAsNote (); // name and save note
        void RevertNote ();

    protected:
        Int16 mFontItemNumber;     // item number of current font in Font menu
        virtualvoid FinishCreateSelf();
        LPrintout * thePrintout; // printer object created by constructor
        FSSpecfileSpec; // file spec used by this note
        LFile * theFile; // file object used by this note
        Boolean mustSaveAs;
        THPrint mPrintRecordH; // handle to print record
};
```

- Creates the scroll bar(s) when the scroller's superview is created.
- Makes itself a listener to its controls (the scroll bar(s)) and then broadcasts a message to its subview to trigger scrolling whenever the user drags a scroll bar thumb.
- Handles vertical or horizontal scrolling triggered by clicking the mouse pointer in a scroll bar or by clicking and holding the mouse pointer in a scroll bar.

Figure 6.2 A PowerPlant object for editing text

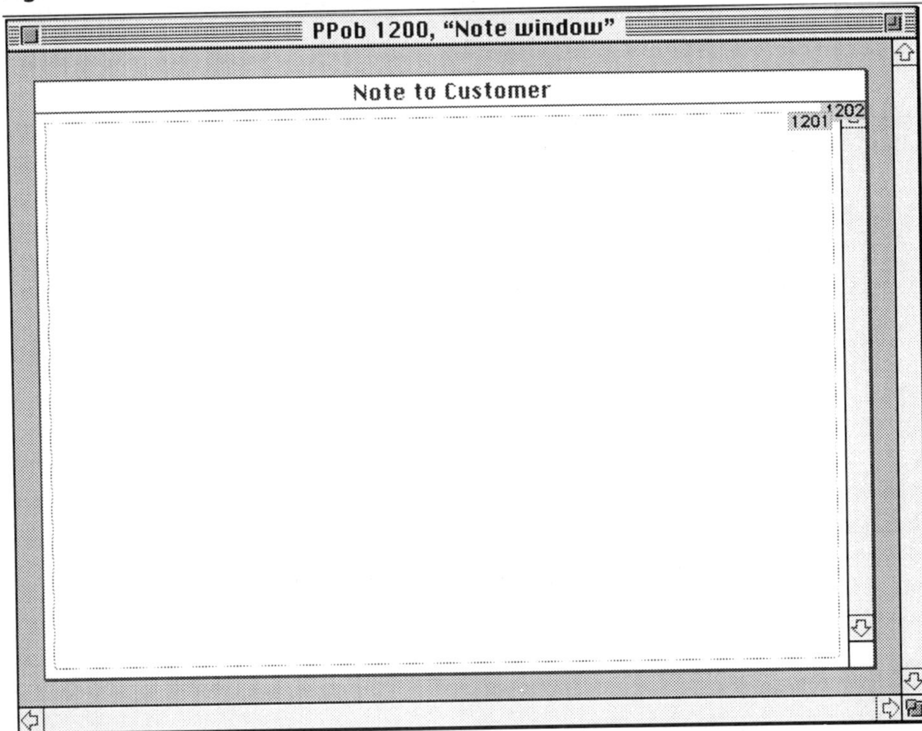

NOTE

LTextEdit is somewhat incomplete. One of the things it doesn't do is autoscroll when the user types below the visible area in a window. When you run the Penultimate Videos program, you'll discover that you can easily do "invisible" typing below the bottom boundary of the note window, and that the only way to expose that hidden text is to use the scroll bar.

- Redraws the scroll bars when the window containing the scroller is resized or moved.

The actual scrolling of the image is performed by the scroller's subview. LScroller expects to find a function named `ScrollImageBy` as one of its subview's member functions. The LScroller object passes in the number of pixels by which the image should be scrolled (horizontal and vertical values) and a Boolean that indicates whether the scrolled view should be redrawn after scrolling. The subview takes care of the rest. As you can see in Listing 6.2, LTextEditM first calls the ToolBox routine `OffsetRect` to change the ToolBox text edit record's view rectangle. In then calls LView's `ScrollImageBy` function, which takes care of redrawing the window.

Listing 6.2 Scrolling text

```
void
LTextEditM::ScrollImageBy(
    Int32   inLeftDelta,// Pixels to scroll horizontally
    Int32   inTopDelta,// Pixels to scroll vertically
    Boolean inRefresh)
{
    OffsetRect(&(**mTextEditH).viewRect, inLeftDelta, inTopDelta);

    LView::ScrollImageBy(inLeftDelta, inTopDelta, inRefresh);
}
```

To create the relationship between a scroller and the pane it will scroll using Constructor, first drag an LScroller into a view (in our example, an object of class LWindow). Then resize it so that it covers the entire area to be scrolled. In this example, the scroller covers all of the LWindow object except its title bar. Finally, you can drag the pane to be scrolled on top of the scroller. If you look back at Figure 6.2, for example, you will see that the LTextEdit object (pane ID 1201) covers most of the LScroller object (pane ID 1202), with the exception of the area occupied by the scroll bar.

An LScroller object's attributes, which are set in its properties window, can be found in Figure 6.3. There are several of these attributes to which you should pay attention when you define a scroller:

- Scrolling View ID: This attribute holds the resource ID between the scroller and the subview whose contents it scrolls. This is the easiest way to set up the relationship between the two.
- Scroll bar indents: The indents indicate how much space should be left between the scroll bars and the edges of the LScroller object. Typically, you'll want to leave 15 pixels at the bottom right to make room for a size box. To suppress a scroll bar, use indents of -1. In Figure 6.3, for example, the scroller will have no horizontal scroll bar because the left and right indents are -1.
- Binding: By default, a scroller is bound on all four sides to its superview. This ensures that the scroller will always fill the same relative position in its superview and will therefore resize properly. In most cases, you won't want to change the binding.

Figure 6.3 LScroller object properties

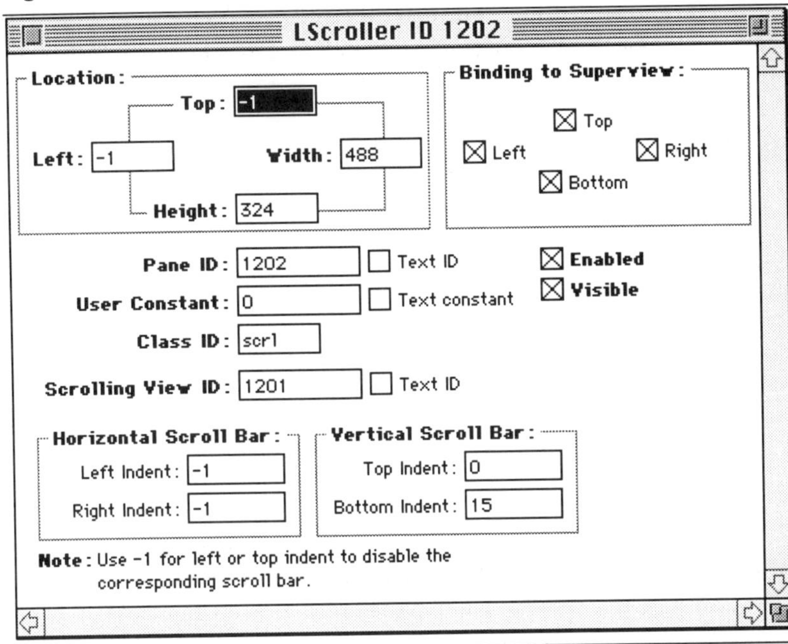

ADDING THE LTEXTEDIT OBJECT

To add an LTextEdit (or LTextEditM) object to a view, drag it into place as you would any other object. Then, open its properties window (Figure 6.4). The attributes with which you are often concerned include the following:

- Location: These values determine the size and position of the pane. In this particular example, the pane is offset six pixels from the top left corner of the scroller to provide a border between the text and the edges of the window. The width and height measurements also leave the same six-pixel border between the bottom of the window and the text, and between the scroll bar and the text.
- Binding: As you know, the binding check boxes determine how the pane will behave when its superview is resized. Because we want a text editing area to resize with the scroller (which resizes along with the window), the text edit pane is bound on all four sides.
- Class ID: By default, an object of class LTextEdit has a class ID of *text*. However, the object defined in this example is actually of class Note, which has been given an ID of *note*. That ID must be attached to the object in the Class ID box so that

Figure 6.4 LTextEdit object properties

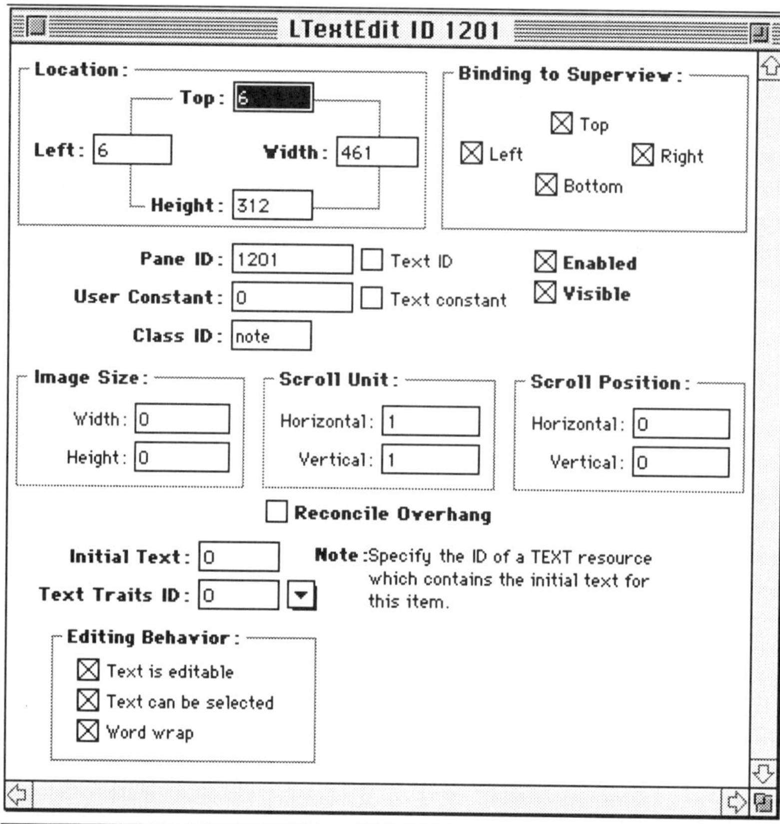

PowerPlant will use the correct `CreateXStream` function when creating an object from this resource.

- Initial Text: If you want the LTextEdit object to contain some text when it initially appears on the screen, you can store that text in a TEXT resource and connect it to the LTextEdit object by entering its resource ID in the Initial Text box.
- Text Traits ID: A text trait is a type specification (font, size, style, alignment, and so on) that you can create using Constructor. To attach a text trait to an LTextEdit object, enter its resource ID in the TextTraits ID box. You will read more about text traits a bit later in this chapter.
- Editing Behavior: These check boxes govern editing and display characteristics of the LTextEdit object. See the following section for details.

Editing Behavior Attributes

Constructor 2.1 provides check boxes for three text editing attributes, all of which are selected by default:

- Text is editable: Removing the X from this check box makes the text in the pane read-only.
- Text can be selected: Removing the X from this check box prevents the user from select a range of text.
- Word wrap: Removing the X from this check box suppresses word wrap in the pane. The user will need to enter a Return to indicate the end of a line.

Before proceeding, a word is in order about word wrap and LTextEdit. Word wrap occurs when the cursor reaches the right edge of the LTextEdit pane. If a user resizes the window, making it wider or narrower, LTextEdit readjusts the word wrap so that no text is hidden horizontally. This is not the way word processors behave, where word wrap depends on the margins you have set for a document rather than the visible area of the document window. As far as LTextEdit is concerned, however, its margins are the physical borders of its pane.

Constructor 1.0 provided *four* editing behavior attributes, collected in the enumerated data type that you can see in Listing 6.3. However, by the time Constructor 2.0 appeared, the multistyled attribute was no longer available. As a matter of fact, the attribute is still a part of an LTextEdit object, but simply isn't accessible through Constructor.

As a result, you can't use Constructor to create a multistyled text edit object. In addition, LTextEdit has never provided any support for multistyled text. This is why a cloned class named LTextEditM was created.

Listing 6.3 LTextEdit object text attributes

```
enum {
    textAttr_MultiStyle= 0x8000,
    textAttr_Editable= 0x4000,
    textAttr_Selectable= 0x2000,
    textAttr_WordWrap= 0x1000
};
```

If you want multistyled text, you have two alternatives. First, you could modify LTextEdit so that it checked the multistyled attribute to determine which type of text edit record was being created. You would then need to create a resource that describes a multistyled LTextEdit object manually using either Rez or Resourcerer. (As mentioned earlier, ResEdit can't handle the complexity of PowerPlant objects.)

Alternatively, you could create a clone of LTextEdit that handled a multistyled text edit record. Objects for that cloned class *could* be created using Constructor. In that case, you would use LTextEdit whenever you wanted monostyled text and the cloned class whenever you wanted multistyled text. Because creating the clone class makes it possible to continue to use Constructor to define objects, the Penultimate Videos program contains the cloned class—LTextEditM—that is used as a base class for the Note class.

Text Traits

As mentioned earlier, a text trait is a specification for the appearance of type. It can affect many objects besides those created from LTextEdit, including buttons, popup menus, display text (captions), and edit fields. If you are working with a monostyled text edit record, then a text trait can also be used to specify the appearance of all text in the text edit record. If you are working with a multistyled text edit record, then a text trait can be used to set the default type style.

Text traits (resources of type Txtr) are most easily created with Constructor. As you can see in Figure 6.5, once you've created the new resource, you can choose the font, size, style, justification, and drawing mode. To set text color, click on the box to the right of Color to display a color wheel. When the text trait is complete, it can then be attached to any object that accepts a text trait by entering its ID in the object's properties window.

The text traits defined for the Penultimate Videos application appear in Figure 6.6. The first four are provided in the PowerPlant starter resource file:

- System Font: Usually Chicago 12, used most commonly for buttons, popup menus, window titles, and so on.
- App Font: Usually Geneva 12, used commonly as the default text font for objects of the LEditField and LTextEdit classes.
- Geneva 9: Used where a smaller variable-spaced font is needed.
- Monaco 9: Used where a small monospaced font is needed.

The remaining two text traits are used by the Penultimate Videos program for printed output (in particular, for the receipt a customer receives when he or she rents something.)

You can change a object's text trait on the fly with a call to `SetTextTraitsID`, which is part of all classes that use text traits. The function's single parameter is the resource ID of the text trait you want to associate with the object.

Figure 6.5 Creating a text trait resource

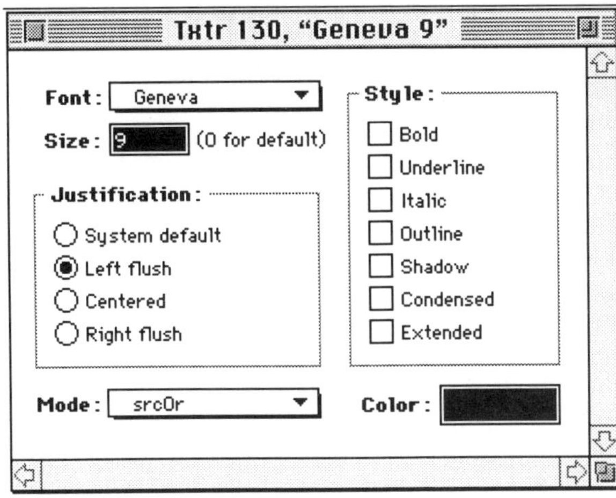

The LTextEdit Class

The declaration of the LTextEdit class can be found in Listing 6.4. Notice first that it is derived from three classes: LView (which provides many of its display management capabilities), LCommander (which manages its activities in the chain of command), and LPeriodical (which handles repeated, automatic events). The class also provides a way for an application program to modify and retrieve the text managed by the object.

In this section you will first be introduced to the text access functions. You will then read about LPeriodical, the base class that handles actions such as blinking the cursor, and how classes derived from it act. Finally, you will see the very tiny code change needed to mutate a monostyled text edit class into a multistyled text edit class.

Text Access Functions

LTextEdit provides four public functions that give you access to the text being maintained by a TextEdit object. The following functions allow you to both change and retrieve entire blocks of text:

Figure 6.6 Text traits in the Penultimate Videos application

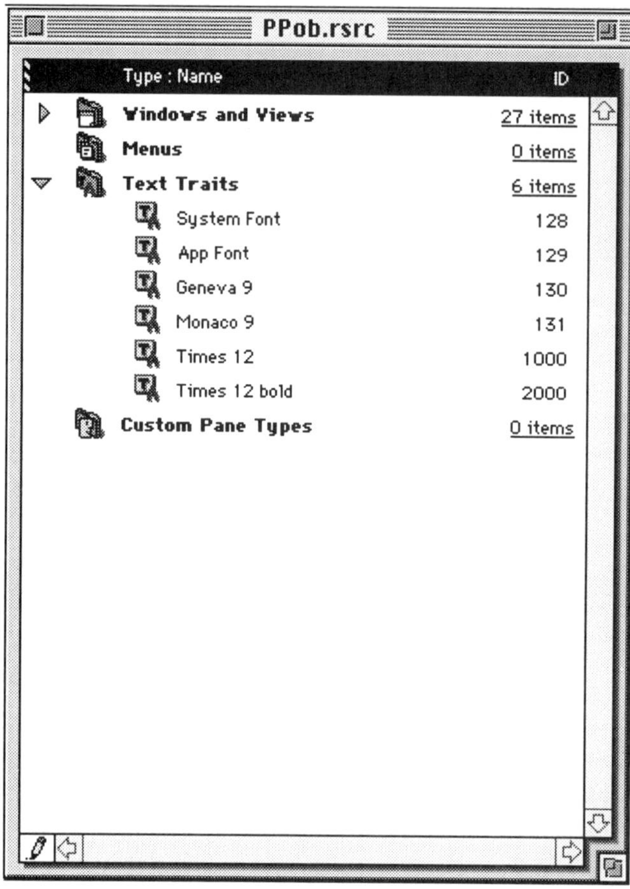

- `SetTextHandle`: Lets you change the entire contents of the block of text being manipulated by passing the text edit record a handle to a replacement block of text.
- `SetTextPtr`: Performs the same action as `SetTextHandle`, working from a pointer to the new text rather than a handle.
- `GetTextHandle`: Retrieves the block of text currently manipulated by a text edit object by returning a handle to the text.
- `GetMacTEH`: Retrieves the handle to the ToolBox text edit record.

Listing 6.4 The declaration of the LTextEdit class

```
class LTextEdit : public LView,
                  public LCommander,
                  public LPeriodical {
    public:
        enum { class_ID = 'text' };
        static LTextEdit* CreateTextEditStream(LStream *inStream);
        LTextEdit();
        LTextEdit(const SPaneInfo &inPaneInfo,
                        const SViewInfo &inViewInfo,
                        Uint16 inTextAttributes,
                        ResIDT inTextTraitsID);
        LTextEdit(LStream *inStream);
        virtual ~LTextEdit();

        virtual void SetTextHandle(Handle inTextH);
        virtual void SetTextPtr(Ptr inTextP, Int32 inTextLen);
        virtual Handle GetTextHandle();
        TEHandle GetMacTEH();

        virtual void SetTextTraitsID(ResIDT inTextTraitsID);
        Boolean HasAttribute(Uint16 inAttribute);

        virtual Boolean ObeyCommand(CommandT inCommand, void *ioParam);
        virtual void FindCommandStatus(CommandT inCommand,
                        Boolean &outEnabled, Boolean &outUsesMark,
                        Char16 &outMark, Str255 outName);
        virtual void SpendTime(const EventRecord &inMacEvent);

        virtual Boolean HandleKeyPress(const EventRecord& inKeyEvent);

        virtual void ResizeFrameBy(Int16 inWidthDelta, Int16 inHeightDelta,
                        Boolean inRefresh);

        virtual void MoveBy(Int32 inHorizDelta, Int32 inVertDelta,
                        Boolean inRefresh);
        virtual void ScrollImageBy(Int32 inLeftDelta, Int32 inTopDelta,
                        Boolean inRefresh);

        virtual BooleanFocusDraw();
        virtual void SelectAll();
        virtual void UserChangedText();
        virtual void AdjustImageToText();

        virtual void SavePlace(LStream *outPlace);
        virtual void RestorePlace(LStream *inPlace);
```

Continued next page

Listing 6.4 (Continued) The declaration of the LTextEdit class

```
    protected:
        TEHandle    mTextEditH;
        ResIDT          mTextTraitsID;
        Uint16          mTextAttributes;

        virtual void DrawSelf();
        virtual void HideSelf();

        virtual void ClickSelf(const SMouseDownEvent &inMouseDown);
        virtual void AdjustCursorSelf(Point inPortPt,
                        const EventRecord &inMacEvent);

        virtual void BeTarget();
        virtual void DontBeTarget();

        virtual void AlignTextEditRects();

        virtual STextEditUndoHSaveStateForUndo();

    private:
        void InitTextEdit(ResIDT inTextTraitsID);
};
```

NOTE

LTextEdit uses the standard ToolBox functions to implement cut, copy, and paste. The ObeyCommand function that provides those capabilities appears in Listing 1.5.

FLASHING THE CURSOR: PERIODIC EVENTS

A Macintosh program has a group of tasks that it performs periodically, either repeatedly during every pass through the event loop (*repeaters*) or whenever the program isn't doing anything else (*idlers*). This includes tasks such as blinking the straight-line insertion point in any area in which a user can enter text for objects of the classes LEditField and LTextEdit, and advancing the play of a Quicktime movie for objects of the class LMovieController. The base class for repeated actions is the abstract base class LPeriodical.

An application maintains one queue of objects that are repeaters and one queue of objects that are idlers. Although a program may use many objects whose classes are derived from LPeriodical, the LPeriodical variables that hold the pointers to the beginning of the repeater and idler queues are `static`. This means that they are "class" variables, that there is only one copy of those variables shared by all objects ultimately derived from LPeriodical.

LPeriodical has two member functions that take care of the members of the repeater and idler queues:

- `DevoteTimeToRepeaters`: This function is called within PowerPlant's main event loop after every event. (See Chapter 1 for details.)
- `DevoteTimeToIdlers`: This function is called by the application's function `UseIdleTime` whenever an idle or mouse-moved event occurs.

In both cases, the application traverses the appropriate queue and calls the `SpendTime` function for each object in the queue.

Any class derived from LPeriodical, such as LTextEdit and LTextEditM, must override LPeriodical's `SpendTime` function. The overriding function should include the action that the subclass should take whenever it receives a chance to perform its periodic action. For example, LTextEdit's `SpendTime` function (Listing 6.5) uses the ToolBox routine `TEIdle` to flash the straight-line cursor in the text edit pane.

Listing 6.5 LTextEdit's SpendTime function

```
void LTextEdit::SpendTime (const EventRecord& * inMacEvent */)
{
    if (FocusDraw() & IsVisible() & HasAttribute(textAttr_Selectable)) {
        ::TEIdle(mTextEditH);
    }
}
```

MAKING IT MULTISTYLED

The first difference between LTextEdit and LTextEditM is remarkably small. (The second difference involves implementing Undo, which is discussed at the end of this chapter.) Look first at the `InitTextEdit` function from LTextEdit (Listing 6.6). Notice that the text edit record is created with a call to the ToolBox routine `TENew`. The result of this call is a monostyled text edit record.

To make the switch to a multistyled text edit record, the `InitTextEdit` function from the LTextEditM class calls `TEStyleNew`, as in Listing 6.7. The result of this change is a text edit record that can handle multiple style characteristics. Note that this particular function also doesn't use the PowerPlant object's text trait, but instead lets the text default to the system's application font.

Listing 6.6 LTextEdit's InitTextEdit function

```
void LTextEdit::InitTextEdit( ResIDT inTextTraitsID)
{
    RectviewRect = {0, 0, 0, 0};
    mTextEditH = ::TENew(&viewRect, &viewRect);

    SetTextTraitsID(inTextTraitsID);

        // If word wrap is on, then the Image width is always the
        // same as the Frame width, which forces text to wrap to
        // the Frame.

        // If the Image width is zero (or negative), the user
        // probably forgot to set it. To accommodate this error,
        // we set the Image width to the Frame width. However, the
        // Image will not change if the Frame resizes.

    if ((mTextAttributes & textAttr_WordWrap) ||
        (mImageSize.width <= 0)) {
        mImageSize.width = mFrameSize.width;
    }
}
```

NOTE

The LTextEditM InitTextEdit function also initializes four variables that are used to support Undo (containerWindow, cutUndoer, pasteUndoer, and clearUndoer). The use of these variables will be discussed at the end of this chapter.

Creating a Note Object

Because most of the work of managing editing text is handled by the Note class, the application object has very little to do when the user requests a note. As you can see in Listing 6.8, the application object creates the note window and calls `SetLatentSub` for the Note pane. The purpose of `SetLatentSub` is to make the Note pane the subcommander that will be on,duty when its commander is put on duty. The effect is that the Note pane becomes the target when the window first appears; the straight-line cursor will then be flashing in the Note pane without requiring the user to click in the pane to activate it.

Listing 6.7 LTextEditM's InitTextEdit function

Here's what makes this one multistyled

```
void LTextEditM::InitTextEdit(ResIDT inTextTraitsID)
{
   RectviewRect = {0, 0, 0, 0};
   // create a multistyled text edit record
   mTextEditH = ::TEStyleNew(&viewRect, &viewRect);

      // If word wrap is on, then the Image width is always the
      // same as the Frame width, which forces text to wrap to
      // the Frame.

      // If the Image width is zero (or negative), the user
      // probably forgot to set it. To accommodate this error,
      // we set the Image width to the Frame width. However, the
      // Image will not change if the Frame resizes.

   if ((mTextAttributes & textAttr_WordWrap) ||
      (mImageSize.width <= 0)) {
      mImageSize.width = mFrameSize.width;
   }

   // set supercommander
   LScroller * theScroller = (LScroller *) LPane::GetSuperView();
   containerWindow = (LWindow *) theScroller->GetSuperView();

   // initialize undoer pointers
   cutUndoer = 0;
   pasteUndoer = 0;
   clearUndoer = 0;
   typingUndoer = 0;
}
```

Listing 6.8 Creating a text editing window

```
void CPPVideoStoreApp::WriteNote()
{
   LWindow * theWindow = LWindow::CreateWindow (WINDOW_NOTE, this);

   LTextEditM * theTE = (LTextEditM *) theWindow->FindPaneByID (NOTE_TE);
   theWindow->SetLatentSub (theTE);
   theWindow->Show;
}
```

Completing the Note Object

Creating the note window also creates objects for all of the window's subpanes, in particular the Note object. Notice in Listing 6.9 that the constructor first calls the base class constructor. It finishes by setting a flag to indicate that the note hasn't been named and that the next Save command should actually trigger Save As.

Listing 6.9 The Note class stream constructor

```
Note::Note (LStream * inStream)
    : LTextEditM (inStream)
{
    mustSaveAs = TRUE; // Must get file spec before saving
}
```

As part of the job of displaying the note window, there are some tasks that can only be performed after the creation of the Note object has been completed. These are handled in the `FinishCreateSelf` function (Listing 6.10), which executes after all subpanes of a pane have been created.

The Note class's `FinishCreateSelf` function first calls its base class's `FinishCreateSelf` function. Then, it saves the handle to the text edit record. Finally, it calls `NameNote`, a class-specific function (also in Listing 6.10) that takes care of giving each unsaved note window a new name.

The first note window is named "untitled note." Then, if the user opens a second unsaved note window, the program gives it the name of "untitled note 1," and so on. The default title and the title to which numbers are added are stored in an STR# resource (Figure 6.7). The `NameNote` function therefore first retrieves the default window name from the resource. It then uses a function from the PowerPlant utility class UWindows to determine if any other window has that name.

Assuming that the name is unique (in other words, this is the first note window to be displayed), `NameNote` obtains a pointer to the window object by first finding the Note object's superview (the LScroller object) and then finding the scroller's superview. At that point, `NameNote` can call `SetDescriptor` to change the window's name.

However, if the note window isn't the first one on the screen, `NameNote` retrieves the second string from the resource and begins adding sequence numbers to it. Each time `NameNote` concatenates a number onto the string, it checks to determine whether a window with the matching name exists. As soon as it finds a unique name, the `while` loop stops so the window can be named.

Listing 6.10 Finishing the creation of a Note object

```
void Note::FinishCreateSelf ()
{
    LTextEditM::FinishCreateSelf();
    mTextEditH = LTextEditM::GetMacTEH(); // get the handle of the text edit record
    NameNote(); // set the note window's name
}

void Note::NameNote ()
{
    Pstring name;
    ::GetIndString (name, STRx_UNTITLED_NOTE, 1);

    long num = 0;
    // need to make sure that no other window has the current name
    while (UWindows::FindNamedWindow (name) != nil)
    {
        ::GetIndString (name, STRx_UNTITLED_NOTE, 2);
        num++;
        Str15 numStr;
        ::NumToString (num, numStr);
        name += numStr;
    }
    LScroller * theScroller = (LScroller *) LPane::GetSuperView();
    LWindow * theWindow = (LWindow *) theScroller->GetSuperView();
    theWindow->SetDescriptor (name);
}
```

Figure 6.7 The STR# resource used to set the note window title

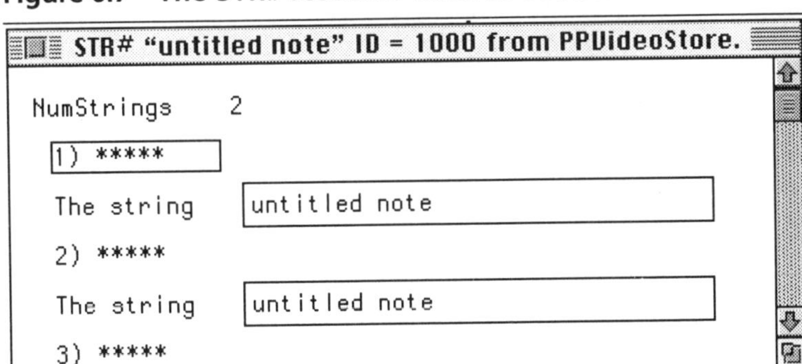

NOTE

The two strings in the STR# resource are identical, so it might seem that you would need only one of them. However, if you decide to change either the default window name (the first string) or the stub to which numbers are added (the second string), it's much easier to change the resource than it is to change program code.

Handling the Text Menus

Most of the work performed by the Note class involves handling the three text menus: Font, Size, and Style. The Font menu in particular presents a special challenge because its menu items aren't fixed, but vary according to the configuration of the computer on which the program is running. PowerPlant refers to such menu items that can't be specified in a resource as *synthetic commands.*

Support for the text menus is provided through a PowerPlant class named UTextMenus, which appeared as a sample file with the original PowerPlant Cookbook tutorials. You can use this file and the techniques demonstrated in the Penultimate Videos program to implement text menus in most programs.

UTextMenusBase and Its Subclasses

UTextMenusBase is a base class for UFontMenu, USizeMenu, and UStyleMenu. The base class (Listing 6.11) provides static (therefore, class) variables for pointers to Font, Size, and Style menu objects and menu handles. It also provides a variety of functions for enabling and disabling menu items.

The subclasses (see Listing 6.12) have several functions in common:

- `Initialize`: Sets up the menu. This function is called once during a program, usually in an application object's constructor.
- `DisableMenu`: Disables the entire menu.
- `EnableMenu`: Enables the entire menu.

UFontMenu and USizeMenu also have `AdjustMenu` functions that change the appearance of the menu while a program is running. In addition, both of these classes have functions that return the font or font size chosen from the menu.

Listing 6.11 UTextMenusBase

```
classUTextMenusBase {

protected:
    static void XAble(LMenu *inMenu, Boolean inEnable);
    static void XAble(ResIDT inMenuID, Boolean inEnable);
    static void XAble(MenuHandle inMenuH, Boolean inEnable);

    static void XAbleEveryItem(LMenu *inMenu, Boolean inEnable,
                    Boolean inUnmarkAll, Boolean inSetStyleNormal);
    static void XAbleEveryItem(ResIDT inMenuID, Boolean inEnable,
                    Boolean inUnmarkAll, Boolean inSetStyleNormal);
    static void XAbleEveryItem(MenuHandle inMenuH, Boolean inEnable,
                    Boolean inUnmarkAll, Boolean inSetStyleNormal);

    static LMenu *sFontMenu;
    static MenuHandle sFontMenuH;
    static LMenu *sSizeMenu;
    static MenuHandle sSizeMenuH;
    static LMenu *sStyleMenu;
    static MenuHandle sStyleMenuH;
};
```

TEXT MENU RESOURCES

The resource for a Style menu (for example, Figure 6.8) is just like most other menus you create for a program. Because it's a standard window, however, you can take advantage of the menu command IDs that have already been established in *PP_Messages.h*. (That is why the command IDs are less than 1000.)

A Size menu often has menu items that don't change, such as "Smaller" or "Larger." However, the bulk of the contents of a Size menu is font sizes. If you decide that the Size menu will only show those font sizes that are appropriate to the chosen font, then you will want to be able to change the items in the menu. Although you could certainly set up a Size menu with unchanging items and therefore with fixed menu command IDs, it is more flexible to use synthetic command numbers for those menu items that might change. In Figure 6.9, for example, all the font sizes have been given an ID of -1. This will signal the program that the menu items aren't fixed and that it must use identify a menu choice by the content of the menu item rather than by a menu command ID.

A Font menu almost never has any fixed items. Its resource (for example, Figure 6.10) has only a title. Because there are no menu items, there are no menu command IDs and therefore no Mcmd resource. As with the Size menu, a program will need to

Listing 6.12 The UTextMenusBase subclasses

```
classUFontMenu : public UTextMenusBase {

public:
    static void Initialize(Boolean inEnabled = true);
    static void AdjustMenu(Int16 inCurrentFont);
    static void DisableMenu();
    static void EnableMenu();
    static void DisableEveryItem();
    static void EnableEveryItem();
    static Int16 GetFontNumber(Int16 inMenuItem);
    static Int16 GetFontItemNumber(Int16inFontNumber);
};

classUSizeMenu : public UTextMenusBase {

public:
    static void Initialize(Int16 inReservedItems, Boolean inEnabled = true);
    static void AdjustMenu(Int16 inMenuItem, Int16 inCurrentSize, Int16 inCurrentFont,
                    Boolean &outEnabled, Boolean &outUsesMark,Char16 &outMark);
    static void DisableMenu();
    static void EnableMenu();
    static void DisableEveryItem();
    static void EnableEveryItem();
    static Int16 GetFontSize(Int16 inMenuItem);

private:
    static Int16 mReservedItems;
};

constInt16kDefaultReservedItems = 5;


classUStyleMenu : public UTextMenusBase {

public:
    static void Initialize(Boolean inEnabled = true);
    static void DisableMenu();
    static void EnableMenu();
};
```

use the menu item itself (in this case, either the name or number of a font) to identify a menu choice.

Figure 6.8 A Style menu resource (Constructor format)

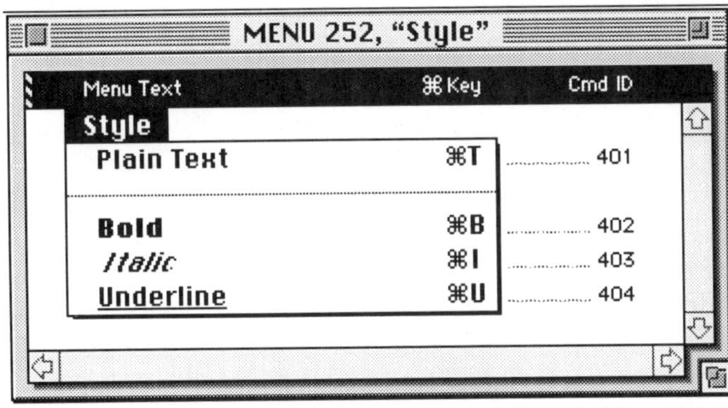

Figure 6.9 A Size menu resource (Constructor format)

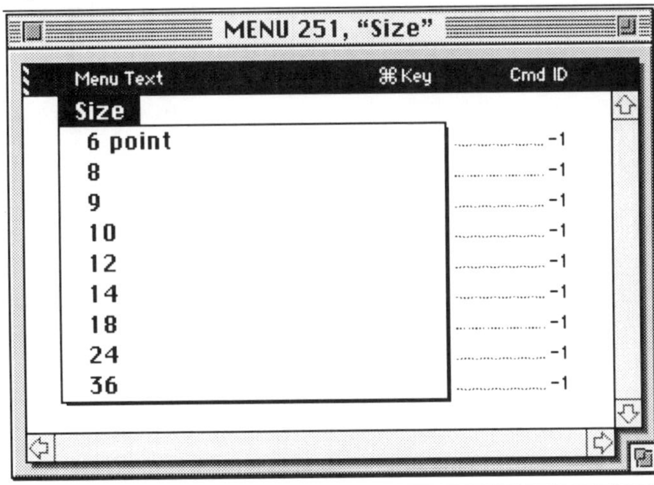

Figure 6.10 A Font menu resource (Constructor format)

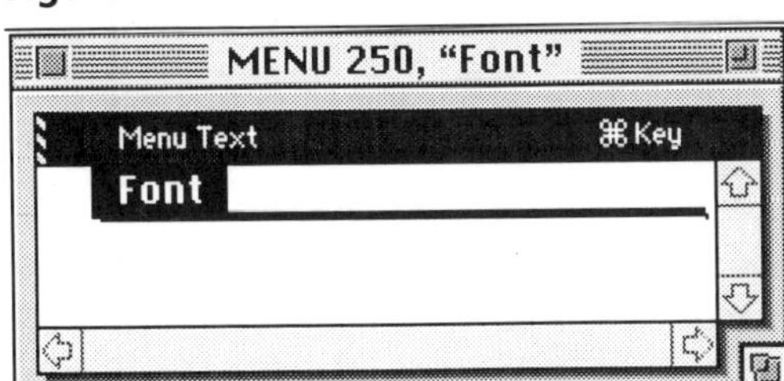

Initializing the Text Menus

The first task that must occur if a program is to support Font, Size, and Style menus is to initialize the menus. (The menu objects themselves are created when the program's LMenuBar object is created.) As mentioned earlier, typically this is handled in the application object's constructor with calls to the three `Initialize` functions:

```
UFontMenu::Initialize (TRUE); // set up the font menu
// zero indicates that there are no items that aren't sizes
USizeMenu::Initialize (0, TRUE);
UStyleMenu::Initialize (TRUE); // set up the style menu
```

The `Initialize` functions operate in the following general way:

- For the Font menu: Calls the ToolBox routine `AppendResMenu` to add the computer's fonts to the menu.
- For all three menus: Stores the menu's handle and a pointer to its object in the appropriate class variable and enables or disables the menu (as appropriate).

Enabling TExt Menus

When running the Penultimate Videos program, you may have noticed that the Font, Style, and Size menus are active only when a note window is present on the screen. This is because the `FindCommandStatus` function that activates those menus belongs to the Note class (Listing 6.13). Much of this code comes from the Menus sample program that was part of the original PowerPlant Cookbook.

The bulk of this `FindCommandStatus` function is broken into two parts. The first detects a synthetic command by calling the LCommander routine `IsSyntheticCommand`. If the command is synthetic, it returns a Boolean indicating that fact along with the menu ID and the menu item number. In that case, the function determines whether the command comes from the Font or Size menu and then uses the `AdjustMenu` function from the appropriate text menu class to change the appearance of the menu. For example, `USizeMenu::AdjustMenu` places a check mark next to the selected size and displays that size using the outline text style. By the same token, `UFontMenu::AdjustMenu` places a check mark next to the chosen font and removes checks from all other fonts in the menu.

If the chosen menu command isn't synthetic, then the command can be enabled like any other menu command. Most menu commands don't use check marks. However, the style commands (plain, bold, underline, and italic) may need check marks if

Listing 6.13 The Note class's FindCommandStatus function

```
void Note::FindCommandStatus (CommandT inCommand, Boolean &outEnabled,
    Boolean &outUsesMark, Char16 &outMark, Str255 outName)
{
    ResIDT menuID;
    Int16 menuItem, mode;
    TextStyle TextStyleRec;

    mode = doFont + doFace + doSize;
    ::TEContinuousStyle(&mode, &TextStyleRec, mTextEditH); // get current style settings

    outEnabled = true; // most of our commands are enabled if we're in
                       // the chain of command
    outUsesMark = true; // most of our command use check marks

    if (IsSyntheticCommand(inCommand, menuID, menuItem))
    {
        if (menuID == MENU_Font)
        {
            UFontMenu::AdjustMenu(mFontItemNumber);
        }
        else if (menuID == MENU_Size)
        {
            USizeMenu::AdjustMenu(menuItem, TextStyleRec.tsSize, TextStyleRec.tsFont,
                outEnabled, outUsesMark, outMark);
        }
        else
            LTextEditM::FindCommandStatus(inCommand, outEnabled, outUsesMark,
                outMark, outName);
    }
    else switch (inCommand)
    {
        case cmd_Plain:
            outMark = (TextStyleRec.tsFace == normal) ? checkMark : noMark;
            break;

            // This is a common idiom for handling the Style menu. It
            // relies on the fact that the command numbers that correspond
            // to the text styles are sequential and in the same order as
            // the constants that represent each bit in the style word.
            // You can see the same idiom in the ObeyCommand() function.

        case cmd_Bold:
        case cmd_Italic:
        case cmd_Underline:
            outMark = TextStyleRec.tsFace &
                (1 << (inCommand - cmd_Bold)) ? checkMark : noMark;
            break;
```

This function call detects a synthetic command

Regular menu commands are processed here

Here's the tricky bit

Continued next page

Listing 6.13 (Continued) The Note class's FindCommandStatus function

```
        case cmd_FontMenu:
        case cmd_SizeMenu:
        case cmd_StyleMenu:
        case cmd_open_note:
        case cmd_save_note:
        case cmd_save_note_as:
        case cmd_revert_note:
            outUsesMark = false;
            break;

// enable printing options when this printable window is visible
        case cmd_Print:
        case cmd_PageSetup:
            outEnabled = TRUE;
            outUsesMark = FALSE;
            break;

        default:
                //  Be sure to call the base class's FindCommanStatus()
                //  member function to get its behavior

            LTextEditM::FindCommandStatus(inCommand, outEnabled, outUsesMark,
                outMark, outName);
            break;
    }
}
```

those styles are in use. The function can detect a plain type style by checking to see if the `tsFace` field of the style record is equal to the constant `normal`.

However, the function resorts to a bit of a trick—found in the Menus sample program mentioned earlier—to figure out whether a mark should be added or removed from one of the other Style menu items. The trick, which appears as the body of the case for bold, italic, and underline in Listing 6.13, depends on the positions of the bits in the style word: Bit 0 represents bold, bit 1 represents italic, and bit 2 represents underline. The command constants associated with the styles are in the same numeric order: 402 for bold, 403 for italic, and 404 for underline. Therefore, when the program subtracts `cmd_Bold` from the input menu command, the result is either 0, 1, or two, which then shifts the 1 into the correct position to identify the chosen style. The statement then performs a logical AND with the style record's `tsFace` field, which returns true if the bit is set and false if it isn't.

Notice that regardless of whether the command is synthetic or regular, the function defaults to calling the base class's `FindCommandStatus` function. This ensures that the program will handle commands that aren't trapped directly by the Note class.

PROCESSING TEXT MENU SELECTIONS

Processing of text menu selections happens in the Note class's `ObeyCommand` function (Listing 6.14). Like the `FindCommandStatus` function, it differentiates between synthetic and regular commands and handles each type separately.

To change a font, the function retrieves the font number with `UFontMenu::GetFontNumber` and then uses that value to set the font in the style record. The style record is then available for use in the call to the ToolBox routine `TESetStyle`. Changing the font size is very similar: `USizeMenu::GetFontSize` inserts the chosen size into the style record, which can then be used when calling `TESetStyle`.

When the command is regular rather than synthetic, processing the command is straightforward: The `switch` traps the command and takes appropriate action. For the Style menu in particular, this means setting the `tsFace` field of the style record and then calling `TESetStyle`.

Implementing Undo

One limitation of LTextEdit is that it doesn't support Undo, although PowerPlant does provide classes for implementing Undo through attachments. To give you an example of using attachments *and* of implementing Undo, we'll look at how LTExtEditM manages the task.

THE ACTION AND UNDOER CLASSES

Before a program can undo something, it needs to have a way of saving whatever the user just did. PowerPlant calls anything that can be undone an *action*, and supports it through the class LAction. Whenever a user does something that can be undone, a program creates an object from a class derived from LAction. (LAction is an abstract base class.) That action is then "posted" to the commander of the object in which the action occurred.

Listing 6.14 The Note class's ObeyCommand function

```
Boolean Note::ObeyCommand (CommandT inCommand, void * ioParam)
{
    ResIDT menuID;
    Int16 menuItem;
    Int32 newSize;
    BooleancmdHandled = TRUE;
    TextStyle TextStyleRec;


    if (IsSyntheticCommand(inCommand, menuID, menuItem))
    {
        if (menuID == MENU_Font)
        {
            //  Set font of currently selected text

            TextStyleRec.tsFont = UFontMenu::GetFontNumber(menuItem);
            ::TESetStyle (doFont, &TextStyleRec, TRUE, mTextEditH);
            mFontItemNumber = menuItem;

        }
        else if (menuID == MENU_Size)
        {

                //  Set the font size for selected text. Since the Size menu
                //  can use the FindCommandStatus() mechanism
                //  to maintain the menu, we don't need to save
                //  the item number of the current size.

            TextStyleRec.tsSize = USizeMenu::GetFontSize(menuItem);
            ::TESetStyle (doSize, &TextStyleRec, TRUE, mTextEditH);
        }
        else
                //  Be sure to call the base class's ObeyCommand()
                //  member function to get its behavior.

            cmdHandled = LTextEditM::ObeyCommand(inCommand, ioParam);
    }
    else switch (inCommand)
    {
        case cmd_Plain:
            TextStyleRec.tsFace = normal;
            ::TESetStyle (doFace, &TextStyleRec, TRUE, mTextEditH);
            break;
```

Continued next page

Listing 6.14 (Continued) The Note class's ObeyCommand function

```
// This is a common idiom for handling the Style menu. It
        // relies on the fact that the command numbers that correspond
        // to the text styles are sequential an in the same order as
        // the constants that represent each bit in the style word.
        // You can see the same idiom in the FindCommandStatus() function.

    case cmd_Bold:
    case cmd_Italic:
    case cmd_Underline:
        TextStyleRec.tsFace = 1 << (inCommand - cmd_Bold);
        ::TESetStyle (doFace + doToggle, &TextStyleRec, TRUE, mTextEditH);
        break;
    case cmd_open_note:
        OpenNote();
        break;
    case cmd_save_note:
        if (mustSaveAs)
            SaveAsNote();
        else
            SaveNote ();
        break;
    case cmd_save_note_as:
        SaveAsNote ();
        break;
    case cmd_revert_note:
        RevertNote();
        break;
    case cmd_Print:
        PrintNote();
        break;
    case cmd_PageSetup:
        ::PrOpen(); // open printer driver
        // Note: mPrintRecordH comes from the LPrintout object, a pointer
        // to which is stored in the note object
        ::PrStlDialog (mPrintRecordH); // display the page setup dialog box
        ::PrClose(); // close the printer driver
    default:
        cmdHandled = LTextEditM::ObeyCommand (inCommand, ioParam);
        break;
    }
    return cmdHandled;
}
```

To help support Undo and Redo in text edit windows, PowerPlant provides the LTETextAction class, which is derived from LAction. LTETextAction has four derived classes of its own: LTEClearAction, LTECutAction, LTEPasteAction, and

LTETypingAction. A program can then use the action-specific classes to capture actions for undoing.

> **NOTE**
>
> *Although LTextEdit doesn't support undo, LEditField does. The code that has been added to LTextEditM to support undo has therefore been modeled after Metrowerk's strategy in implementing Undo for LEditField.*

In addition to objects created from classes derived from LAction, a program must create an object of class LUndoer, an attachment that takes care of triggering the undo or redo of actions that have been posted to a commander and managing the Undo menu item. The LUndoer object is added as an attachment to an object derived from LCommander.

The LUndoer object uses several functions from LAction-derived classes to manage undo and redo operations:

- `CanRedo`: Determines whether an action can be redone.
- `CanUndo`: Determines whether an action can be undone.
- `Undo`: Calls `UndoSelf` to reverse the action.
- `Redo`: Calls `RedoSelf` to redo the action.

> **NOTE**
>
> *If you need to undo something other than a text edit action, you will need to create your own subclass of LAction. Your derived class should include overriding Undo, UndoSelf, Redo, and RedoSelf functions.*

Implementing the Undo and Redo

Adding support for Undo and Redo to the note window requires code in several places:

- The class must provide variables to hold pointers to the action objects and a pointer to the window object. Although LTextEditM could retrieve a pointer to the window object each time an action occurs, it is more efficient to obtain that pointer once and store it in the LTextEditM object. If you'll look back at Listing 6.7, you'll see that the `InitTextEdit` function finds the pane's immediate supercommander (an object of class LScroller) and then the scroller's supercommander (the window). Note that this function also initializes the action object pointers to 0.

- An LUndoer object must be created and attached to the note window when the window is created.
- Because cut, clear, and paste are implemented in LTextEditM's `ObeyCommand` function, that function must create action objects and post actions to the window's commander.
- Because keystrokes are handled by the `HandleKeypress` function, undo typing code must be added to that function.

Setting Up the LUndoer Attachment

The note window is created in the application object's `WriteNote` function (Listing 6.15). Once the window object has been created, the function creates an LUndoer object. Then it calls the LCommander function `AddAttachment` to add the LUndoer object to the window object's list of attachments. (Keep in mind that you can add attachments only to objects whose classes are derived from LCommander.)

Listing 6.15 Adding an LUndoer object as an attachment to a window

```
void CPPVideoStoreApp::WriteNote()
{
    LWindow * theWindow = LWindow::CreateWindow (WINDOW_NOTE, this);

    // enable undo operations in this window
    LUndoer *undoer = new LUndoer;
    theWindow->AddAttachment(undoer, nil, TRUE);

    LTextEditM * theTE = (LTextEditM *) theWindow->FindPaneByID (NOTE_TE);
    theWindow->SetLatentSub (theTE);
    theWindow->Show;
}
```

If you were to run the program with just the LUndoer object attached to the window object, you would discover that the Undo option in the Edit menu responds properly to what the user has done. For example, when the user chooses Cut, the menu option reads Undo Cut; when the user chooses undo, the menu option changes to Redo Cut. The LUndoer object is managing the menu option, taking the strings for the menu option from *PP Action Strings.rsrc*. However, no undoing or redoing would occur, because actions for the undoer object to handle haven't been posted to the window.

Handling the Action Objects for Copy, Clear, and Paste

When support for Undo and Redo is part of a class, code in the class's `ObeyCommand` function changes considerably. As you can see in Listing 6.16 (LTextEditM's `ObeyCommand` function), the `switch` statement contains the same `case`s as that of LTextEdit (first seen in Listing 1.5), along with some new `case`s that interaction with action objects. Of the four text editing operations—cut, copy, paste, and clear—only copy contains any ToolBox calls. This is because copy is generally not an undoable operation.

To handle Undo and Redo, each undoable/redoable action does the following:

- Creates a new action object to hold whatever the user has just done and store a pointer to that object.
- Posts the action to the commander (in this example, the note window).

Posting the action using the `PostAction` function executes the action by running all the attachments belonging to the commander receiving the post. In this particular example, the single attachment is the undoer object, which calls the action object's `Redo` function. This has the effect of performing the action for the first time. Because LUndoer operates in this way, the `ObeyCommand` function doesn't need the code to perform the undoable/redoable text editing tasks; those tasks are handled by the action object.

Notice that the `ObeyCommand` function in Listing 6.16 traps five action commands. The first four (cut, paste, clear, and typing) call the `UserChangedText` function, which by default does nothing. However, you could override this function in a derived class to make customized changes in the text edit record. The final action command (cmd_ActionDeleted) handles the situation where the action object that records typing has been deleted. Resetting the pointer to 0 (or nil) ensures that the next keypress creates a new typing action object and therefore prevents the program from attempting to access a nonexistent object.

Handling Undo Typing

Undoing and redoing typing presents a special challenge because typing isn't a single action like cutting, clearing, or pasting. Instead, it's a series of individual keypresses, each of which can represent a character for display, cursor movement (for example, the Home and End keys), or character removal (the Delete and Del keys). This means that once an action object has been created for typing, the code that handles keypresses must add to or remove from the action object, storing keypresses until another operation (a cut, clear, or paste) interrupts typing.

Listing 6.16 LTextEditM's ObeyCommand function

```
Boolean LTextEditM::ObeyCommand (CommandT inCommand, void * ioParam)
{
    Boolean cmdHandled = true;

    switch (inCommand) {
        case cmd_Cut:
            cutUndoer = new LTECutAction (mTextEditH, containerWindow, this);
            // Important note: posting the action performs the action!
            PostAction (cutUndoer);
            AdjustImageToText();
            UserChangedText();
            break;

        case cmd_Copy:
            ::TECopy(mTextEditH);
            ::ZeroScrap();
            ::TEToScrap();
            break;

        case cmd_Paste:
            pasteUndoer = new LTEPasteAction (mTextEditH, containerWindow, this);
            PostAction (pasteUndoer);
            AdjustImageToText();
            UserChangedText();
            break;

        case cmd_Clear:
            clearUndoer = new LTEClearAction (mTextEditH, containerWindow, this);
            PostAction (clearUndoer);
            AdjustImageToText();
            UserChangedText();
            break;

        case cmd_ActionCut:
        case cmd_ActionPaste:
        case cmd_ActionClear:
        case cmd_ActionTyping:
            UserChangedText();
            break;

        case msg_TabSelect:
            if (!IsEnabled()) {
                cmdHandled = false;
                break;
            }
        case cmd_ActionDeleted:
            if ((LTETypingAction *) ioParam == typingUndoer)
                typingUndoer = 0;
                break;
```

Continued next page

Listing 6.16 (Continued) LTextEditM's ObeyCommand function

```
        case cmd_SelectAll:
            SelectAll();
            break;

        default:
            cmdHandled = LCommander::ObeyCommand(inCommand, ioParam);
            break;
    }

    return cmdHandled;
}
```

To support this requirement, LTETypingAction includes special functions to modify an action object's contents:

- `InputCharacter`: Handles a character for display.
- `BackwardErase`: Handles the use of the Delete key.
- `ForewardErase`: Handles the use of the Del key.

These functions are called from LTextEditM's `HandleKeyPress` function (Listing 6.17). The general strategy is to check the content of the variable that points to the typing action object (`typingUndoer`). If the variable contains 0, then there is no existing typing action object and a new one must be created. When a typing action object exists, the keypress is sent to the appropriate LTETypingAction function, which performs the action and then modifies the action object to include the effect of the action.

Listing 6.17 LTextEditM's HandleKeyPress function

```
Boolean LTextEditM::HandleKeyPress (const EventRecord&inKeyEvent)
{
    Boolean keyHandled = true;
    EKeyStatustheKeyStatus = keyStatus_Input;
    Int16   theKey = inKeyEvent.message & charCodeMask;

    if (inKeyEvent.modifiers & cmdKey) {// Always pass up when the command
        theKeyStatus = keyStatus_PassUp;//   key is down
    } else {

        theKeyStatus = UKeyFilters::PrintingCharField(inKeyEvent);
    }

    shortlineCount = (**mTextEditH).nLines;

    switch (theKeyStatus) {

        case keyStatus_Input:
            FocusDraw();
            if (typingUndoer == 0)
            {
                typingUndoer = new LTETypingAction (mTextEditH, this, this);
                PostAction (typingUndoer);
            }

            if (typingUndoer != 0)
                typingUndoer->InputCharacter (theKey);
            else
                ::TEKey (theKey, mTextEditH);

            UserChangedText();
            break;

        case keyStatus_TEDelete:
            FocusDraw();
            if ((**mTextEditH).selEnd > 0)
                if (typingUndoer == 0)
                {
                    typingUndoer = new LTETypingAction (mTextEditH, this, this);
                    PostAction (typingUndoer);
                }

            if (typingUndoer != 0)
                typingUndoer->BackwardErase();
            else
                ::TEKey(theKey, mTextEditH);

            UserChangedText();
            break;
```

Continued next page

Listing 6.17 (Continued) LTextEditM's HandleKeyPress function

```
case keyStatus_TECursor:
        FocusDraw();
        ::TEKey(theKey, mTextEditH);
        break;

    case keyStatus_ExtraEdit:
        switch (theKey)
        {
            case char_Home:
                FocusDraw();
                ::TESetSelect (0,0,mTextEditH);
                break;

            case char_End:
                FocusDraw();
                ::TESetSelect (max_Int16, max_Int16, mTextEditH);
                break;

            case char_FwdDelete:
                FocusDraw();
                if ((**mTextEditH).selStart < (**mTextEditH).teLength)
                {
                    if (typingUndoer == 0)
                    {
                     typingUndoer = new LTETypingAction (mTextEditH, this, this);
                     PostAction (typingUndoer);
                    }
                    if (typingUndoer != 0)
                     typingUndoer->ForwardErase();
                    else
                    {
                     if ((**mTextEditH).selStart == (**mTextEditH).selEnd)
                     ::TESetSelect((**mTextEditH).selStart,
                     (**mTextEditH).selStart + 1, mTextEditH);
                    ::TEDelete (mTextEditH);
                    }
                    UserChangedText();
                    break;
                }

          default:
              keyHandled = LCommander::HandleKeyPress(inKeyEvent);
        }
        break;

    case keyStatus_Reject:
        // +++ Do something
        SysBeep(1);
        break;
```

Continued next page

Listing 6.17 (Continued) LTextEditM's HandleKeyPress function

```
        case keyStatus_PassUp:
            if (theKey == char_Return) {
                FocusDraw();
                ::TEKey(theKey, mTextEditH);
                UserChangedText();
            } else {
                keyHandled = LCommander::HandleKeyPress(inKeyEvent);
            }
            break;
    }

    if (lineCount != (**mTextEditH).nLines) {
        AdjustImageToText();
    }

    return keyHandled;
}
```

CHAPTER 7

Dialog Box and Control Resources

Dialog boxes are a staple of Macintosh programs. We use them to collect information a program needs, such as the name of a file to open, properties to be applied to a graphic object, or data that the program will manipulate in some way. In this chapter you will be introduced to creating resources for dialog boxes. In most cases, dialog boxes are populated with a variety of controls, such as buttons, popup menus, radio buttons, and check boxes. This chapter therefore also provides a logical place to introduce the way in which PowerPlant control resources are defined. (The code needed to handle dialog boxes and their controls is discussed in Chapter 8.)

Dialog boxes (and the items you place on them) are most easily defined as PowerPlant objects using Constructor. As we look at the resources and code needed to support dialog boxes, we will be using two examples. The first is the dialog box used to modify data stored about a film (Figure 7.1). As you can see in Figure 7.2, the resource contains objects of class LCaption, LEditField, LStdPopupMenu, and LStdButton.

The second example we will be using is the dialog box used to enter data about a video copy (Figure 7.3). The resource (seen in Figure 7.4) adds check boxes and radio

Figure 7.1 The Modify/Delete Movie dialog box

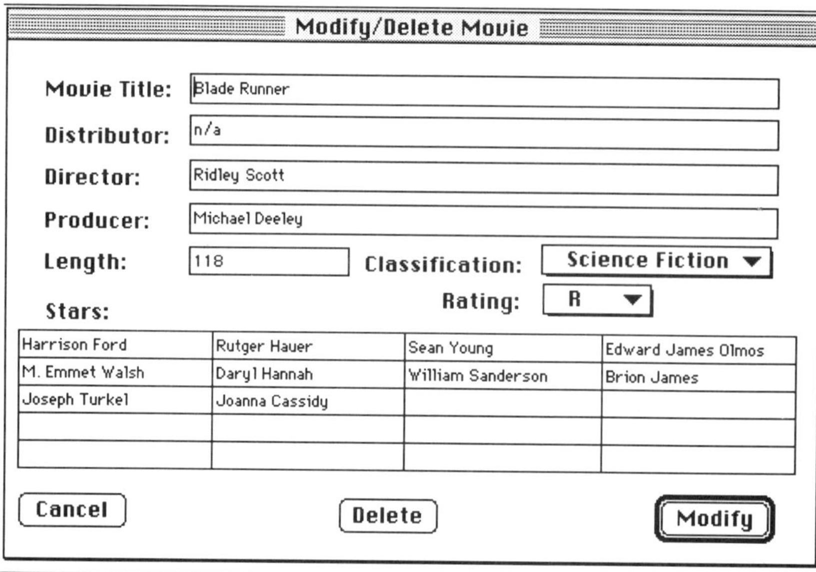

Figure 7.2 The Constructor view of Figure 7.1

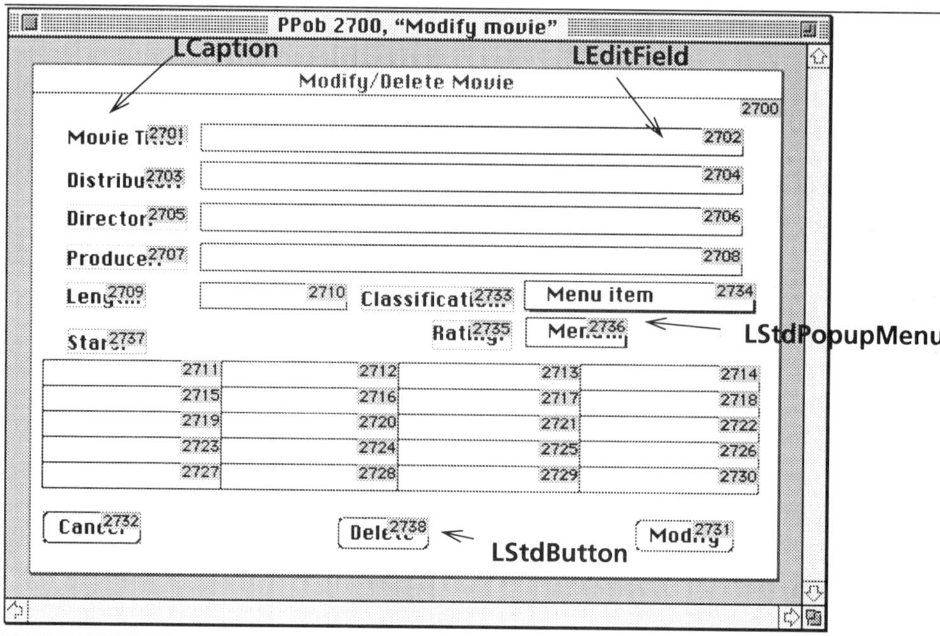

buttons to a popup menu and standard buttons. The scrolling list of titles is an object of class LListBox and will be discussed in Chapter 9.

Figure 7.3 The Enter New Video Copy dialog box

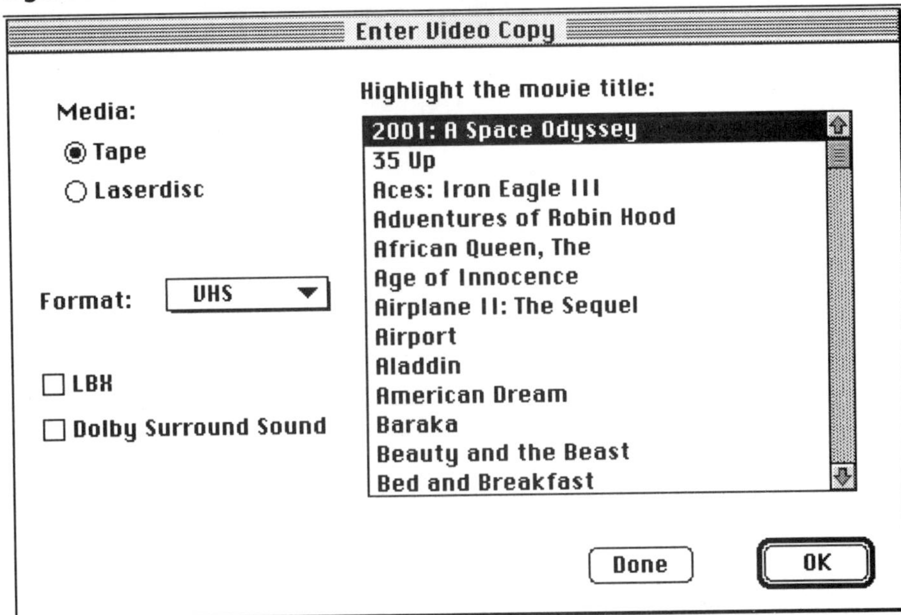

Creating Dialog Box Resources

The class LDialogBox is derived from LWindow and LListener and is therefore a PowerPlant view. When you create a new LDialogBox resource, you therefore choose a PowerPlant view as the resource type and LDialogBox as the view type (for example, Figure 7.5). As with other resources, you also give it a name and a resource ID. Constructor then creates an empty LDialogBox resource (Figure 7.6).

To change the dialog box's attributes, double-click anywhere on the dialog box to display its properties window. In Figure 7.7, for example, you can see the properties window for the Modify/Delete Movie dialog box.

Figure 7.4 The Constructor view of Figure 7.3

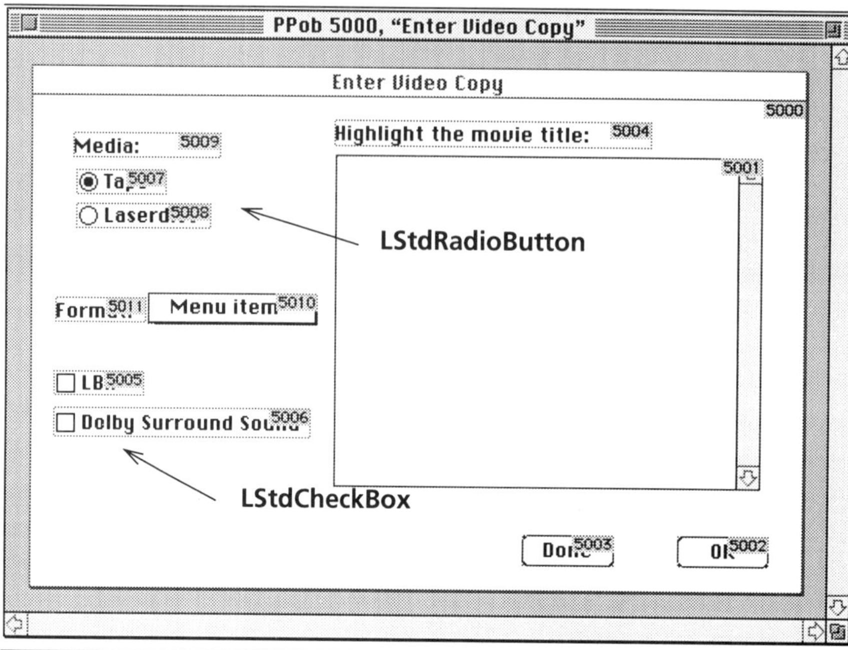

Figure 7.5 Creating a new LDialogBox resource

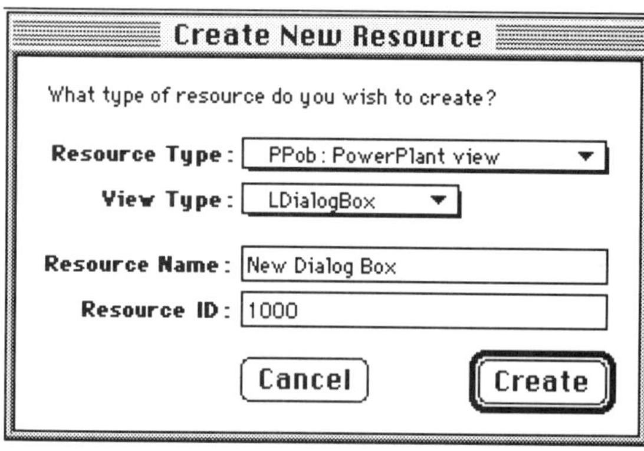

Configuring the Window Type

By default, Constructor creates a standard modal dialog box. However, you have complete control over the appearance of the window. For example, the dialog boxes

Figure 7.6 An empty LDialogBox resource

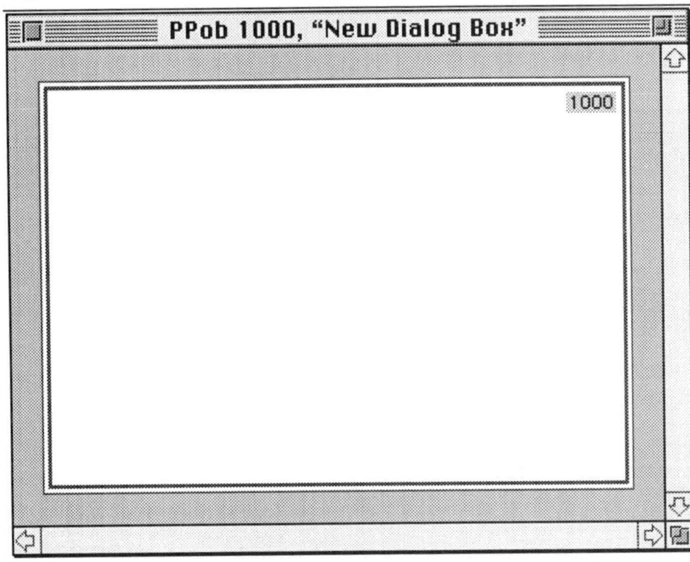

used as examples in this chapter are document windows with title bars that are nonmodal and centered on the main screen.

To change the window type, choose the type from the Window Kind popup menu. As you can see in Figure 7.8, although we are working with an object of class LDialogBox, the dialog box can look like a standard document window as well as like any of the classic dialog boxes.

Should you choose a window type that has a title bar, you can then enter the title in the Window Title box, as was done in Figure 7.7. Use the check boxes at the left of the Window Type area to set characteristics such as whether the window has a size box, zoom box, or close box and whether the window is resizable.

The Auto Position popup menu (Figure 7.9) determines where the window will appear on the screen when it is drawn by a program. By default, Auto Position is off. However, the Modify/Delete Movie dialog box has been modified so that it is centered on the main screen.

The third popup in the Window Type area —Window Layer in Figure 7.10—determines how the window behaves relative to other windows on the screen. As you can see, PowerPlant supports not only modal and nonmodal windows, but also floating palettes.

Figure 7.7 The LDialogBox properties window

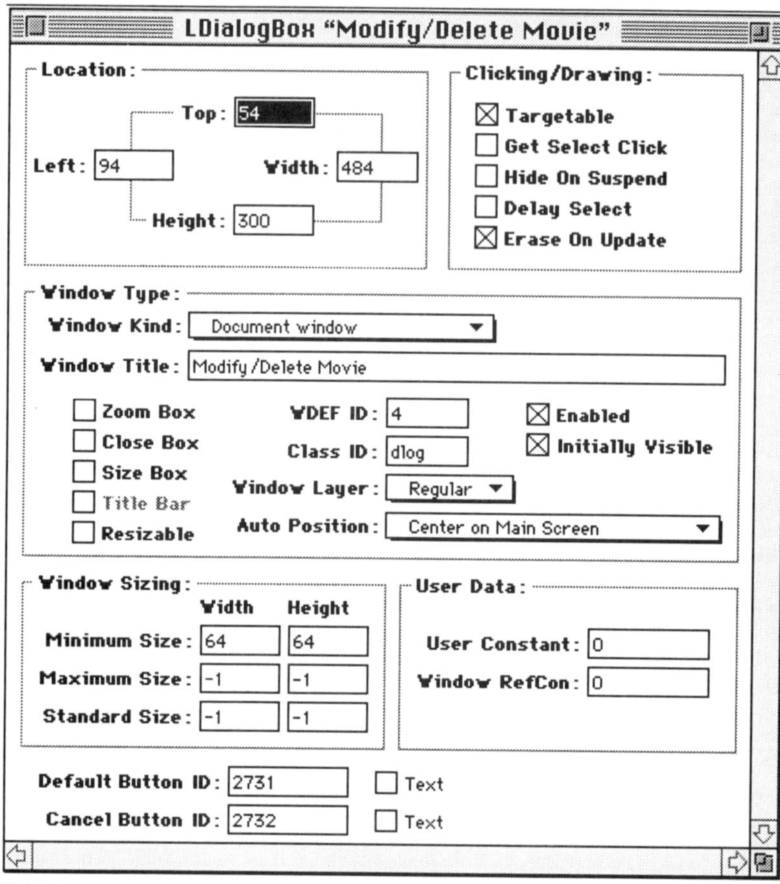

Figure 7.8 PowerPlant object window types

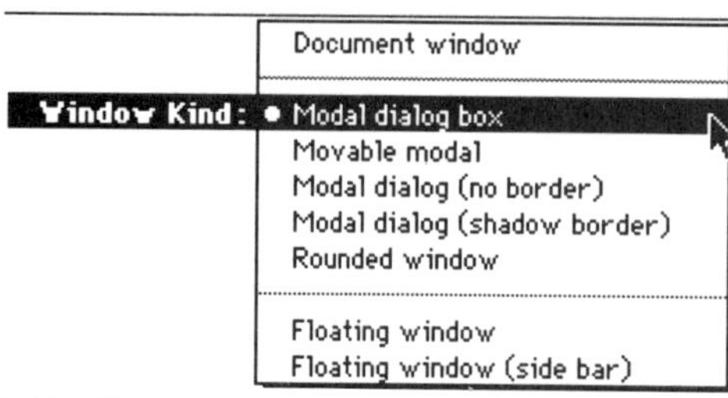

Figure 7.9 Setting a window's autoposition

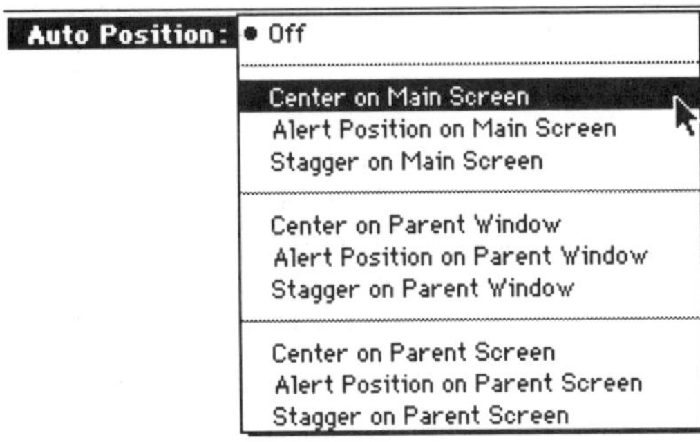

Figure 7.10 Setting a window's layer

USER DATA

Like most PowerPlant objects, a window has two attributes that you can set and use for your own purposes: `User Constant` and `Window RefCon`. Both are long integers and can be an alternative to using global variables for sharing values between objects. You will see an example of how these are used when we look at the code that supports the Modify/Delete Movie dialog box.

BUTTON MESSAGES

If you look back at Figure 5.6 (LWindow properties) and compare it to Figure 7.7, you'll notice that most of dialog box's properties are inherited from LWindow. However, at the bottom of Figure 7.7, there is space to record the resource IDs of the dialog box's default button and Cancel button. This links the buttons to the dialog box so that the dialog box will listen automatically to those buttons. You will leave these boxes blank until you have added buttons to the dialog box object.

Adding Display Text and Edit Fields

Although most of what you place on a dialog box are controls, dialog boxes also often contain two types of text: static text for display only (objects of class LCaption) and editable text (objects of class LEditField). In this section we will look at configuring both types of objects.

Objects of Class LCaption

The LCaption class provides display text. Although a program can change the text, the user cannot. To add a caption, drag an object of LCaption from the Tools palette onto a window and resize it as necessary. Then, double-click on the object to display its properties window.

As you can see in Figure 7.11, a caption is given its own unique ID, some initial text, and a text traits ID to set the font characteristics in which its text will appear. If you will be setting the text in the caption in a program, you can leave the Caption Text field empty.

Figure 7.11 LCaption properties

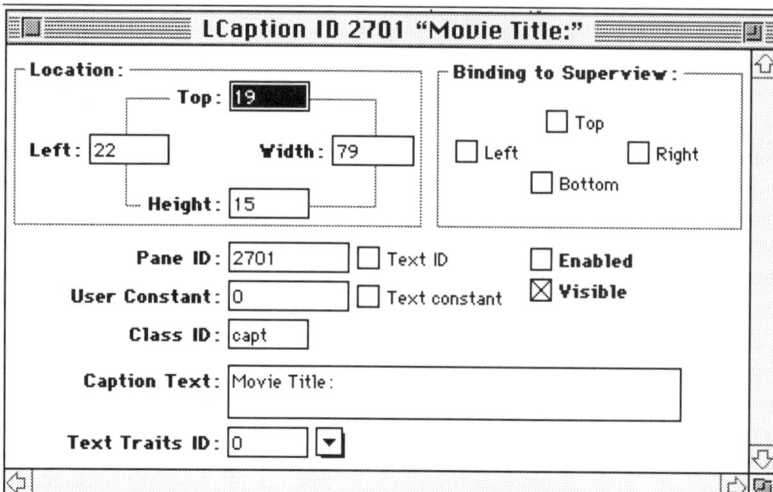

OBJECTS OF CLASS LEDITFIELD

The class LEditField is in many ways a smaller version of LTextEdit. although an object of LEditField usually appears surrounded by a border and cannot be placed in a Scroller. LEditField supports cut, copy, paste, and clear in the edit field. Unlike LTextEdit, it provides support for undo operations. All you have to do is attach an LUndoer to the dialog box containing the LEditField.

To add an edit field to a window, drag an object of LEditField from the Tools palette onto the window. Resize and reposition it as you like. Then double-click on it to open its properties window (for example, Figure 7.12).

Figure 7.12 LEditField properties

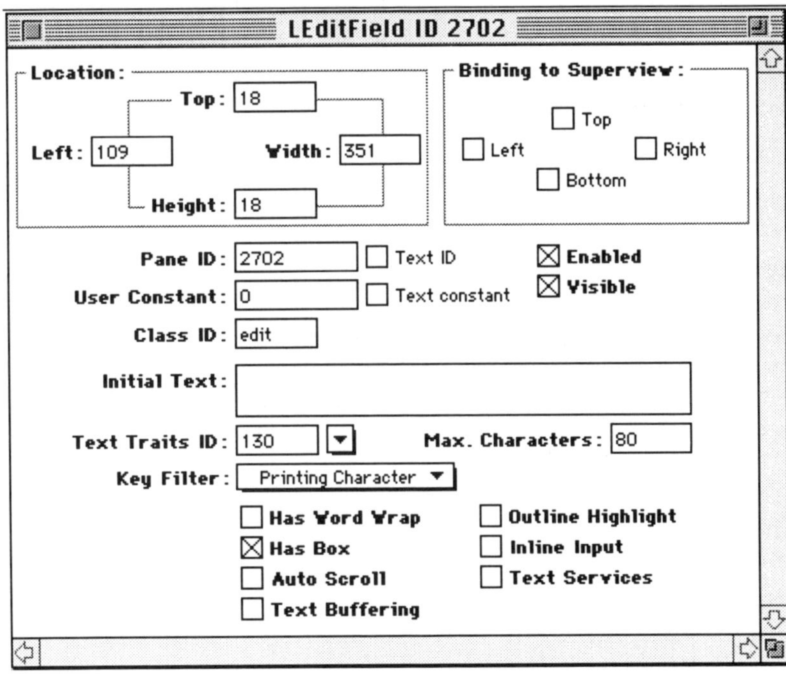

Use the properties window to give the object a unique resource ID, some initial text (if any), and a text traits ID. Use the Max. Characters box to limit the total number of characters that will be allowed in the field. (This can be particularly handy if you will be capturing the data as a string and want to make sure that you don't overflow your string storage.) At runtime, the Mac's speaker will beep if the user attempts to enter more than the maximum number of characters.

Additional error checking on the value entered in the edit field can be applied by using a Key Filter (Figure 7.13). By default, no key filter is applied and anything the user types is acceptable. However, you can restrict the value to an integer (handy for fields such as the length of a movie), an alphanumeric, or any printing character.

Figure 7.13 Key filters

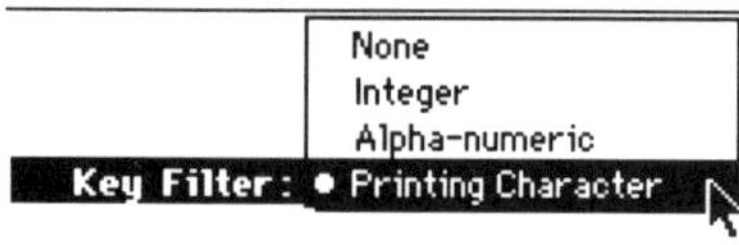

The check boxes at the bottom of the properties window control a variety of edit field characteristics, including the following:

- Has Word Wrap: When checked, performs word wrap if the text entered won't fit on a single line.
- Has Box: When checked, displays a box around the edge of the field.
- Auto Scroll: When checked, automatically scrolls the text as the user types beyond the bottom border of the box.
- Outline Highlight: When checked, draws an outline around selected text when the window on which the edit field has been placed is inactive.
- Text Buffering and Inline Input: Provide support for non-Roman (particularly 2-byte) character sets.

Adding a Tab Group

A tab group (an object of class LTabGroup) defines a group of panes between which the user can move by pressing the Tab key. Each top-level view, such as a dialog box, can have one tab group.

To create a tab group, first place all the edit fields on the window. Then, choose Make Tab Group from the Arrange menu. PowerPlant places all panes (including captions and buttons) in the tab group. Although the tab group actually contains every pane in the window, only objects of LEditField and LTextEdit (the only objects in which a straight-line cursor can appear) are affected when the user presses Tab.

NOTE

If you modify a PowerPlant object, removing or adding LEditField and LTextEdit objects, you should re-create the tab group by choose the Make Tab Group menu option again.

To see the elements of a window that have been added to a tab group, display Constructor's hierarchy window, as was done to generate Figure 1.4. Because a tab group isn't a pane, you can't see in a Constructor resource window.

Edit Fields versus Tables

If you look back at Figure 7.2, you'll be able to count a *lot* of edit field objects (25 of them, to be precise). Since PowerPlant provides a class called LTable, couldn't a table with columns and rows be used to hold the names of up to 20 movie stars rather than 20 individual edit fields? Using a table would be a great idea, but PowerPlant tables are for display only. In fact, they are much more closely related to list boxes than they are to edit fields. To provide editable text, you must resort to objects of class LEditField.

Adding Control Resources

In this section you will learn about four of the most commonly used types of controls (buttons, popup menus, radio buttons, and check boxes). As you read, you will begin to discover the consistent threads that run through all controls supported by PowerPlant.

Buttons

Buttons are typically created from the class LStdButton. Once you've dragged an object onto a window, double-click on the button to display its properties window (for example, Figure 7.14). Give the button its unique resource ID and enter the button title (the text that should appear inside the button).

You must also give the button a "Value Message," the value that will be sent to the window that listens to the button whenever the user clicks the button. When working with dialog boxes, there are two rules you must keep in mind about value messages:

Figure 7.14 LStdButton properties

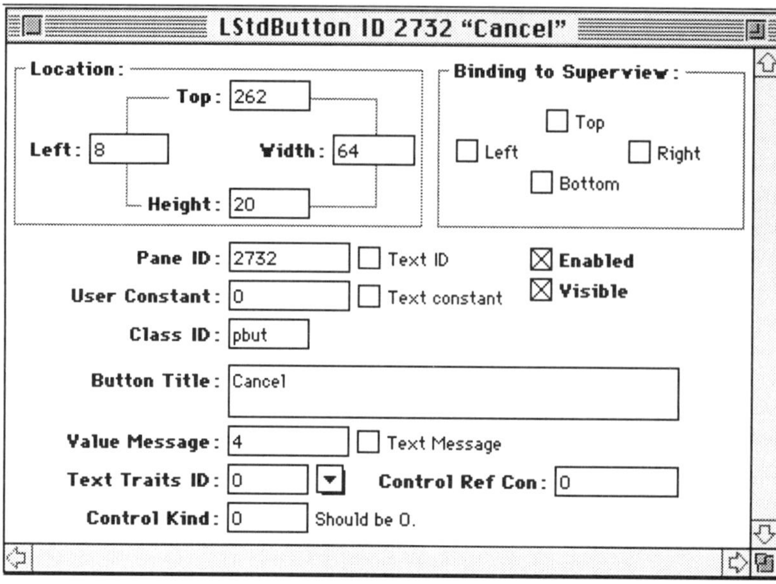

- LDialogBox expects the Cancel button (regardless of what text appears in the button) to have a value message of 4. In other words, when an object of class LDialogBox receives a message of 4, it closes the dialog box without saving any changes made.
- Other than the Cancel message of 4, LDialogBox responds only to *negative* value messages. To make this easy to handle, you may want to give buttons in dialog boxes value messages that are the negative of their resource IDs. For example, if a button has a resource ID of 2733, give it a value message of –2733.

NOTE

When you are working with a dialog box, don't forget to go back to the dialog box's properties window and enter the resource IDs of the Cancel and default buttons. Otherwise, the dialog box won't respond to them.

If the window in which you have placed a button is resizable, you will also need to consider binding the button to its superview. If you want the button to stay in a fixed position relative to one corner of the window, bind the button on either the top and left or the bottom and right. If you want the button to stay in a fixed position relative to one side of the window, bind it on just that side. However, don't bind the button on more than two adjacent sides. Doing so would force a change in the button's size when the superview is resized, causing a distortion in the appearance of the button.

> **NOTE**
> *By default, a dialog box only listens to two buttons. If your dialog box has more, as does the Modify/Delete Movie dialog box, you will need to explicitly tell the dialog box to listen to the additional button(s). Adding listeners is discussed in Chapter 8, where we will cover the code necessary to support dialog box interactions.*

POPUP MENUS

A popup menu requires two resources: an object of class LStdPopupMenu that you create using Constructor, and a MENU resource to contain the menu items. There's no reason you can't use Constructor to create the MENU resource. However, popup menus don't need accompanying Mcmd resources. You will therefore end up with an unnecessary (but harmless) resource if you use Constructor.

To avoid the unnecessary Mcmd resource, the Penultimate Videos program uses MENU resources created with ResEdit for its popup menu items. For example, in Figure 7.15 you can see the resource used to supply the items for the movie type popup in the Modify/Delete Movie dialog box. (This resource is also used in the Enter Movie dialog box.)

Figure 7.15 A MENU resource for a popup menu (ResEdit format)

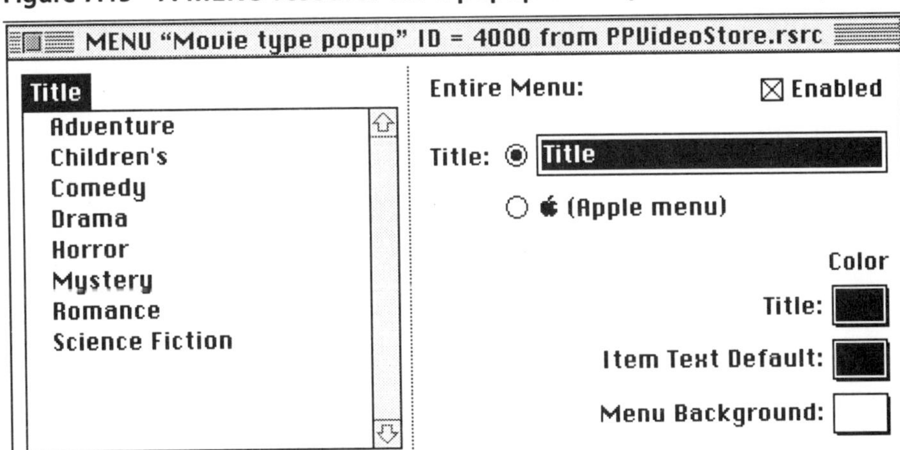

Once you have a resource containing menu items, you can add an object of LStd-PopupMenu to your window, which has the properties seen in Figure 7.16. If you do nothing else with the object, be sure to enter the ID of the MENU resource in the MENU ID box.

Figure 7.16 LStdPopupMenu properties

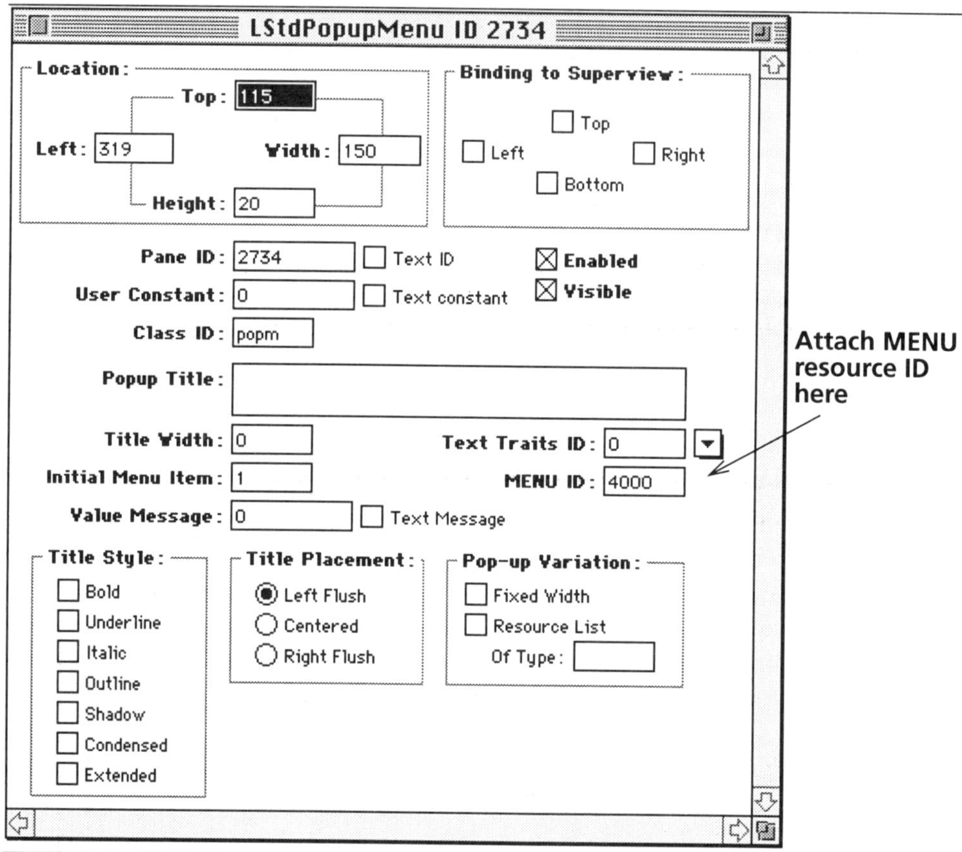

When it comes to popup titles, you have two choices. You can enter the title in the LStdPopupMenu properties window and use the Title Style check boxes to set its style and the Title Placement radio buttons to determine its alignment. Alternatively, you can use an object of class LCaption as a title, leaving the Popup Title box empty. The latter gives you a bit more flexibility because you can change the LCaption object while the program is running.

PowerPlant numbers the items in a popup menu beginning with 1, counting from the top of the MENU resource's item list. To set a default value for the popup, enter the number of the default item in the Initial Menu Item box.

If your window is resizable, you should also pay attention to binding the popup menu to its superview. In most cases, you will bind it either to the top left or bottom right of the window.

RADIO BUTTONS

Dialog boxes often contain one or more groups of radio buttons that allow a user to choose one option from a group of mutually exclusive options. The Enter Video Copy dialog box in Figure 7.3, for example, uses radio buttons to allow the user to select whether a copy is a tape or a laserdisc.

You add a radio button to a view by dragging an object of LStdRadioButton from the Tools palette onto a window. Using its properties window (for example, Figure 7.17), you can set the following object characteristics:

Figure 7.17 LStdRadioButton properties

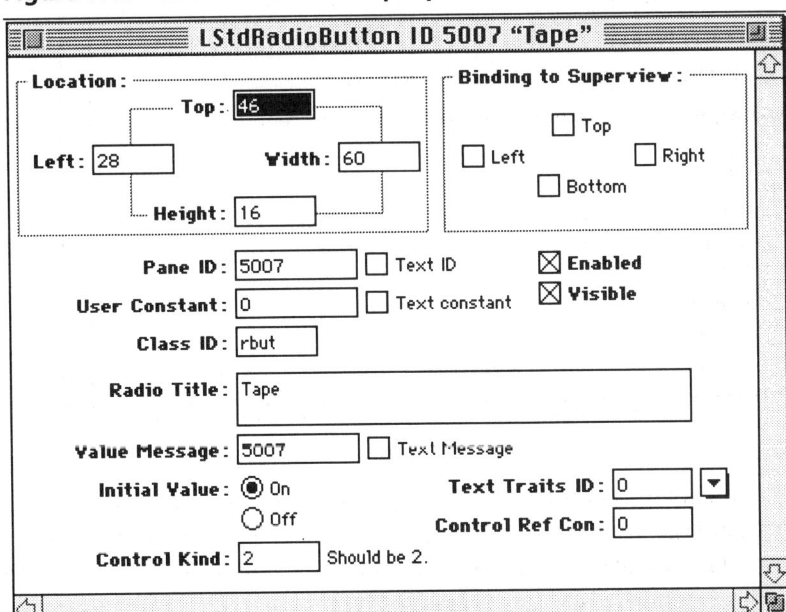

- The unique resource ID.
- The button title, which always appears to the right of the button.
- A text traits ID for the button title.
- A value message that the button sends when it is clicked. This message is detected and handled by the LStdRadioButton class.
- The button's initial value.

A special note should be made about a button's initial value. Only one radio button in any group of radio buttons should be "on." It is therefore up to you to make sure that you only give one radio button in any given group of radio buttons an initial value of "on."

Grouping Radio Buttons

When a radio button is added to a view, it exists as a stand-alone object. However, we need radio buttons to act as part of a group. You must therefore create an object of class LRadioGroup for each separate group of radio buttons.

To define a radio group, select all the radio buttons that should be part of a single group. Then, choose Make Radio Group from the Arrange menu or press ⌘-G. Constructor adds an object of class LRadioGroup to your view. Because an object of class LRadioGroup isn't a pane, it won't show up on the view you are creating. However, if you look at the view's object hierarchy (for example, Figure 7.18), you can see the radio group object followed by a list of the resource IDs of the radio buttons that are part of that group.

Check Boxes

A check box provides a simple way for users to enter binary data (yes/no, on/off, and so on). As with any other control you've seen to this point, you add a check box to a view by dragging an object of class LStdCheckBox onto a window. Then, you set the properties found in Figure 7.19, which include the following:

- The check box's unique resource ID.
- The check box's title, which always appears to the right of the check box.
- A text traits ID for the check box's title.
- A unique value message that the check box sends back to the class LStdCheckBox when the box is clicked.
- An initial value (either "on" or "off").

Figure 7.18 A view hierarchy including a radio group

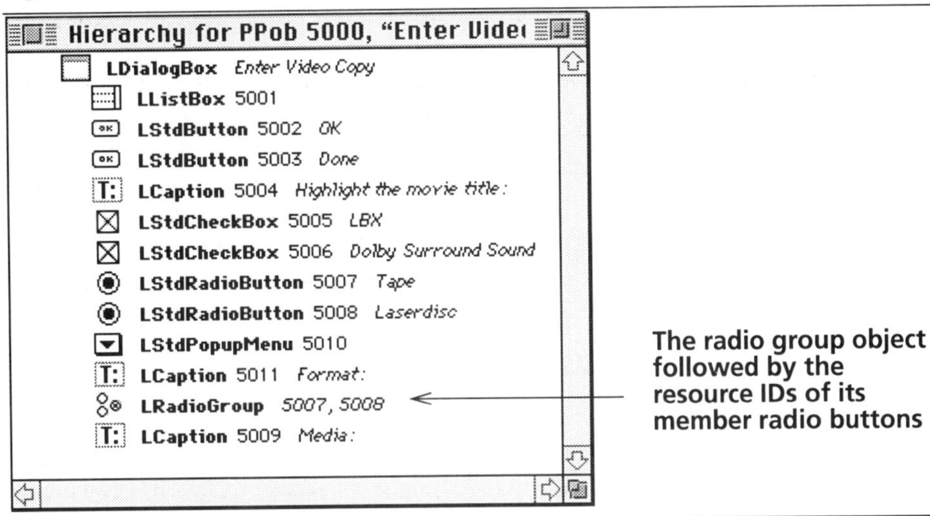

Figure 7.19 LStdCheckBox properties

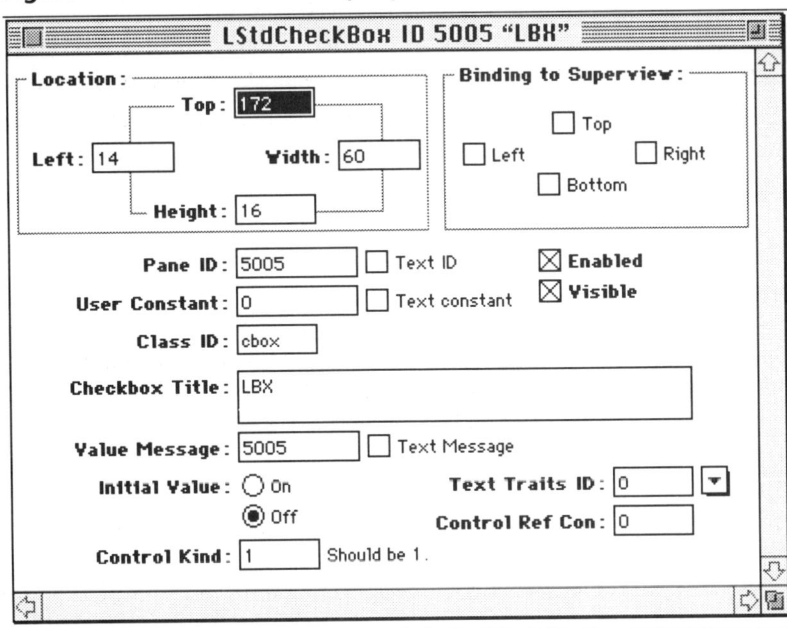

RidL Resources

Whenever you use Constructor to create a view that contains controls, Constructor automatically adds the resource IDs of those controls to a RidL (Resource ID list) resource. As you can see in Figure 7.20, the RidL resource for the New Video Copy dialog box contains the resource IDs of the radio buttons, check boxes, popup menus, and standard buttons that appear on the window.

Figure 7.20 The RidL resource for the New Video Copy dialog box

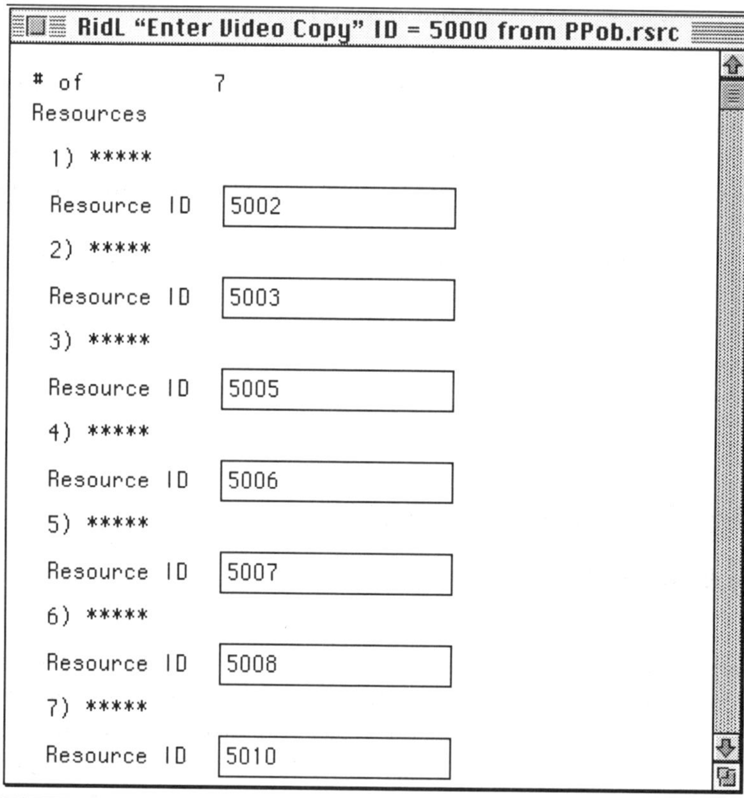

An RidL resource is used by the class LDialogBox to connect controls, which are broadcasters, to the listener that will respond to them using the function `UReanimator::LinkListenerToControls`. This function makes repeated calls to

AddListener and can therefore simplify the task of getting a window to listen to many controls. The function call has the following general format:

```
UReanimator::LinkListenerToControls (* listener_object,
        * pane_containing_controls, resource_ID_of_RidL);
```

An important note is warranted here with regard to when you need to add a listener for a control. In many cases, you don't care about the value of a control at the time the user changes that value. For example, in the Modify/Delete Movie dialog box, the program doesn't need to respond to any of the popup menus right away; it only needs to capture their values when the user uses the Modify button. Therefore, the dialog box only needs to listen to its three buttons.

By the same token, the New Video Copy dialog box doesn't need to listen to its radio buttons, check boxes, popup menu, or list of video titles. The current settings in all of those subpanes can be captured when the user clicks the OK button.

However, if you want a control to have an immediate effect, then you must make sure that some object listens to it. In Chapter 8, for example, we will look at a window that contains check boxes to which a program respond as soon as a use changes the state of a control. In addition, in Chapter 9, you will see that a dialog box must listen to an LListBox if the program is to respond to a double-click in the list. In both cases, the windows containing the controls must explicitly add them to their lists of broadcasters.

Preparing Resource and Message Constants

PowerPlant programs make extensive use of the resource IDs and value messages that are part of the resources we have been discussing. It is ironic that an object-oriented environment that should be adhering to the ideas of data encapsulation is so closely tied to global constants. Nonetheless, because the Macintosh is designed to use resource IDs, we are stuck with needing to deal with a large number of constants. Typically, we make life much easier by collecting these constants into header files so they can be easily found, and if necessary, modified.

Like many other PowerPlant programs of any appreciable size, the Penultimate Videos program maintains a header file for resource IDs (*ResourceConstants.h*) and a resource file for value messages (*MenuCommands.h*). In Listing 7.1, for example, you will find the resource constants for the two dialog boxes we have been using as examples in this chapter. Notice that there is a constant for the dialog box resource and every object on the dialog box from which the program must retrieve a value. As far as buttons are concerned, a program that uses a dialog box needs to be concerned only with buttons other than the default and Cancel buttons. The Enter Video Copy resource constants therefore don't need to include any buttons. However, the Modify/Delete Movie dialog box has a third button—Delete—that the program will need to manipulate directly. This button must therefore have a constant for the program to use.

Listing 7.1 Sample resource constants for the Penultimate Videos program

```
const ResIDT WINDOW_NEW_VCOPY = 5000;
// The following are constants for all the controls on the dialog box,
// everything from which the program must retrieve a value.
    const ResIDT VCOPY_LIST_BOX = 5001;
    const ResIDT VCOPY_RB_TAPE = 5007;
    const ResIDT VCOPY_RB_LD = 5008;
    const ResIDT VCOPY_FORMAT = 5010;
    const ResIDT VCOPY_CB_LBX = 5005;
    const ResIDT VCOPY_CB_DSS = 5006;

const ResIDT WINDOW_MOD_MOVIE = 2700;
// The following are all the edit fields and popup menus on the dialog box.
// There are constants for every pane from which the program must retrieve a value.
    const ResIDT MOD_MOVIE_TITLE = 2702;
    const ResIDT MOD_MOVIE_DIST = 2704;
    const ResIDT MOD_MOVIE_DIRECT = 2706;
    const ResIDT MOD_MOVIE_PRODUCE = 2708;
    const ResIDT MOD_MOVIE_LENGTH = 2710;
    const ResIDT MOD_MOVIE_CLASS = 2734;
    const ResIDT MOD_MOVIE_RATING = 2736;
    const ResIDT MOD_MOVIE_STAR1 = 2711;
    const ResIDT MOD_MOVIE_STAR2 = 2712;
    const ResIDT MOD_MOVIE_STAR3 = 2713;
    const ResIDT MOD_MOVIE_STAR4 = 2714;
    const ResIDT MOD_MOVIE_STAR5 = 2715;
    const ResIDT MOD_MOVIE_STAR6 = 2716;
    const ResIDT MOD_MOVIE_STAR7 = 2717;
    const ResIDT MOD_MOVIE_STAR8 = 2718;
    const ResIDT MOD_MOVIE_STAR9 = 2719;
    const ResIDT MOD_MOVIE_STAR10 = 2720;
    const ResIDT MOD_MOVIE_STAR11 = 2721;
    const ResIDT MOD_MOVIE_STAR12 = 2722;
    const ResIDT MOD_MOVIE_STAR13 = 2723;
    const ResIDT MOD_MOVIE_STAR14 = 2724;
```

Continued next page

Listing 7.1 (Continued) Sample resource constants for the Penultimate Videos pro-

```
    const ResIDT MOD_MOVIE_STAR15 = 2725;
    const ResIDT MOD_MOVIE_STAR16 = 2726;
    const ResIDT MOD_MOVIE_STAR17 = 2727;
    const ResIDT MOD_MOVIE_STAR18 = 2728;
    const ResIDT MOD_MOVIE_STAR19 = 2729;
    const ResIDT MOD_MOVIE_STAR20 = 2730;
// Only the Delete button appears hear because the dialog box handles
// the Cancel button and the default button automatically
    const ResIDT MOD_MOVIE_DELETE = 2738;
```

Message constants should exist for every message a program will trap. For example, Listing 7.2 contains the message constants needed for the two sample dialog boxes. Messages sent by radio buttons, check boxes, and the Cancel button are handled by LStdRadioButton, LStdCheckBox, and LDialogBox, respectively. However, the program must trap the default buttons and the Modify/Delete Movie's Delete buttons. The program therefore needs constants for those messages.

Listing 7.2 Sample message constants for the Penultimate Videos program

```
const MessageT cmd_OK_new_video_copy = -5002;

const MessageT cmd_Modify_movie = -2731;
const MessageT cmd_Delete_movie = -2738;
```

NOTE

PowerPlant has constants for messages that its classes recognize (for example, the message of 4 for a Cancel button) stored in PP Messages.h.

CHAPTER 8

Programming for Dialog Boxes and Controls

In Chapter 7 you read about creating the resources necessary to support dialog boxes and the items that appear on them. This chapter first extends that discussion by looking at the code needed to display dialog boxes, trap user actions with dialog box buttons, and capture and modify dialog box item values. The initial discussion of controls looks at situations where a program reads the values of controls (other than buttons) after the user has finished working with the dialog box.

However, a window or dialog box can also respond immediately to changes made in controls such as radio buttons and check boxes. For example, you might use a check box to display or hide a pane. An example of this type of "live" control can be found at the end of this chapter.

Deciding Whether to Subclass

It is often possible to create objects directly from LDialogBox without creating a subclass because many dialog boxes behave in a standard manner. Assuming that you aren't planning to add any custom functionality to a dialog box, should you go ahead and create a subclass anyway?

As you read earlier in this book, there are a number of issues involved with making that decision. When a listener such as LDialogBox is concerned, there is one additional consideration: LDialogBox, like all listeners, has a function called `ListenToMessage`. This is where it traps messages from its broadcasters. As written, the function handles a dialog box's Cancel and default buttons. (To be completed accurately, LDialogBox traps the default button's message and then passes the message to its supercommander's `ProcessCommand` function.)

If you create a subclass for a dialog box, you can override `ListenToMessage` so that you can add code to it to handle messages from all the controls you place on the dialog box. If you don't create a subclass, all the code to handle control messages is usually part of the dialog box's supercommander (in its `ListenToMessage` or `ObeyCommand` function). In the case of the Penultimate Videos program, the application object is the supercommander of all dialog boxes because it is the commander object that creates the dialog box objects. The result is a very large, but centrally located, `ObeyCommand` function.

The bottom line? If your dialog box will include only standard behaviors, choose whichever structure makes maintaining the program easier for you and the programming team with which you may be working.

Should you choose to subclass, there are some programming issues with which you will need to contend, including the decision as to which base class functions to override. The window that is used as a demonstration of "live" controls at the end of this chapter is therefore implemented as a subclass. This provides an example of setting up a listener, linking it to its controls, and trapping user actions with those controls.

Displaying a Dialog Box

To display a dialog box, a program needs to create an object of class LDialogBox and then call the object's `Show` function. In Listing 8.1, for example, you will find the function that displays the New Video Copy dialog box. Most of the code in this function builds the scrolling list of titles. In fact, displaying the dialog box on the screen requires only two actions:

Listing 8.1 Displaying the New Video Copy dialog box

```
void CPPVideoStoreApp::SetUpNewVideoCopy()
{
    LDialogBox * theDialog;
    LListBox * theList;
    ListHandle theListHandle;  // handle to list of movies

    theDialog = (LDialogBox *) LWindow::CreateWindow (WINDOW_NEW_VCOPY, this);

// This code sets up the scrolling list of items.
// We'll discussion of it until Chapter 9.

    theList = (LListBox *) theDialog->FindPaneByID (VCOPY_LIST_BOX);
    theListHandle = theList->GetMacListH(); // get the list box's list handle
    ::LAddColumn (1, 0, theListHandle); // add a column to the empty list

    MerchItr traversal;
    int Type, row = 0;
    Merchandise_Item * currentOne;
    char * Title;
    StringPtr pascalString;
    // a cell (row & column number) and a pointer to the variable
    Cell theCell, * theCellPtr;

    theCellPtr = &theCell;

    for (traversal.Init (Items); !traversal; ++traversal)
    {
        currentOne = traversal();
        Type = currentOne->getItem_type();
        if (Type == FILM || Type == OTHER)
        {
            Title = currentOne->getTitle();
            ::LAddRow (1, row, theListHandle); // add a row to the list
            // initialize the coordinates of the cell just added
            ::SetPt (theCellPtr, 0, row++);
            ::LSetCell (Title, strlen(Title), theCell, theListHandle); // add the data
        }
    }
    theList->SetValue (0); // make sure first item is highlighted
// End of list-building code

    theDialog->Show();
}
```

- Call the `CreateWindow` function, typecasting the LWindow pointer returned by the function to an LDialogBox pointer:

```
theDialog = (LDialogBox *) LWindow::CreateWindow (WINDOW_NEW_VCOPY, this);
```

- Call the `Show` function:

```
theDialog->Show();
```

As you know, the `CreateWindow` function initiates a sequence of actions that creates the dialog box object itself along with objects for all of its subpanes (the items that appear on the dialog box).

Enabling Undo

If a dialog box contains edit fields and you want undo operations to work, you should attach an LUndoer to the dialog box:

```
LUndoer * theUndoer = new LUndoer;
theDialog->AddAttachment(theUndoer, nil, TRUE);
```

One undoer object will take care of all the edit fields on any given dialog box.

Adding Listeners for Other Controls

By default, a dialog box listens only to its Cancel and default buttons. If a dialog box contains anything else to which it should listen—such as another button or a double-click in a scrolling list—a program must explicitly add that object to the dialog box's list of listeners. For example, the Modify/Delete Movie dialog box must add the Delete button as a listener. Doing so requires two lines of code:

```
LStdButton * deleteButton = (LStdButton *)
      theDialog->FindPaneByID (MOD_MOVIE_DELETE);
deleteButton->AddListener (theDialog);
```

The `FindPaneByID` function, which you will use frequently, retrieves a pointer to a subpane of a view. Its single parameter is the subpane's resource ID, which in the preceding example is represented by the constant `MOD_MOVIE_DELETE`. By default, `FindPaneByID` returns a pointer to an object of class LPane because the function is inherited from LPane. You must therefore typecast it to the specific class from which the object whose pointer you want has been created.

Once a program has a pointer to the pane in question (in this example, a button), that pane can add itself to a list of broadcasters to which another object listens. As nonintuitive as it might seem, the `AddListener` function is called by the broadcaster (the button) rather than the listener. (If it helps to keep this straight, you might want to think of the `AddListener` function as "Add to listener.")

Positioning the Insertion Point

When a dialog box contains more than one edit field, as does the Modify/Delete Movie dialog box, the straight-line insertion point ends up in the last edit field created. However, in most cases you want the cursor to appear in the top edit field on the dialog box so the user can then tab "down" the dialog box as he or she works. In other words, you want to make sure that the first edit field is the current target.

To explicitly switch the target, you need a pointer to the pane that should become the target. Then you can use the `SwitchTarget` function:

```
theEditField = (LEditField *) theDialog->FindPaneByID (MOD_MOVIE_TITLE);
firstEditField = theEditField;

// some other stuff goes on in here, perhaps

// do this before turning control over to the user
firstEditField->SwitchTarget (firstEditField);
```

The `SwitchTarget` function belongs to the LCommander class. The object that calls the function must be a commander. The function's single parameter is a pointer to the object that wants to become the target. By having the object that wants to become the target pass itself into the function, the object says,"Make me the target."

Trapping Button Actions

A program traps actions in a dialog box in an `ObeyCommand` function. The class to which that function belongs depends on the structure of the program. If the dialog box is being created directly from LDialogBox, without a subclass, then actions in that dialog box are trapped in the `ObeyCommand` function of the class that created the dialog box. In the Penultimate Videos program, for example, that class is the application class (a subclass of LApplication). However, if the dialog box was created from a subclass of LDialogBox, then the `ObeyCommand` function that traps dialog box actions is typically part of the subclass.

In Listing 8.2 you will find the `case` from the Penultimate Video's `ObeyCommand` function that traps the OK button on the New Video Copy dialog box. Notice that the function that handles the action (`ProcessNewVideoCopy`) has a single parameter: the structure `ioParam`, which is typecast to a dialog response structure (`SDialogResponse`). This dialog response structure contains a pointer to the dialog box with which the user most recently interacted. A PowerPlant program therefore usually doesn't need to store dialog box pointers once a dialog box has been displayed.

Listing 8.2 Trapping the click of an OK button

```
case cmd_OK_new_video_copy:
        ProcessNewVideoCopy ((SDialogResponse *) ioParam);
        break;
```

NOTE

There is an informal naming scheme used in the functions that handle the Penultimate Videos dialog boxes. Those function names that begin with "SetUp" display dialog boxes; those that begin with "Process" trap dialog box actions and process the contents of the dialog box in some way.

Removing a Dialog Box

When the user clicks a dialog box's Cancel button, LDialogBox takes care of removing the dialog box from the screen. However, if the user clicks the default button or interacts with any other controls that your program traps, it is up to you to remove the dialog box. To do so, simply delete the dialog box object:

```
delete theDialog;
```

The dialog box will be removed from the screen and deleted from memory.

Handling Edit Fields

Once a program has trapped an action with a control, the program must process the contents of the dialog box in some way. In this section we will look at retrieving the contents of edit fields, as well as how to place data into edit fields.

Retrieving Data from Edit Fields

When a user activates the Modify button on the Modify/Delete Movie dialog box, the program traps the button press and then calls the `ModifyMovie` function, which retrieves data from the dialog box's edit fields and uses those values to change a Film object in memory.

A portion of `ModifyMovie` can be found in Listing 8.3. As you can see, the first step is to obtain a pointer to the edit field object with a call to `FindPaneByID`. Then, you can use one of two functions to capture the contents of the edit field:

- `GetDescriptor`: Returns the contents of the edit field as a Pascal string.
- `GetValue`: Returns the integer value of the contents of the edit field. Use this function only when you know that the edit field contains an integer.

The running time of a movie is an integer. Therefore, the Penultimate Videos program can use `GetValue` only with the Length variable. The program must use `GetDescriptor` to retrieve the contents of the rest of the edit fields on the dialog box.

Putting Data in Edit Fields

The Penultimate Videos program's `SetUpItemModify` function retrieves the merchandise item being modified and displays its data in a dialog box for the user to change. When the item is a movie, the program uses the Modify/Delete Movie dialog box.

In Listing 8.4, you can see that the process is the opposite of retrieving data. First, you use `FindPaneByID` to get a pointer to the edit field object, and then you use one of the following two functions to replace the object's contents:

- `SetDescriptor`: Replaces an edit field's contents with a new Pascal string.
- `SetValue`: Replaces an edit field's contents with an integer. Use this function only when you are dealing with an integer.

Listing 8.3 Retrieving data from edit fields

```
// must first check to see if title has been modified.
// if so,  must delete from title tree and reinsert
    LEditField * theEditField = (LEditField *)
        theDialog->FindPaneByID (MOD_MOVIE_TITLE);
    theEditField->GetDescriptor(pascalValue);
    convertPascal255 (pascalValue, ANSIValue);
    currentTitle = theFilm->getTitle();
    if (strcmp (ANSIValue, currentTitle) != 0)
    {
        // FALSE in call to Delete prevents copies from being deleted
        Items->Delete (FALSE, theFilm, Copies);
        theFilm->setTitle (ANSIValue);  // modify title
        theFilm->setLeftName (0);  // reset pointers for title tree
        theFilm->setRightName (0);
        Items->Insert (theFilm, ANSIValue, FALSE);  // reinsert
    }

    theEditField = (LEditField *) theDialog->FindPaneByID (MOD_MOVIE_DIST);
    theEditField->GetDescriptor(pascalValue);
    convertPascal255 (pascalValue, ANSIValue);
    theFilm->setDistributor (ANSIValue);
    theEditField = (LEditField *) theDialog->FindPaneByID (MOD_MOVIE_DIRECT);
    theEditField->GetDescriptor(pascalValue);
    convertPascal255 (pascalValue, ANSIValue);
    theFilm->setDirector (ANSIValue);
    theEditField = (LEditField *) theDialog->FindPaneByID (MOD_MOVIE_PRODUCE);
    theEditField->GetDescriptor(pascalValue);
    convertPascal255 (pascalValue, ANSIValue);
    theFilm->setProducer (ANSIValue);
    theEditField = (LEditField *) theDialog->FindPaneByID (MOD_MOVIE_LENGTH);
    intValue = theEditField->GetValue();
    theFilm->setLength (intValue);
```

Clearing Edit Fields

When a user is entering new data using the Penultimate Videos program, he or she will probably be entering more than one object's data at a time. It therefore makes sense to leave the dialog box with which the user is working on the screen after processing one object's data. Rather than deleting the dialog box object and recreating it, a program can simply clear the contents of edit fields.

The code fragment in Listing 8.5 is taken from the `ProcessNewMovie`. To retrieve data from an edit field and then reset the field for the next object, the code does the following:

Listing 8.4 Placing data in edit fields

```
theDialog = (LDialogBox *) LWindow::CreateWindow (WINDOW_MOD_MOVIE, this);
theEditField = (LEditField *) theDialog->FindPaneByID (MOD_MOVIE_TITLE);
firstEditField = theEditField;
theEditField->SetDescriptor (pascalString);
theEditField = (LEditField *) theDialog->FindPaneByID (MOD_MOVIE_DIST);
pascalString = theMovie->getDistributor ();
theEditField->SetDescriptor (pascalString);
theEditField = (LEditField *) theDialog->FindPaneByID (MOD_MOVIE_DIRECT);
pascalString = theMovie->getDirector ();
theEditField->SetDescriptor (pascalString);
theEditField = (LEditField *) theDialog->FindPaneByID (MOD_MOVIE_PRODUCE);
pascalString = theMovie->getProducer ();
theEditField->SetDescriptor (pascalString);
theEditField = (LEditField *) theDialog->FindPaneByID (MOD_MOVIE_LENGTH);
int how_long = theMovie->getLength ();
theEditField->SetValue (how_long);
```

Listing 8.5 Clearing an edit field

```
LEditField * theFirstEditField = (LEditField *) theDialog->FindPaneByID (MOVIE_TITLE);
theFirstEditField->GetDescriptor (pascalString);
convertPascal255 (pascalString, iTitle);
theFirstEditField->SetDescriptor (null);

// other stuff goes here

// Make the top edit field on the dialog box the target
theFirstEditField->SwitchTarget (theFirstEditField);
```

- Gets a pointer to the edit field object with `FindPaneByID`.
- Retrieves the contents of the edit field with `GetDescriptor`.
- Converts the contents to a C string so it can be processed.
- Sets the contents of the edit field to *null* with `SetDescriptor`.

After the contents of all edit fields and controls on the dialog box have been handled, the function makes the dialog box's top edit field the target. This leaves the dialog box in the same state it was when it was first created.

Working with Check Boxes

A check box represents a Boolean value (0 for checked, 1 for not checked). To capture a check box setting, you therefore use the `GetValue` function. As you can see in Listing 8.6, the code first obtains a pointer to the check box object and then retrieves its value. To set a check box's value, send a 0 for checked or a 1 for not checked to the check box using its `SetValue` function, as in Listing 8.7.

Listing 8.6 Reading a check box's setting

```
LStdCheckBox * theCheckBox = (LStdCheckBox *) theDialog->FindPaneByID(VCOPY_CB_LBX);
iLBX = theCheckBox->GetValue();

theCheckBox = (LStdCheckBox *) theDialog->FindPaneByID(VCOPY_CB_DSS);
iDolby = theCheckBox->GetValue();
```

Listing 8.7 Changing a check box's setting

```
// set the check boxes
theCheckBox = (LStdCheckBox *) theDialog->FindPaneByID(MOD_VC_CB_LBX);
theCheckBox->SetValue(saveVideoCopy->getLBX());
theCheckBox = (LStdCheckBox *) theDialog->FindPaneByID(MOD_VC_CB_DSS);
theCheckBox->SetValue(saveVideoCopy->getDolby());
```

NOTE

The LStdCheckBox class does have GetDescriptor and SetDescriptor functions. However, in this case GetDescriptor returns the title of the check box (the text that appears to the right of it) and SetDescriptor changes the title of the check box.

Working with Radio Buttons

Like a check box, a radio button returns its value (represented by the PowerPlant constants `Button_On` and `Button_Off`) through its `GetValue` function (for example, Listing 8.8). However, because there can be more than two buttons in a radio group, you may need to check more than one button before you can determine which one is highlighted. To set the value in a radio button, as in Listing 8.9, pass either `Button_On` or `Button_Off` through the button's `SetValue` function.

Listing 8.8 Reading radio button settings

```
LStdRadioButton * theRadioButton = (LStdRadioButton *)
    theDialog->FindPaneByID(VCOPY_RB_TAPE);
RadioButtonValue = theRadioButton->GetValue();
if (RadioButtonValue == Button_On)
    strcpy (iMedia,"Tape");
else
    strcpy (iMedia,"Laserdisc");
```

Listing 8.9 Changing radio button settings

```
// set the media radio buttons
property = saveVideoCopy->getMedia();
if (strcmp (property, "Tape") == 0)
    theRadioButton = (LStdRadioButton *) theDialog->FindPaneByID(MOD_VC_RB_TAPE);
else
    theRadioButton = (LStdRadioButton *) theDialog->FindPaneByID(MOD_VC_RB_LD);
theRadioButton->SetValue(Button_On);
```

NOTE

Like check boxes, radio buttons also have GetDescriptor and SetDescriptor functions that affect the title of the button.

Handling Popup Menus

Dealing with popup menus is only slightly more involved than handling check boxes or radio buttons. PowerPlant numbers the items in a popup menu's MENU resource beginning with 1. A popup's `GetValue` function returns the currently selected item. Once you have that value, you can either process the value directly or look it up in a table to retrieve the item text or a constant you've assigned to the item. In Listing 8.10, for example, popup menu items are stored in arrays that can be used as lookup tables to retrieve the item text.

Listing 8.10 Reading a popup menu choice

```
ANSIstring classPopup [] = {"Adventure", "Children's", "Comedy", "Drama", "Horror",
    "Mystery","Romance","Science Fiction"};
ANSIstring ratingPopup [] = {"G","PG","PG-13","R","NR-17","X","XXX"};

LStdPopupMenu * thePopup = (LStdPopupMenu *) theDialog->FindPaneByID (MOD_MOVIE_CLASS);
int menuChoice = thePopup->GetValue () - 1;
theFilm->setClass(classPopup[menuChoice]);

thePopup = (LStdPopupMenu *) theDialog->FindPaneByID (MOD_MOVIE_RATING);
menuChoice = thePopup->GetValue () - 1;
theFilm->setRating (ratingPopup[menuChoice]);
```

NOTE

It's probably not wise to use the position of a popup menu item in the popup as data that represents that item. If you ever change the popup menu's associated MENU resource, the item's position in the popup will change, invalidating at least some of your code.

To set a popup menu's value, you must pass the popup's `SetValue` function an integer that corresponds to the item that should be selected. For example, in Listing 8.11 the Penultimate Videos program finds the stored value in a lookup table (an array) and then uses that value to set the selected item in the popup menu.

Listing 8.11 Setting a popup menu choice

```
ANSIstring classPopup [] = {"Adventure","Children's","Comedy","Drama","Horror","
   Mystery","Romance","Science Fiction"};
ANSIstring ratingPopup [] = {"G","PG","PG-13","R","NR-17","X","XXX"};

property = theMovie->getRating ();
for (i = 0; i < 7; i++)
    if (strcmp (property, ratingPopup[i]) == 0)
        break;
thePopup = (LStdPopupMenu *) theDialog->FindPaneByID (MOD_MOVIE_RATING);
thePopup->SetValue (i+1);

property = theMovie->getClass ();
for (i = 0; i < 8; i++)
    if (strcmp (property,classPopup[i]) == 0)
        break;
thePopup = (LStdPopupMenu *) theDialog->FindPaneByID (MOD_MOVIE_CLASS);
thePopup->SetValue (i+1);
```

Manipulating Display Text

The text you display in a view using an object of LCaption isn't necessarily fixed. Although we often simply display the text without modification, it's also common to change that text on the fly. For example, the Penultimate Videos program uses an object of class LCaption to display the customer number on a rental receipt (Listing 8.12). The initial value of the caption contains the stub "Customer #:". All the program needs to do is concatenate the actual customer number on the end.

Listing 8.12 Manipulating a caption

```
itoaC (cust_numb, cust_numbString); // convert integer to C string
displayString = cust_numbString; // initialize pascal string object with integer
LPane * theCaption = (LPane *) receiptDialog->FindPaneByID (RECEIPT_CUST_NUMB);
theCaption->GetDescriptor(currentString);
currentString += displayString; // concatenate renter number
theCaption->SetDescriptor (currentString);
```

To manipulate the caption, the program does the following:

- Converts the customer number (an integer) to a C string using one of the program's global utility functions (`itoaC`).
- Translates the C string to a Pascal string, which is required for setting the caption's value.
- Obtains a pointer to the caption.
- Uses the `GetDescriptor` function to retrieve the caption's current text as a Pascal string.
- Concatenates the string version of the customer number onto the caption's current string.
- Replaces the caption's current text with the concatenated string using the `SetDescriptor` function.

A Complete Dialog Box Example

To help you put all the things you've read about so far in this chapter into context, let's take a look at the complete code for creating and processing a dialog box that is created directly from LDialogBox, without a subclass. The dialog box in question is the one used to enter data about miscellaneous videos, which you first saw in Figure 2.2.

The dialog box is set up by the code in Listing 8.13. As with any other dialog box that behaves in a standard manner, the process is fairly straightforward. First, the program creates the dialog box object. Then, it attaches an undoer to support undo in the dialog box's edit fields. Finally, it issues a call to `Show` to make sure the dialog box appears on the screen.

Listing 8.13 Setting up a dialog box for entering data about a miscellaneous video

```
void CPPVideoStoreApp::SetUpNewMisc()
{
    LDialogBox * theDialog;
    theDialog = (LDialogBox *) LWindow::CreateWindow (WINDOW_NEW_MISC, this);

    LUndoer * theUndoer = new LUndoer;
    theDialog->AddAttachment(theUndoer, nil, TRUE);

    theDialog->Show();
}
```

When the user clicks the dialog box's OK button, the application object traps the action and calls the function in Listing 8.14 to process the user's action. Although there is a lot of code in Listing 8.14, you'll notice that the logic isn't complex: The program retrieves the value from each edit field or control, one at a time. Once all the data have been retrieved, the program creates a new Other video object, passing the data collected from the dialog box to the object's constructor.

Because this is a data entry dialog box, the program leaves the dialog box on the screen until the user closes it with the Done button (the "Cancel" button). Therefore, after retrieving the value of an edit field or control, the program clears out the data entry areas. Each edit field receives a null; each control receives its original default value. The final task is to make the first edit field on the dialog box the target. The dialog box will then look as it did when it first appeared on the screen.

Listing 8.14 Processing values from the Enter Miscellaneous Video dialog box

```
void CPPVideoStoreApp::ProcessNewMisc(SDialogResponse * dialogResponse)
{
    ANSIstring miscPopup[] = {"Documentary","Instructional","Nature"};
    LEditField * theEditField, * theFirstEditField;
    Other * newOther;
    int Title_numb, iLen;
    ANSIstring iTitle, iDistributor, iDirector, iProducer, iClass;
    Str255 pascalString;

    Title_numb = Items->inclastTitle_numb();

    LDialogBox * theDialog = dialogResponse->dialogBox;

    theFirstEditField = (LEditField *) theDialog->FindPaneByID (MISC_TITLE);
    theFirstEditField->GetDescriptor (pascalString);
    convertPascal255 (pascalString,iTitle);
    theFirstEditField->SetDescriptor (null);

    theEditField = (LEditField *) theDialog->FindPaneByID (MISC_DIST);
    theEditField->GetDescriptor (pascalString);
    convertPascal255 (pascalString,iDistributor);
    theEditField->SetDescriptor (null);

    theEditField = (LEditField *) theDialog->FindPaneByID (MISC_PRODUCE);
    theEditField->GetDescriptor (pascalString);
    convertPascal255 (pascalString,iProducer);
    theEditField->SetDescriptor (null);

    theEditField = (LEditField *) theDialog->FindPaneByID (MISC_DIRECT);
    theEditField->GetDescriptor (pascalString);
    convertPascal255 (pascalString,iDirector);
    theEditField->SetDescriptor (null);

    theEditField = (LEditField *) theDialog->FindPaneByID (MISC_LENGTH);
    iLen = theEditField->GetValue ();// grab a value and translate to an integer
    theEditField->SetDescriptor (null);

    // popup menu returns the integer position of the value chosen
    LStdPopupMenu * thePopup = (LStdPopupMenu *) theDialog->FindPaneByID (MISC_CLASS);
    int menuChoice = thePopup->GetValue () - 1;
    strcpy (iClass, miscPopup[menuChoice]);
    thePopup->SetValue (1);
```

Continued next page

Listing 8.14 (Continued) Processing values from the Enter Miscellaneous Video dialog

```
    Try_
    {
        newOther = new Other (Title_numb, iTitle, iDistributor, iDirector, iProducer,
            iClass, iLen, Items, ItemsByNumb);
        Other_count++;
    }

    Catch_ (inErr)
    {
        Throw_(inErr);
    } EndCatch_

    theFirstEditField->SwitchTarget (theFirstEditField);
    save_flag = FALSE;
}
```

Responding to "Live" Controls

Throughout this chapter, you have been reading about the use of controls in situations where the values of the controls aren't read until the user clicks a button to signal that he or she has finished working with a dialog box. (A button is always a "live" control.) However, there are situations in which you want to read the value in a control as soon as the user makes a change in the control, and then take some action based on the user's choice. When that is the case, you must make sure that the window in which the controls appear listens for the controls.

As an example, we will be looking at the classes and code that support the Penultimate Videos inventory statistics window (Figure 8.1). The check boxes control the display of data in the Total Items and Percent of Total columns. When the boxes are checked, the data appear; when the boxes are not checked, the data disappear. The window responds immediately to any changes the user makes in the check boxes.

NOTE

Yes, yes … the percentages don't add up to quite 100 percent. That's because the arithmetic truncates the fractional portions of the percentages to two digits rather than rounding them. (Even with rounding, it still might not come out to exactly 100 percent!)

The PowerPlant object that the Penultimate Videos program uses for the window in Figure 8.1 appears in Figure 8.2. Most of the panes in the window are captions.

Figure 8.1 The Inventory Statistics window

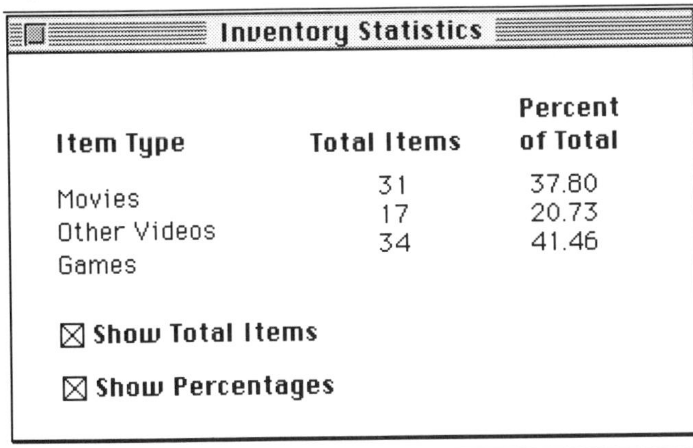

However, there are also the two check boxes and an object of the class LTable. (We will be discussing tables in great depth in Chapter 9, and will therefore leave the discussion of the implementation of this table and the subclass that supports it until then.)

Figure 8.2 PowerPlant resource for the Inventory Statistics window

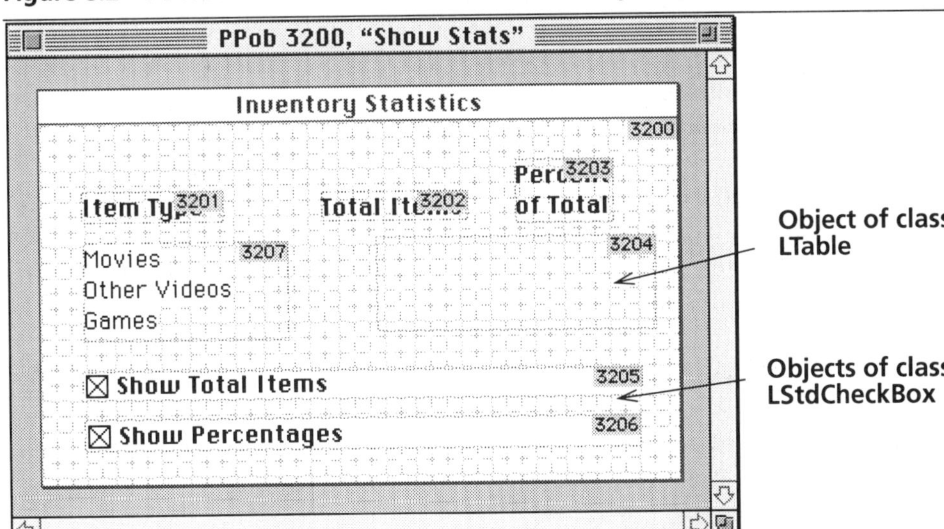

To make the code a bit more interesting, the inventory statistics window isn't based on LDialogBox, but on a subclass of LWindow., which means that it isn't automatically a listener. It must therefore be derived not only from LWindow, but LListener as well.

The header file for the derived class—StatsWindow—can be found in Listing 8.15. This class has the requisite constructors (a default constructor and a stream input constructor), destructor, and `CreateXStream` function. In addition, it overrides two LWindow functions—`ObeyCommand` and `FinishCreateSelf`—as well as one LListener function (`listenToMessage`). The `ObeyCommand` function passes commands to LWindow. It is present to simplify later enhancements that might be made to the class.

Listing 8.15 The StatsWindow class

```
#include <LWIndow.h>
#include <LListener.h>

class StatsTable;

class StatsWindow : public LWindow, public LListener
{
    public:
        enum { class_ID = 'SWin' };
        static StatsWindow * CreateStatsWindowStream (LStream * inStream);
        StatsWindow ();
        StatsWindow (LStream * inStream);
        ~StatsWindow ();
        virtual Boolean ObeyCommand (CommandT inCommand, void * ioParam);
        void ListenToMessage (MessageT inMessage, void * ioParam);
    protected:
        StatsTable * theTable; // pointer to table object
        virtual void FinishCreateSelf();
};
```

Among other things, `FinishCreateSelf` (Listing 8.16) takes care of initializing the table that displays the inventory statistics. Because this activity involves one of the window's subpanes, it must wait until after the window has been completely created. For our current discussion, however, the important part of `FinishCreateSelf` is the function call that tells the window to listen for messages sent by the check boxes:

```
UReanimator::LinkListenerToControls (this, this, WINDOW_STATS);
```

Listing 8.16 The StatsWindow FinishCreateSelf function

```
void StatsWindow::FinishCreateSelf()
{
    UReanimator::LinkListenerToControls (this, this, WINDOW_STATS);

    theTable = (StatsTable *) FindPaneByID (STATS_TABLE);
        // save pointer to table object

    TableCellT theCell;

    for (int i = 1; i <= 3; i++)
        for (int j = 1; j <= 2; j++)
        {
            theCell.row = i;
            theCell.col = j;
            theTable->SetTableCell (theCell);
        }
}
```

The three parameters are a pointer to the listener, a pointer to the view that contains all the control panes to be linked as broadcasters, and the resource ID of the RidL resource that identifies the controls. In this particular example, the listener and the view containing the controls are the same (the current object). Because Constructor gives the RidL resource the same ID as the window (the view containing the controls), the program can use the constant that identifies the window as the third parameter.

Once the controls have been linked to the listener, the listener must use its `ListenToMessage` function to trap and act upon changes in the controls. The Inventory Statistics window responds to the messages sent by both check boxes. For simplicity, their value messages were set equal to their resource IDs and assigned constants in *MenuCommands.h*.

As you can see in Listing 8.17, a `ListenToMessage` function contains a `switch` that traps the messages to which the listener should respond. The StatsWindow `ListenToMessage` function does the following:

- Determines which check box broadcast the message.
- Obtains a pointer to the check box object.
- Retrieves the state of the check box before the user acted on it (0 = checked, 1 = not checked).
- Based on the state in which the check box will be after the user's action is completely processed, either clears or displays data in the table.

Listing 8.17 The StatsWindow ListenToMessage function

```
void StatsWindow::ListenToMessage (MessageT inMessage, void * ioParam)
{
    int currentState, i;
    LStdCheckBox * theCheckBox;
    TableCellT theCell;

    switch (inMessage)
    {
        case cmd_stats_total_cb:
            theCheckBox = (LStdCheckBox *) FindPaneByID (STATS_TOTAL_CB);
            currentState = theCheckBox->GetValue();
            theCell.col = 1;
            for (i = 1; i <= 3; i++)
            {
                theCell.row = i;
                if (!currentState)
                    theTable->ClearTableCell (theCell);
                else
                    theTable->SetTableCell (theCell);
            }
            break;
        case cmd_stats_percent_cb:
            theCheckBox = (LStdCheckBox *) FindPaneByID (STATS_PERCENT_CB);
            currentState = theCheckBox->GetValue();
            theCell.col = 2;
            for (i = 1; i <= 3; i++)
            {
                theCell.row = i;
                if (!currentState)
                    theTable->ClearTableCell (theCell);
                else
                    theTable->SetTableCell (theCell);
            }
            break;
    }
    theTable->DrawSelf();
    theTable->Refresh();
}
```

The function finishes with two function calls—`DrawSelf` and `Refresh`—that make sure that the table displays correctly.

Because most of the work of managing the Inventory Statistics window is handled by the StatsWindow class, the application object needs to do only the following:

- Activate the menu command that displays the Inventory Statistics window in its `FindCommandStatus` function.
- Trap the menu command and create an object of the class StatsWindow in its `ObeyCommand` function:

```
case cmd_stats:
      StatsWindow * theStatsWindow = (StatsWindow *)
            LWindow::CreateWindow (WINDOW_STATS, this);
      break;
```

CHAPTER 9

List Boxes and Tables

One of the fixtures of the Macintosh user interface is a scrolling list of items. A user picks from that list either by double-clicking on an item in the list or by selecting an item and then clicking a button. PowerPlant provides support for scrolling lists with the class LListBox. In this chapter you will see how to create list boxes, using a combination of PowerPlant class features and calls to the ToolBox List Manager.

PowerPlant tables are closely related to scrolling lists, in that they are for display only and can report back to the program the cell in the table that is currently selected. This chapter therefore also looks at the PowerPlant class LTable, a simple class that maintains a grid of columns and rows.

List Boxes

An object of class LListBox provides a simple way to support a list with scroll bars. Although you can create a subclass of LListBox, if your list box will behave in a standard manner, you can create the object directly from LListBox without a subclass. As an example, we will be looking at the listing of titles managed by the Penultimate Videos program, which you first saw in Figure 2.6.

List Box Resources

The easiest way to create a list box is to define the object using Constructor. Whatever you choose for the list box's superview, the superview must be derived from LListener. (It it's not, it won't be able to respond to double-clicks in the list.) You can derive a class from LWindow and LListener, or you can use an LDialogBox object. The title list, for example, is based on a dialog box.

The resource that contains the list box of titles can be found in Figure 9.1. This resource contains only two objects: the LDialogBox object that is the superview, and the LListBox object. In this case, the scroll bars are part of the LListBox object rather than an additional LScroller object.

As you can see in Figure 9.2, a list box has some properties in common with any other pane. In particular, it has a unique resource ID and a value message (in this case, the "double click message"). Because the list box in this example has a dialog box as its superview, the double click message is negative. (Remember that dialog boxes only listen to negative messages.)

In addition, you can use the properties window to determine which, if any, scroll bars appear in the list box. You can also set a text traits ID for the list box's items, whether the list will have a grow box, and whether a selected item will retain a focus box when the window is inactive.

Building the Contents of a List Box

An LListBox object is somewhat incomplete when it is created: It has no columns or rows. You must add then using ToolBox List Manager calls before adding any items to the list. Once you've added a column and rows, you can then place data in the list's cells and display the list.

NOTE

Although there is technically nothing to prevent you from creating an LListBox with more than one column, the class only supports single-column lists. If you need a multi-column list, you will need to use a table, which you can place in a scroller.

Figure 9.1 A resource containing an LListBox object

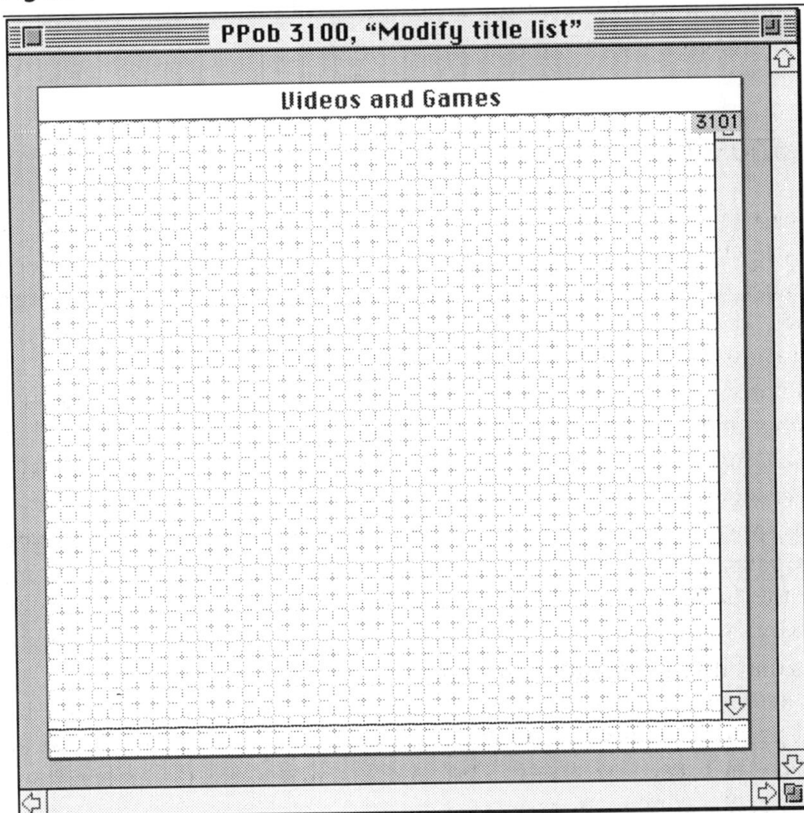

The title list resource that we are using as an example can display games, other videos, or movies. To initiate the building of the correct list, the Penultimate Videos program first traps the user's menu selection in the application object's `ObeyCommand` function, a portion of which appears in Listing 9.1. Each menu selection calls the application object's `ItemList` function with the type of item the user wants to modify as an input parameter.

The complete `ItemList` function can be found in Listing 9.2. To build the list it does the following:

- Creates the dialog box (`theDialog`).
- Retrieves a pointer to the LListBox object (`theList`).

Figure 9.2 LListBox properties

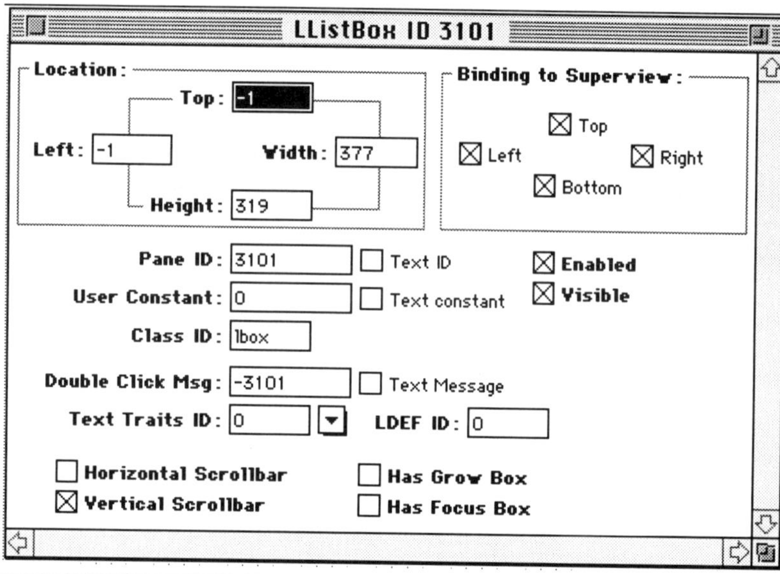

Listing 9.1 Trapping menu selections that produce the item list

```
:
:
// For modifying and deleting merchandise items
        case cmd_mod_movie:
            ItemList (FILM);
            break;
        case cmd_mod_misc:
            ItemList (OTHER);
            break;
        case cmd_mod_game:
            ItemList (GAME);
            break;
:
:
```

- Uses the type of merchandise input parameter to determine what the title of the dialog box's window should be and sets the title by calling the dialog box's `SetDescriptor` function.
- Retrieves the handle to the list box's list of items (`theListHandle`) by calling the list box's function `GetMacListH`.
- Adds one column to the list with the ToolBox function `LAddColumn`.

Listing 9.2 Setting up the list of titles

```
void CPPVideoStoreApp::ItemList (int item_type)
{
    LDialogBox * theDialog;
    LListBox * theList;

    theDialog = (LDialogBox *) LWindow::CreateWindow (WINDOW_MOD_LIST, this);
    theList = (LListBox *) theDialog->FindPaneByID (MOD_LIST_BOX);

    if (item_type == FILM)
        theDialog->SetDescriptor ("\pChoose Movie to Modify/Delete");
    else if (item_type == OTHER)
        theDialog->SetDescriptor ("\pChoose Video to Modify/Delete");
    else
        theDialog->SetDescriptor ("\pChoose Game to Modify/Delete");

    ListHandle theListHandle = theList->GetMacListH(); // get the list box's list handle
    ::LAddColumn (1, 0, theListHandle); // add a column to the empty list

    MerchItr traversal;
    int Type, row = 0;
    Merchandise_Item * currentOne;
    char * Title;
    Cell theCell, * theCellPtr;
        // a cell (row & column number) and a pointer to the variable
    theCellPtr = &theCell;

    for (traversal.Init (Items); !traversal; ++traversal)
    {
        currentOne = traversal();
        Type = currentOne->getItem_type();
        if (Type == item_type)
        {
            Title = currentOne->getTitle();
            ::LAddRow (1, row, theListHandle); // add a row to the list
            ::SetPt (theCellPtr, 0, row++);
                // initialize the coordinates of the cell just added
            ::LSetCell (Title, strlen(Title), theCell, theListHandle);
                // add the data
        }
    }
    theList->AddListener (theDialog);
        // add listener so message will be sent on double-click
    theDialog->SetUserCon (item_type); // save type of item being modified
    theDialog->Show();
}
```

- Creates an in-order iterator for the merchandise item tree that is organized alphabetically by item title (`traversal`).
- Sets up a variable of type Cell (`theCell`) and a variable that contains a pointer to the cell (`theCellPtr`). The Cell data structure has two integer members: `Cell.row`, which contains the row number, and `Cell.col`, which contains the column number. Because you are working with the ToolBox List Manager, row and column numbering begins with 0.
- Traverses the merchandise item tree. If an item is of the type that is to be displayed in the list box, add a row to the list box with the ToolBox routine `LAddRow`. Initialize the cell pointer to the row just added using the ToolBox routine `SetPt`. Then, add the item title to the new cell with the ToolBox routine `LSetCell`.
- Adds the list box to the dialog box's list of listeners using the `AddListener` function.
- Sets the dialog box's `UserCon` variable to the type of item being displayed with the dialog box's `SetUserCon` function. The function that traps a double-click in the list box will then be able to retrieve this value to determine which Modify dialog box to display.
- Displays the dialog box by calling its `Show` function.

Finding the Selected List Item

As with other controls, a window can actively listen for changes in a list box or can tap the value of the list box when the user signals that he or she is finished (for example, by clicking a button.) The New Video Copy dialog box works in exactly this way. The user highlights the title of the item, makes changes in the other controls in the dialog box, and clicks the OK button. The program must then figure out which item in the list box has been highlighted.

To do so, a function must first obtain a pointer to the list box object. Then, it can use the list box's `GetDescriptor` function, which returns the text of the first highlighted item in the list:

```
LListBox * theList = (LListBox *) theDialog->FindPaneByID
      (VCOPY_LIST_BOX);
theList->GetDescriptor (pascalString); // get first highlighted item
```

Capturing a Double-Click in a List Box

To actively listen for user actions in a list box, a program waits for a double-click. When the user double-clicks in a scrolling list provided by an LListBox object, the object broadcasts its double-click message. If you have created a subclass for the window in which the list box appears, the subclass will have a `ListenToMessage` function that will include the double-click message. However, if you have not created a subclass and the application object "owns" the window in which the list box appears, as is the case in our example, then the application object's `ObeyCommand` function can trap the double-click.

To handle a selection in an LListBox object, a program needs to know the item on which the user double-clicked. In Listing 9.3, for example, you will find a portion of the function that processes a selection in the title list dialog box. [The remainder of this long function (`SetUpItemModify`) displays one of three Modify dialog boxes, depending on the type of item identified by the dialog box's `UserCon` attribute.]

Listing 9.3 Handling list box selections

```
:
:
LDialogBox * theDialog = dialogResponse->dialogBox;
int item_type = theDialog->GetUserCon(); // retrieve item type

LListBox * theList = (LListBox *) theDialog->FindPaneByID (MOD_LIST_BOX);
theList->GetDescriptor (pascalString); // get first highlighted item
convertPascal255 (pascalString, Title);

saveItem = Items->find (Title); // get and save pointer to item
delete theDialog;
:
:
```

To process the selection and obtain enough information to display the Modify dialog box, the `SetUpItemModify` function does the following:

- Retrieves a pointer to the dialog box in which the double-click occurred (`theDialog`).
- Retrieves the item type using the dialog box's `GetUserCon` function.
- Obtains a pointer to the list box object (`theList`).
- Gets the text of the selected item with the list box's `GetDescriptor` function. The text is returned as a Pascal string.
- Converts the Pascal string to a C string using the program's global utility function `convertPascal255`.

NOTE

The ToolBox does provide a Pascal-to-C conversion routine. However, it modifies the source string, which isn't always desirable. Therefore, the Penultimate Videos program provides its own conversion routines that leave the source string intact.

- Searches the merchandise item tree, which is organized alphabetically by item title to locate a pointer to the selected item.
- Removes the dialog box from the screen by deleting the dialog box object.

At this point, the `SetUpItemModify` function has all the information it needs to display the correct Modify dialog box and retrieve information about the object being modified, using the procedures you saw in Chapter 8.

Tables

Probably the biggest limitation of LListBox is that it supports only single-column lists. If you need a list with multiple columns, you will need to use a PowerPlant table. The basic table class is LTable, which supports an unlimited number of equal-sized columns and rows. The columns and rows are numbered beginning with 1, unlike the rows and columns in a list box, which are numbered beginning with 0.

NOTE

At the time this book was written, Metrowerks was working on a more flexible table class—LTableView—that allows for columns of different widths in the same table. With CW 8, it can be found in the In Progress folder. If LTable is too restrictive for your needs, you may want to experiment with LTableView and the other table classes Metrowerks has been building.

The example we will be using for this discussion is the receipt that is given to a Penultimate Videos customer whenever he or she rents merchandise. As you can see in Figure 9.3, titles and their due dates are added to the table at the bottom of the receipt. Because table cells are the same width and the receipt window needs to have enough room to display a long item title, the actual table extends past the right edge of the window. As long as the contents of the second column (the column in which the date due appears) don't extend past the right edge of the dialog box, the overly wide table presents no problem.

Figure 9.3 The rental receipt window

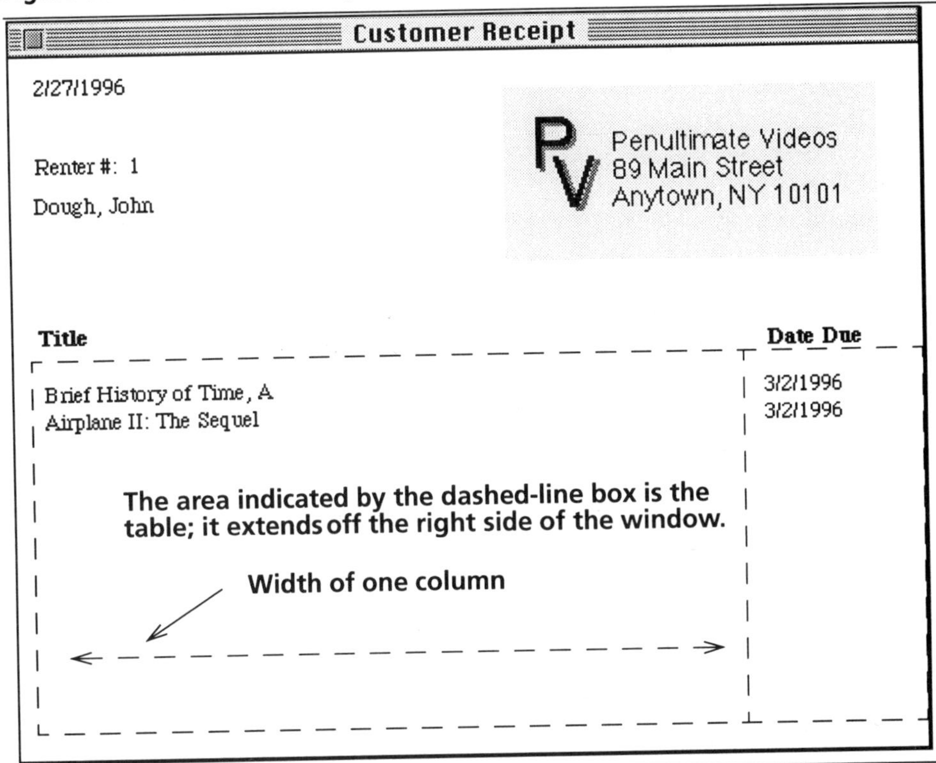

NOTE

As you will see in Chapter 11, we can take the panes in the receipt window and install them in a printing view without modification, making it easy to print the receipt for the user.

TABLE RESOURCES

As you might expect, the receipt window resource is defined as a PowerPlant object using Constructor. In Figure 9.4, for example, you can see that the resource contains some display text, the LTable object, and an LPicture object to contain the company's logo. (We will talk about that logo shortly.)

Figure 9.4 A view containing an LTable object

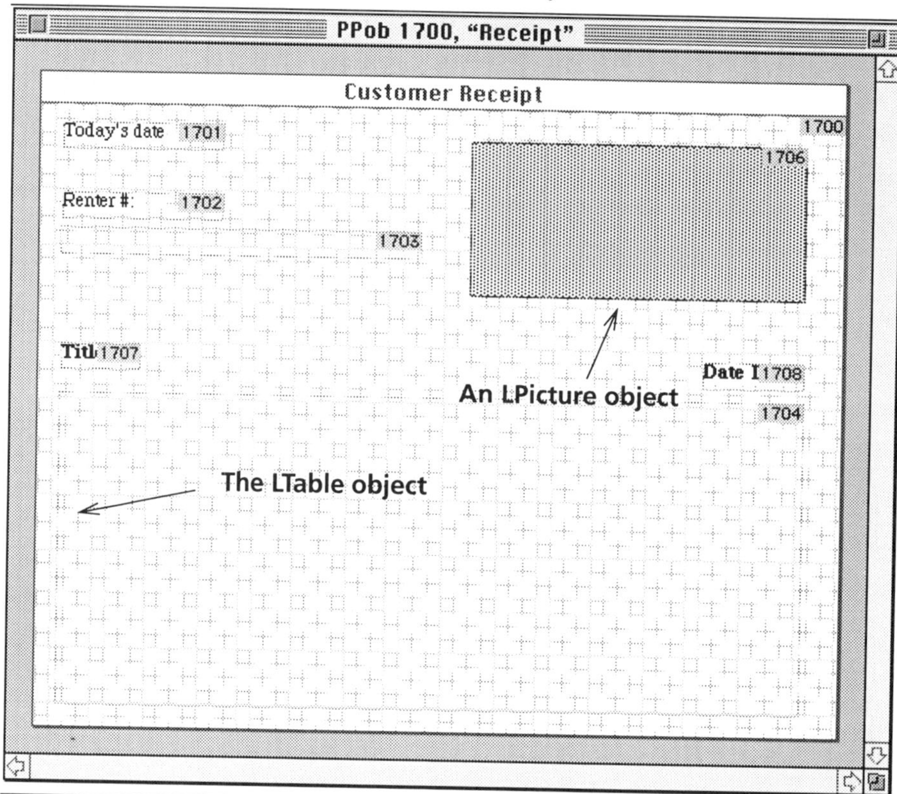

You specify the characteristics of an LTable object in its properties window (Figure 9.5). The important values for configuring a table appear in the five boxes at the bottom of the window:

- Number of Rows: Enter the number of rows in the table.
- Number of Columns: Enter the number of columns in the table.
- Row Height: Enter the height, in pixels, of the table's rows.
- Column Width: Enter the width, in pixels, of the table's columns.
- Cell Data Size: Enter the number of bytes of storage that should be set aside for each cell in the table.

NOTE

If you leave the Cell Data Size set to the default of 0, PowerPlant won't allocate any storage for cell data.

Figure 9.5 LTable properties

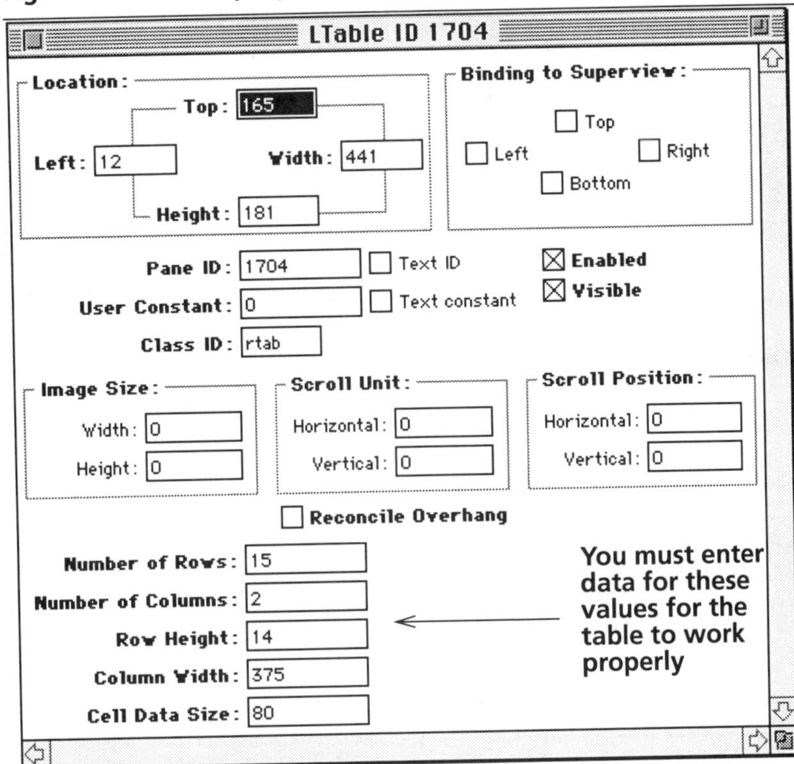

Adding the Logo (LPicture Objects)

Although it may seem out of sequence, this is as good a spot as any to take a quick aside to look at adding a graphic to a window for display purposes. The Penultimate Videos logo, which appears in the upper right corner of the receipt, is stored as a PICT resource (Figure 9.6). The receipt window can therefore use an object of class LPicture to display it.

To set up an LPicture object, drag the object onto a window from Constructor's Tools palette. Position and resize the object as necessary. Then, double-click to open its properties window (Figure 9.7). Give the object its own unique resource ID and enter the resource ID of the PICT resource in the PICT resource ID box at the very bottom of the window. Assuming that the PICT resource is linked to the LPicture object in this way, the program will retrieve and display the graphic whenever the window is created.

Figure 9.6 A PICT resource that can be attached to an LPicture object

Figure 9.7 LPicture properties

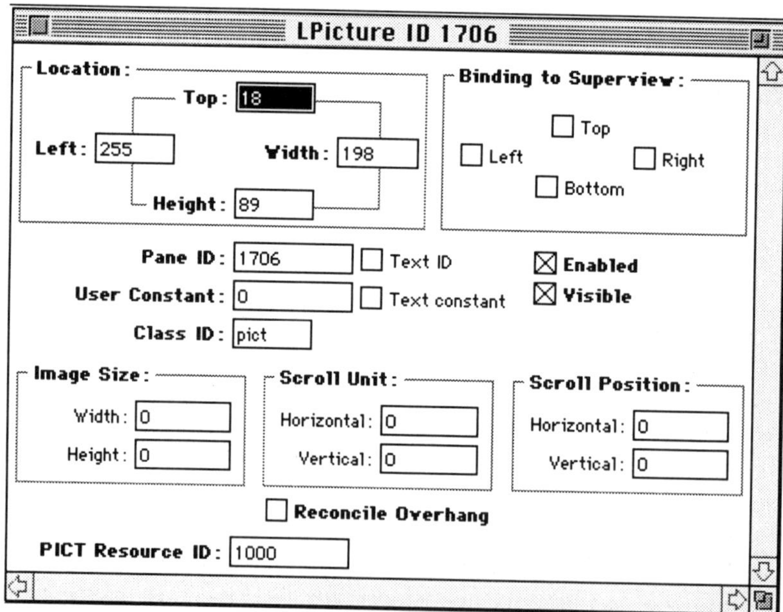

Table Subclasses

Unlike a list box, where you have a choice whether to create a subclass, you *must* create a subclass whenever you want to use a table. LTable contains two functions—

DrawSelf and DrawCell—that are specific to a given table. In many cases DrawSelf's default behavior will be acceptable. However, the LTable DrawCell function displays the cell column and row numbers. You must therefore override this function to display whatever data you want to appear in a table cell.

The class that supports the table on the receipt window can be found in Listing 9.4. It contains constructors, a destructor, a Create*X*Stream function, and the two overridden functions: DrawCell and DrawSelf. The remainder of the class's behavior and attributes can be inherited directly from LTable.

Listing 9.4 The ReceiptTable class

```
#include <LTable.h>

class ReceiptTable : public LTable
{
    public:
        enum { class_ID = 'rtab' };
        static ReceiptTable * CreateReceiptTableStream(LStream *inStream);
        ReceiptTable();
        ReceiptTable(LStream *inStream);
        virtual ~ReceiptTable();
        virtual void DrawSelf ();
    protected:
        virtual void DrawCell (const TableCellT &inCell);
};
```

INITIALIZING TABLE STORAGE

The LTable class creates an object of class LDynamicArray to hold a table's data. However, although the storage is created for you, LTable doesn't initialize that storage. This means that unless you explicitly take care of clearing out the cells in a table, any empty cells may display garbage.

The easiest place to intialize table storage is in a table class's stream input constructor. As an example, take a look at the ReceipTable class's constructor in Listing 9.5. The function first obtains a pointer to a null string. It then calls the LDynamic Array function GetCount to retrieve the number of cells in the table. (Yes, you do know how many cells there are in the table because you created the resource for it. However, this strategy is more flexible than using a constant because you can modify the table resource at any time without having to modify your code.) The constructor finishes by calling SetItemAt to place the null string in each table cell.

Listing 9.5 Initializing table storage

```
ReceiptTable::ReceiptTable(
    LStream * inStream)
        : LTable(inStream)
{
    // null out the table storage array
    PString nullString = "";
    unsigned char * theString = nullString.getmString();
    int numbItems = mCellData->GetCount();
    for (int i = 1; i <= numbItems; i++)
        mCellData->SetItemAt (i, theString);
}
```

NOTE

As you will see in Chapter 10, LDynamicArray has many functions in common with LList. This is because LList is derived from LDynamicArray.

BUILDING THE CONTENTS OF A TABLE

Unlike a list box, where you must build the contents of the list using ToolBox calls, a class derived from LTable takes care of adding columns and rows itself. LTable also makes it possible to place data in a cell and retrieve data from a cell without issuing a ToolBox call.

NOTE

From the "Guaranteed to make you nuts" department: A scrolling list based on an LListBox object numbers its rows beginning with 0. However, columns and rows in an object derived from LTable are numbered starting with 1. In particular, the coordinates of the cell in the upper-left corner of a table are 1,1, not 0.0.

Whenever the user enters a rental, the Penultimate Videos program adds a row to the table on the receipt window and then redraws the table. The code to manage adding data to a table cell can be found in Listing 9.6. This code uses a variable named `theCell`, which is of type `TableCellT`. Like the cell structure used with the list box, it has two components, `col` and `row`.

To place data in the storage allocated for a table cell, first obtain a pointer to the table object. (`FindPaneByID` will do the trick.) Then, initialize a `TableCellT` structure with the column and row into which you want to place the data. Finally, use the table's `SetCellData` function to pass the cell and the data to the table storage. Note that the data for the table cell must be stored as a Pascal string.

Listing 9.6 Setting table data

```
:
:
// put item into receipt table array
int Title_numb = whichItem->getTitle_numb();
Merchandise_Item * whichTitle = ItemsByNumb->find (Title_numb);
PString itemTitle = whichTitle->getTitle();
PString dueDate =  whenDue->showDate(Tdate);
theCell.col = 1;
theTable->SetCellData (theCell, itemTitle);
theCell.col = 2;
theTable->SetCellData (theCell, dueDate);
theCell.row++;

// draw the table
theTable->DrawSelf();
theTable->Refresh(); // make sure everything shows up
:
:
```

It is important to realize that the SetCellData function merely places data into the data structure set aside to hold the contents of the table: It doesn't display the table. To make changes appear, you will need to call the table's DrawSelf function and then, depending on how windows are layered on the screen, perhaps the Refresh function. Refresh is inherited from LPane. Its purpose is to generate an update event, which forces the entire pane to be redrawn.

DRAWING TABLE CELLS

A table class's DrawSelf function should determine which cells need to be updated and then draw those cells by calling DrawCell. In Listing 9.7 you will find the receipt table's DrawSelf function, which is largely unmodified from that found in LTable. To determine which cells need updating, the function does the following:

- Obtains the handle of the current update region, expressed in local coordinates, by calling GetLocalUpdateRgn. This function is inherited from LView.
- Retrieves an update rectangle in local coordinates from the rgnBox variable that is the bounds of the update structure.
- Uses the ToolBox routine DisposeRgn to get rid of the update region.
- Finds the cell at the top of the update rectangle. Doing so requires two steps. First, the function translates the local coordinates to image coordinates using Local-

Listing 9.7 The ReceiptTable class's DrawSelf function

```
void ReceiptTable::DrawSelf()
{
        // Determine cells that need updating. Rather than checking
        // on a cell by cell basis, we just see which cells intersect
        // the bounding box of the update region. This is relatively
        // fast, but may result in unnecessary cell updates for
        // non-rectangular update regions.

    RgnHandle localUpdateRgnH = GetLocalUpdateRgn();
    Rect    updateRect = (**localUpdateRgnH).rgnBBox;
    ::DisposeRgn(localUpdateRgnH);

                        // Find cell at top left of update rect
    SPoint32 topLeftUpdate;
    TableCellT topLeftCell;
    LocalToImagePoint(topLeft(updateRect), topLeftUpdate);
    FetchCellHitBy(topLeftUpdate, topLeftCell);
    if (topLeftCell.row < 1) // Lower bound is cell (1,1)
        topLeftCell.row = 1;
    if (topLeftCell.col < 1)
        topLeftCell.col = 1;

                        // Find cell at bottom right of update rect
    SPoint32 botRightUpdate;
    TableCellT botRightCell;
    LocalToImagePoint(botRight(updateRect), botRightUpdate);
    FetchCellHitBy(botRightUpdate, botRightCell);
                        // Upper bound is cell (mRows,mCols)
    if (botRightCell.row > mRows)
        botRightCell.row = mRows;
    if (botRightCell.col > mCols)
        botRightCell.col = mCols;

                        // Draw each cell within the update rect
    TableCellT cell;
    for (cell.row = topLeftCell.row; cell.row <= botRightCell.row; cell.row++) {
        for (cell.col = topLeftCell.col; cell.col <= botRightCell.col; cell.col++) {
            DrawCell(cell);
        }
    }
}
```

ToImagePoint. Then, it calls FetchCellHitBy, an LTable function that returns the cell that contains a given image coordinate.

- Makes sure that the cell returned by FetchCellHitBy is within the table by adjusting the cell so that it is no less than 1,1.

- Finds the cell at the bottom right of the update region, using the same procedure as that used to find the cell at the top left corner.
- Makes sure that the bottom right cell is within the table by checking it against `mCols` and `mRows`, LTable variables that store the number of columns and rows, respectively.
- Performs a `for` loop that draws the cells in the update region. The body of the loop is a call to `DrawCell`.

Given a reference to a cell, the `DrawCell` function (see Listing 9.8) takes care of

Listing 9.8 The ReceiptTable class's DrawCell function

```
void ReceiptTable::DrawCell (const TableCellT &inCell)
{
    PString displayValue;
    Rect cellFrame;
    if (FetchLocalCellFrame(inCell, cellFrame)) {
        ::TextFont(times);
        ::TextSize(12);
        ::TextStyle(plain);
        ::MoveTo(cellFrame.left + 4, cellFrame.bottom - 4);
        GetCellData (inCell, displayValue);
        ::DrawString(displayValue);
    }
}
```

making the contents of a cell appear. The function does its drawing only if the cell's image coordinates are within the view's frame by calling `FetchLocalCellFrame`. This LTable function converts the cell to local coordinates and returns a Boolean indicating whether the cell is within the view.

Assuming the cell lies within the view's frame, then `DrawCell` can proceed with its drawing. As you can see in Listing 9.8, the function first sets the display text characteristics and moves the pen to the location where drawing should begin (four pixels offset from the bottom left corner of the cell). Then, it calls the LTable function `GetCellData` to retrieve the data stored in the cell. Finally, it draws the text.

NOTE

If you are interested in a table class that is designed to show icons rather than text, experiment with the SmallIconTable class, found in CW 8's In Progress folder.

Finding the Selected Cell

In the example you have just seen, a table is being used to simplify formatting a display. However, in some cases you can also use a table in place of a list box. In other words, a user can highlight a table cell by clicking on it, and a program can identify the highlighted cell.

When you want to find the selected cell after a user signals you by clicking a button, use the LTable function `GetSelectedCell`:

```
TableCellT theCell;
theTable->GetSelectedCell (theCell);
```

The function call returns the cell number in the `theCell` variable. You can then use that cell to retrieve its contents.

CHAPTER 10

Strings, Lists, and Files

PowerPlant includes a collection of classes for nongraphic objects such as strings, lists, and files. Although the user never sees objects created from these classes, they provide considerable support for program actions. For example, PowerPlant itself makes extensive use of linked lists to keep track of attachments and subpanes. In this chapter we will look at these important support classes, focusing on how you can take advantage of them in your own programs.

Strings

Strings can be the bane of a Macintosh C++ programmer. Because of the Macintosh's Pascal heritage, many of the ToolBox routines require Pascal, not C, strings. To make matters worse, even if you store everything as a Pascal string, you're still faced with needing to call functions for even the simplest string manipulation. The traditional solution has been to create a string class that overloads assignment, concatenation, and comparison operators. PowerPlant includes a class (LString) that does just that for Pascal strings. As you will see shortly, the Penultimate Videos program has extended that idea by creating a companion class for C strings.

LString and LStr255

The base class for PowerPlant Pascal strings is LString. An abstract base class, it supports a string of any length. The functions and operators it provides are summarized in Table 10.1. The string comparison operators (==, <, >, <=, >=, and !=) are declared as global functions.

Table 10.1 LString capabilities

Function/Operator	Purpose
`Length`	Returns number of characters in the string
`ConstStringPtr` `StringPtr`	Return a pointer to the Pascal string being managed
`Int32`	Converts string to a long integer
`double_t`	Converts string to a floating point number
`FourCharCode`	Converts a string to a four character code, such as a type or creator string
`[ ]`	Returns the character at the position within the brackets
=	Assigns one string to another. Overloaded to support several types of input.
+=	Concatenates something onto an LString object.
+	Concatenates either two LString objects, an LString object and a Pascal string, or an LString object and a char. Overloaded to work with the LString on either side of the operator.
`Assign`	Assigns a value to an LString object. Overloaded to support input in the forms supported by the = operator. The = operator functions call `Assign`.
`Append`	Concatenates something with an LString object. Overloaded to support input in the forms supported by the += and + operators. The += and + operator functions call `Append`.

Table 10.1 (Continued) LString capabilities

Function/Operator	Purpose
`CompareTo`	Performs a comparison between an LString object and another LString object, a Pascal string, or a character. Called by the comparison operator functions.
`Find`	Searches for a substring within an LString object, beginning at the character position specified in the function call and searching toward the end of the string. Overloaded to support input from an LString object, a Pascal string, or a character.
`ReverseFind`	Searches for a substring within an LString object, beginning at the character position specified in the function call and searching toward the beginning of the string.
`BeginsWith`	Checks to see if an LString object begins with a given string.
`EndsWith`	Check to see if an LString object ends with a given string.
`FindWithin`	Similar to Find, but always starts its search with the first character in the string.
`ReverseFindWithin`	Similar to ReverseFind, but always starts its search with the last character in the string.
`( )`	Returns a substring starting at a specified position in the LString object and containing a specified number of characters.
`Insert`	Inserts a substring into an LString object beginning at a specified position.
`Remove`	Removes a substring from an LString object beginning at a specified position and with a specified length.
`Replace`	Replaces a substring of an LString object with another string.

LString is an abstract base class. You therefore have two choices if you want to use it. First, you can create a subclass, which PowerPlant has already done with LStr255. Alternatively, you can use PowerPlant's string template class (TString).

NOTE

LString, LStr255, and TString can all be found in LString.h and LString.cp.

LStr255 is a subclass of LString that handles a Pascal string of up to 255 characters. It therefore comes in handy for a number of ToolBox calls, particularly because you can use an LStr255 object anywhere a function requires a parameter of Str255. Using a string object also makes string handling easier because you can, in most cases, write simpler code that avoids explicit function calls. In particular, you can perform string assignment, concatenation, and comparison using the typical operators.

There is one limitation to the overloaded string operators of which you should be aware. While most of the overloading allows you to place the string object on either side of most operators, the [ ] operator only returns a character at a given position in the string; it cannot be used on the left side of an assignment operator to change a character. For example, the following code is valid:

```
LStr255 myString;
char oneLetter;

myString = "Sample String";
oneLetter = myString[6];
```

However, the code below won't work because the compiler expects a pointer (the location where the character is stored) but instead receives an integer:

```
LStr255 myString;
myString[7] = 'z';
```

SUBCLASSING LSTRING: PSTRING

The Penultimate Video's class PString is a subclass of LString that is very similar to LStr255. However, it has a couple of additions to ease conversions between C and Pascal strings, and in particular, the Penultimate Videos class CString. As you can see in Table 10.1, the class contains constructors that transform a variety of types of input (Pascal strings, PString objects, C strings, integers, floating point numbers, and characters) into a PString. The remainder of its functions, including the overloaded operators for assignment, concatenation, and comparison, are either global or inherited from LString.

The class also contains a variable called `mString`, which acts as storage for the string being managed by an object of this class. LString does not provide any string storage; you *must* make it part of a derived class.

The first addition to the PString class is another constructor, which takes a CString object and converts it to a PString. This constructor is particularly important for Penultimate Videos because it stores its data as C strings.

Listing 10.1 The PString class

```
class PString : public LString
{
    public:
        // constructors : unfortunately, they aren't inherited
        PString ();
        PString (const PString& inOriginal);
        PString (const LString& inOriginal);
        PString (ConstStringPtr inStringPtr);
        PString (Uchar inChar);
        PString (const char * inCString);
        PString (const void * inPtr, Uint8 inLength);
        PString (Handle inHandle);
        PString (ResIDT inResID, Int16 inIndex);
        PString (Int32 inNumber);
        PString (double_t inNumber, Int8 inStyle, Int16 inDigits);
        PString (FourCharCode inCode);

        PString & operator= (const LString& inString)  // All this is based on LStr255
            {
                LString::operator=(inString);
                return *this;
            }

        PString & operator= (ConstStringPtrinStringPtr)
            {
                LString::operator=(inStringPtr);
                return *this;
            }

        PString & operator= (Uchar inChar)
            {
                LString::operator=(inChar);
                return *this;
            }

        PString & operator= (const char* inCString)
            {
                LString::operator=(inCString);
                return *this;
            }
        PString & operator= (Int32 inNumber)
            {
                LString::operator=(inNumber);
                return *this;
            }
```

Continued next page

Listing 10.1 The PString class

```
        PString & operator= (FourCharCode inCode)
            {
                LString::operator=(inCode);
                return *this;
            }

        // Constructor added to handle CString objects
        PString (CString); // source is a CString object
        // Function added to return string pointer; alternative is to assign
        // the pointer to mStringPtr and use the LString operator StringPtr.
        unsigned char * getmString();

    protected:
        Str255      mString;
};
```

The second addition is a function called `getmString`, which returns a pointer to the Pascal string being handled by a PString object. The CString class needs this so that it can accept a PString object as input and translate the contents into CString format. There are actually two ways to provide this pointer. LString contains a variable called `mStringPtr`, which is returned by the `ConstStringPtr` and `StringPtr` functions. The derived class can assign the address of its string storage (in the case of the PString class, `mString`) to `mStringPtr` in its constructors. Alternatively, a derived class can add a simple function that returns a pointer to `mString`, without involving `mStringPtr` at all.

ADDING A CLASS FOR C STRINGS: CSTRING

Because Penultimate Videos makes such extensive use of C strings, the program can be simplified considerably if it has a class for a C string that interacts seamlessly with a PowerPlant class for Pascal strings. The CString class (Listing 10.2), is a complete C string class that includes a large number of overloaded operators that work with the CString object on either side of the operator. The overloading supports CString objects, PString objects, and standard C strings (`char *`).

A CString object can be used anywhere a function expects a `char *` parameter. This capability is provided by the overloaded operator `char*`, whose implementation simply returns the address of the CString variable `cString`, a 255-character C string.

Listing 10.2 The CString class

```
class CString
{
    // operators overloaded as friend functions

    // equal to
    friend int operator== (CString, char *);
    friend int operator== (char *, CString);
    friend int operator== (CString, PString);
    friend int operator== (PString, CString);

    // not equal to
    friend int operator!= (CString, char *);
    friend int operator!= (char *, CString);
    friend int operator!= (CString, PString);
    friend int operator!= (PString, CString);

    // greater than
    friend int operator> (CString, char *);
    friend int operator> (char *, CString);
    friend int operator> (CString, PString);
    friend int operator> (PString, CString);

    // greater than or equal to
    friend int operator>= (CString, char *);
    friend int operator>= (char *, CString);
    friend int operator>= (CString, PString);
    friend int operator>= (PString, CString);

    // less than
    friend int operator< (CString, char *);
    friend int operator< (char *, CString);
    friend int operator< (CString, PString);
    friend int operator< (PString, CString);

    // less than or equal to
    friend int operator<= (CString, char *);
    friend int operator<= (char *, CString);
    friend int operator<= (CString, PString);
    friend int operator<= (PString, CString);

    private:
        char cString[256]; // 255 character C string
    public:
        CString (); // create and initialize to null
        CString (CString &);
        CString (char *);
        CString (PString);
        char * getcString (); // return pointer to the string itself
        int len (); // get length of string
```

Continued next page

Listing 10.2 (Continued) The CString class

```
    // overloaded operators

        // assignment
        void operator= (CString *); // assignment between two C string objects
        void operator= (char *); // assignment from a literal
        void operator= (PString *); // assignment and conversion from PString

        // relationship
        int operator== (CString);
        int operator> (CString);
        int operator>= (CString);
        int operator< (CString);
        int operator<= (CString);
        int operator!= (CString);

        // concatenation
        void operator+= (CString);
        void operator+= (char *);
        void operator+= (PString);

        // character access
        char operator[] (int); // program sends in array index; use on right side of =

        // type conversion (lets you use CString in place of char *)
        operator char*();
};
```

The CString class suffers from the same limitation as PString: The [ ] operator can be used only to retrieve a character from a given position in the string. It can't be used as the target of an assignment.

NOTE

PString and CString can be found in the files stringobjects.h and stringobjects.cpp.

USING THE STRING CLASSES

Using the PString and CString classes can greatly simplify string handling in a program where you are mixing the two types of strings. As an example, look at the block of code that appears in Listing 10.3, which has been taken from the Penultimate Video application object's `DisplayTitleInfo` function.

The program first declares an object of class PString. It then identifies the dialog box that triggered the function call and retrieves a pointer to the dialog box's list box.

Listing 10.3 Using PString and CString objects

```
// Declare a PString object
PString pascalString;

LDialogBox * theDialog = dialogResponse->dialogBox;
LListBox * theList = (LListBox *) theDialog->FindPaneByID (TITLE_LIST_BOX);

// Use the PString object to receive the highlighted item
theList->GetDescriptor (pascalString); // get first highlighted item

// Copy the PString object to a CString object, making the conversion from
// a Pascal string to a C string
CString cTitle = pascalString;

// Use the CString object in place of a C string
Parent = Items->find (cTitle); // find item with that title
```

Then it calls `GetDescriptor` to retrieve the text of the highlighted item in the list box. However, unlike the examples you saw in Chapter 8, in this case the parameter in which the descriptor is to be returned is a PString object rather than a variable of type Str255. (Remember, you can use a PowerPlant Pascal string object anywhere a function requires a Pascal string of the same length.)

Because the purpose of the `DisplayTitleInfo` function is to display a collection of information about the selected merchandise item, the function must retrieve a pointer to the selected item. The Penultimate Videos program stores all its data as C strings. Therefore, the PString object that contains the descriptor from the list box must be converted to a CString before it can be used in a search of the binary tree of titles. To make the conversion, all the program needs to do is create a CString object and assign the contents of the PString object to it. The CString object can then be used in the `find` function in place of a C string.

Lists

As you read earlier, PowerPlant makes extensive use of linked lists to relate objects within the PowerPlant environment. The same classes that PowerPlant uses for its own internal purposes are available to help you manage objects within your own program.

The list class hierarchy begins with the class LIteratedList, an abstract base class that provides support for connecting iterators to and removing iterators from a list.

It does not provide storage for or access to the members of a list. That must be provided by another class—LDynamicArray. The single derived class provided by PowerPlant—the one used for many of PowerPlant's internal data structures— is LList.

CREATING AND MAINTAINING A LIST

LList stores items of any type. As you might expect, typically those items are pointers to objects. Once you've created the LList object, the class provides the following iterations with the list:

- Retrieval of the number of items in the list using the `GetCount` function.
- Retrieval of an item at a specified position (index) in the list using the `FetchItemAt` function. The items in a list are numbered beginning with 1.
- Insertion of one or more items at a specified index in the list using the `InsertItemsAt` function.
- Removal of one or more items at a specified index in the list using the `RemoveItemsAt` function.

You may also find some of the `FetchIndexOf` function—which is inherited from LDynamicArray—to be useful. It returns the position in the list of an item. In other words, `FetchIndexOf` performs a search of the list using a pointer to the item you want to find.

The Penultimate Videos program uses an object of class LList to connect rented merchandise items to the customer who rented them. To support the list, the Customer class contains a pointer to an LList object (`Items_rented`). The list object is created in the class's constructors with the following statement:

```
Items_rented = new LList();
```

This particular constructor sets up a list of unknown length and unknown item size. Alternatively, you can pass a constructor the size of the item and the number of spaces to allocate for the list. In both cases, you have defined an empty list. However, if the items for the list happen to be available, you can pass yet a third constructor the size of the items and a handle to where they are stored, generating a list that is already populated.

Whenever a Penultimate Videos customer rents an item, a pointer to that item is inserted into the linked list of rentals for that customer (see Listing 10.4). In the Rent function, the program retrieves a pointer to the customer renting the item and then calls the customer object's `InsertRentedItem` function to actually perform the insertion. As you can see in Listing 10.4, `InsertRentedItem` contains just a call to the LList function `InsertItemsAt`.

Listing 10.4 Functions to insert an object into an LList object

```
date * Item_copy::Rent (Customer * theRenter, int rentalPeriod)
{
    DateTimeRec todayRec;
    date * today;

    ::GetTime (&todayRec); // call ToolBox routine to get current date and time
    today = new date (todayRec);
    *Date_due = (*today) + rentalPeriod; // uses overloaded operators
    Renter_numb = theRenter->getRenter_numb();

    // put item into customer's LList of rented items
    theRenter->InsertRentedItem (this);

    In_stock = FALSE;
    return Date_due;
}

void Customer::InsertRentedItem (Item_copy * rentedItem)
{
    Items_rented->InsertItemsAt (1, arrayIndex_Last, &rentedItem);
}
```

To insert an item, you must specify three things:

- The number of items to be inserted (in this case, just one).
- The list position after which the new item(s) are to be inserted. In this example, the function call uses a constant that indicates that the item is to be placed at the end of the list.
- The address of the item being inserted. Notice in Listing 10.4, for example, that the item being inserted is a pointer stored in the variable `rentedItem`. The function call therefore includes the address of the pointer variable rather than its contents.

Removing an item from a list means you must find the item first and find its position in the list. We will leave finding the item for a moment, because it provides a good place to provide an example of using a list iterator. Therefore, assuming that you do know an item's list index, you can remove it with

```
theList->RemoveItemsAt (1, index);
```

The first parameter specifies the number of items to remove. The second is the starting index in the list.

Using a List Iterator

You might want to use a list iterator for several reasons. The most obvious is to traverse the list to access each member. However, you might also want to traverse the list to search it based on some value other than a pointer to the item (the only type of search supported by LList through its inherited `FetchIndexOf` function) or to find the location for inserting an item when you are keeping the list in some order.

Basic list iteration is provided by the class LListIterator. It supports iteration from the first or last item in the list, as well as from a specified index position. The four functions you are most likely to use are these:

- `Current`: Returns the current item.
- `Next`: Moves to the next item in the list.
- `Previous`: Moves to the previous item in the list.
- `ResetTo`: Changes the current index to a specified position.

The first three functions, which actually access items in the list, each return a Boolean that indicates whether the access was successful. For example, if `Next` or `Prior` returns false, you have reached the end of the list.

The beauty of an LListIterator object is that it can keep track of its position in the list even if the list changes. In other words, if you insert items into or remove items from a list while an iterator is attached to the list, the iterator remains valid. In fact, if the associated list object has been deleted, the iterator will gracefully handle the situation.

The problem with an LListIterator object is that it can't tell you where it is: It can return the current object, but can't return that object's index. If you happen to be keeping the list in some order or need to search by something other than a pointer to the object, then you desperately need to be able to know that index. Admittedly, given that an iterator adjusts to changes in a list, the possibility exists that an index returned during a list traversal could be invalid when you try to use it. However, if you can be certain that the list *won't* change in the interval between finding the item and using the index of that item, then it would be extremely useful to have an iterator that returned the index.

To solve the problem, the Penultimate Videos program uses a subclass of LListIterator (IndexAccessIterator in Listing 10.5). This class adds a single function to LListIterator that simply returns the value in the iterator object's `mCurrIndex` variable.

This iterator can then be used in any situation in which there is no chance that the list will change before the retrieved index is used.

Listing 10.5 The IndexAccessIterator class

```
class IndexAccessIterator : public LListIterator
{
    friend class LIteratedList;

    public:
        IndexAccessIterator (LIteratedList &inList, ArrayIndexT inPosition);
        ~IndexAccessIterator();

        getCurrentIndex();
};
```

To see a list iterator in action, take a look at Listing 10.6, the function that removes an item from a customer's linked list of rented items. Although a pointer to the item is available, for demonstration purposes the search uses the item's inventory number. The function first creates an iterator object from the IndexAccessIterator class. It then gets the first item in the list. If the list is empty, the variable `search_result` will contain false; otherwise, `search_result` is true and `listItem` contains a pointer to the first item in the list.

The function continues to iterate through the list by placing a call to the `Next` function in a `while`. The loop will stop as soon as the function encounters an item with the correct inventory number or there are no more items in the list. At that point, the function can remove the item from the linked list by placing a call to the `getCurrentIndex` function in the call to `RemoveItemsAt`.

Files

PowerPlant provides the class named LFile that acts as a wrapper for File Manager calls. You can use it to manage the entire data and/or resource fork of a file. Although LFile includes code for opening both the data and resource forks, it only includes code for reading and writing the data fork; you will need to add your own code for handling the resource fork.

Listing 10.6 Using a list iterator

```
void Customer::RemoveRentedItem (Item_copy *  rentedItem)
{
    Item_copy * listItem;
    Boolean search_result;

    // create list iterator
    IndexAccessIterator * RIList = new IndexAccessIterator (*Items_rented, 1);

    search_result = RIList->Current (&listItem); // get first item

    while (rentedItem->getInventory_numb() != listItem->getInventory_numb()
        && search_result)
            search_result = RIList->Next (&listItem); // get next item in list

    if (!search_result)
    {
        // alert goes here
    }
    else
        // remove item found
        Items_rented->RemoveItemsAt (1, RIList->getCurrentIndex());
}
```

To demonstrate how an LFile object can simplify file handling, we'll be looking at code that opens and saves the contents of a Note object. In Listing 10.7, for example, you will find code that opens a file containing a note and places the text that has been read from the note into a Note object.

The `OpenNote` function first uses the standard GetFile dialog box to obtain a FileSpec for the file to be opened. In particular, notice that the call to the ToolBox routine `StandardGetFile` is bracketed by calls to two UDesktop routines: `Deactivate` and `Activate`. You should use these functions whenever your program will be displaying a modal dialog box, such as the GetFile dialog box. `Deactivate` makes the front window inactive and lets the modal dialog box take over event trapping. You should therefore call it just before displaying a modal dialog box. `Activate` makes the front window active again and should be called immediately after a modal dialog box has been closed.

Although there are several ways to initialize an LFile object, probably the easiest is to use a FileSpec. As you can see in Listing 10.7, the `OpenNote` function retrieves the FileSpec from the data structure returned when the GetFile dialog box is closed. It then uses that FileSpec as input to a constructor when creating a new LFile object. Creating the object opens the file. If no file matches the file specified by the FileSpec,

Listing 10.7 Opening a note

```
void Note::OpenNote ()
{
    StandardFileReply replyStruct;
    SFTypeList typeList;
    short numTypes = 1;
    Str63 fileName;

    typeList[0] = 'TEXT'; // read just text files

    UDesktop::Deactivate();
    ::StandardGetFile (nil, numTypes, typeList, &replyStruct);
    UDesktop::Activate();

    if (!replyStruct.sfGood) return; // user cancelled

    fileSpec = replyStruct.sfFile;

    Try_
    {
        theFile = new LFile (fileSpec);
        theFile->OpenDataFork (fsRdWrPerm);
        Handle tempTextH = theFile->ReadDataFork();
        SetTextHandle (tempTextH);
        ::DisposeHandle (tempTextH);

        LScroller * theScroller = (LScroller *) LPane::GetSuperView();
        LWindow * theWindow = (LWindow *) theScroller->GetSuperView();
        theWindow->SetDescriptor(replyStruct.sfFile.name);
    }

    Catch_ (inErr)
    {
        Throw_(inErr);
    } EndCatch_
}
```

no file will be opened. As you will see shortly, when you want a new file, you must create it explicitly.

Once the file has been opened, `OpenNote` opens the file's data fork for both reading and writing with the LFile function `OpenDataFork`. Then, the function can use the function `ReadDataFork` to load the entire contents of the data fork into memory, returning a handle to where the data are located.

NOTE

LFile contains a function related to OpenDataFork—OpenResourceFork—to open the resource fork of a file. However, there is no file analogous to ReadDataFork for the resource fork. As mentioned earlier, you will need to code resource fork reads yourself using File Manager calls.

The next step is to insert the text into the text edit record being managed by a Note object. To do so, `OpenNote` calls the LTextEdit function `SetTextHandle`, which modifies the Note object so that it uses the handle to the text loaded from the file to locate a note's contents. Finally, the function disposes of the handle it created when loading data and sets the note window's title to the name of the file from which data were just loaded.

Saving something in a file's data fork is almost precisely the opposite of reading the data fork. As you can see in Listing 10.8, there are two functions that handle saving a note. `SaveNote` takes care of writing to the file; `SaveAsNote` handles naming a new file.

Because saving a file always involves doing a Save As at least once, let's look first at the `SaveAs` function. To save a file under a new name, the function does the following:

- Deactivates the front window.
- Displays the standard PutFile dialog box to obtain a FileSpec.
- Reactivates the front window.
- Sets the name of the note window to the file name chosen by the user.
- Assuming the user wants to create a new file (rather than replace an existing file of the same name), creates the file with the LFile function `CreateNewDataFile`. Notice that this function requires the creator string, the file type string, and a constant for the script system that should be used to display the file name. The 0 in Listing 10.8 indicates a Roman script.
- Calls the `SaveNote` function to write the data to the file.

NOTE

Constants for script systems can be found in Script.h.

The `SaveNote` function begins by deleting an existing LFile object, which closes the file. Then it creates a new object using the stored FileSpec and opens the file's data fork. To prepare for writing, `SaveNote` gets the handle to the text to be written and locks that handle. Finally, it can use the LFile function `WriteDataFork` to write the entire note to the file at once. Notice that `SaveNote` passes `WriteDataFork` a pointer to the text along with the number of bytes to be written.

Listing 10.8 Saving a note

```
void Note::SaveNote ()
{
    delete theFile; // remove existing file object
    theFile = new LFile (fileSpec); // create new object
    theFile->OpenDataFork (fsRdWrPerm);

    Handle tempTextH = GetTextHandle ();
    StHandleLocker theLock(tempTextH);
    theFile->WriteDataFork (*tempTextH, GetHandleSize (tempTextH));
}

void Note::SaveAsNote ()
{
    StandardFileReply replyStruct;
    LStr255 prompt = "Save note as:";
    LStr255 fileName;

    UDesktop::Deactivate();
    ::StandardPutFile (prompt, fileName, &replyStruct);
    UDesktop::Activate();

    if (!replyStruct.sfGood) return; // user cancelled

    fileSpec = replyStruct.sfFile;

    LScroller * theScroller = (LScroller *) LPane::GetSuperView();
    LWindow * theWindow = (LWindow *) theScroller->GetSuperView();
    theWindow->SetDescriptor(replyStruct.sfFile.name);

    if (!replyStruct.sfReplacing)
        theFile->CreateNewDataFile ('VidS', 'TEXT', 0);
    SaveNote();

    mustSaveAs = FALSE;
}
```

NOTE

In the CW8 InProgress folder, you will find a class called LStreamable. When complete, this class will act as a mix-in base class for any class whose data values you want to store in a file. Using overloaded operators inherited from LStream, you will be able to use the stream insertion and extraction operators to read from and write to a file. Doing so will be much like using ANSI stream I/O, although somewhat simpler because you won't need to worry about things such as placing nulls at the end of C strings and skipping over blanks that follow numbers and precede strings. Keep an eye out for when this class graduates from "in progress" to becoming a useful part of PowerPlant.

CHAPTER 11

Repeated Actions: Periodicals

In Chapter 6, where we looked at editing text, you were introduced to the idea of a *periodical*, a class whose objects receive attention at regular intervals, either after every event (*repeaters*) or after every idle event (*idlers*). The most widely visible use of a periodical in a Macintosh program, of course, is the flashing straight-line insertion point. However, that isn't the only instance in which an object needs to receive attention regularly.

In this chapter we'll take a more in-depth look at periodicals so you can set up your own periodicals as needed. The example we'll be using is the Penultimate Videos memory monitor window (Figure 11.1), which displays the amount of memory available to the program at any given time. Once the window has been opened, the program updates it whenever the amount of free memory changes.

NOTE

Although you probably wouldn't make this type of information available to users of a rcal-world video store management program, the window nonetheless serves as a good example of a periodical. Because Penultimate Videos is totally memory-based—its data

Figure 11.1 The memory monitor window

are all stored in main memory—it also comes in handy when working on the program as a warning when memory shortages are likely to occur.

The LPeriodical Class

LPeriodical is a mix-in class: You add it to a derived class to provide additional functionality to whatever the derived class is inheriting from other its other base class(es). If the class that should receive regular attention is a pane, then it will inherit from at least the pane class and LPeriodical; if the class is a window, then it will inherit from at least LWindow and LPeriodical.

The LPeriodical class maintains two linked lists (objects of class LList): one of repeaters and one of idlers. The class stores pointers to the list objects. Because these pointers are stored in `static` variables, a program maintains only one copy of those variables, which is shared by all objects that are derived from LPeriodical.

To request that a program give time to a periodical, the program must insert the periodical into one or both of the periodical lists, using the following functions:

- `StartIdling`: Inserts a periodical into the idlers list.
- `StartRepeating`: Inserts a periodical into the repeaters list.

To stop giving time to a periodical, a program removes them from the appropriate list using the following functions:

- `StopIdling`: Removes a periodical from the idlers list.
- `StopRepeating`: Removes a periodical from the repeaters list.

As you may remember from Chapter 1, where we looked at PowerPlant's event trapping mechanism, an application object's `ProcessNextEvent` function (Listing

1.3) contains two functions that traverse the periodical lists and handle all periodicals on those lists: UseIdleTime takes care of idle events, including a call to the LPeriodical function DevoteTimeToIdlers, which takes care of objects in the idler list; DevoteTimeToRepeaters is an LPeriodical function that handles the repeater list.

Both DevoteTimeToIdlers and DevoteTimeToRepeaters traverse the appropriate list and execute each object's SpendTime function, a pure virtual function that you must override in a subclass. SpendTime should perform whatever actions need to occur each time the object gets a chance to execute.

Subclassing to Create a Periodical

As you have read, a subclass that inherits from LPeriodical must also inherit from at least one other class. The memory monitor window class, for example, inherits from both LPeriodical and LWindow (see Listing 11.1). The class includes a FinishCreateSelf function (overriding the LPane function) and a SpendTime function (overriding the LPeriodical function). The FindCommandStatus function takes care of deactivating the Memory Monitor menu item when a window is open on the screen so that no more than one memory monitor window appears at any given time.

Listing 11.1 The MemoryMonitor class

```
class MemoryMonitor : public LWindow, public LPeriodical
{
    public:
        static MemoryMonitor * CreateMemoryMonitorStream (LStream * inStream);
        MemoryMonitor();
        MemoryMonitor (LStream * inStream);
        ~MemoryMonitor();
        void FindCommandStatus(CommandTinCommand, Boolean &outEnabled,
            Boolean &outUsesMark,Char16 &outMark,Str255 outName)

        void FinishCreateSelf();
        void SpendTime (const EventRecord & inMacEvent);
    private:
        LPane * FreeMemCaption;
        long previousFree;
};
```

The class's FreeMemCaption variable holds a pointer to the LCaption object that displays the number of bytes of free memory; the previousFree variable holds the previous reading of the amount of free memory for determining whether the window needs to be updated.

Several important things need to happen in a periodical's member functions. As you can see in Listing 11.2, the FinishCreateSelf function inserts an object into both the idler and repeater lists. The destructor removes the object from the lists, a step that is essential to ensuring that the program doesn't attempt to access a nonexistent object.

Of course, most of the work occurs in the SpendTime function, which begins by calling the ToolBox routine FreeMem to retrieve the number of bytes of memory available to the program. The function could then immediately update the caption that displays the free memory. However, doing so causes the display to flicker. SpendTime therefore checks to see if the amount of free memory has changed since the last time the function was executed and updates the caption only if a change has occurred.

Programming Support for a Periodical

The Penultimate Videos application object activates the Memory Monitor menu item in its application object's FindCommandStatus function. It then traps selection of that menu item in its ObeyCommand function, which simply creates the memory monitor window:

```
LWindow * theMonitorWindow =
        LWindow::CreateWindow (WINDOW_MEMORY_MONITOR, this);
```

Because the memory monitor object's FinishCreateSelf function takes care of installing the object into the periodical lists, there is nothing else the application object needs to do.

Listing 11.2 The MemoryMonitor class's member functions

```
MemoryMonitor * MemoryMonitor::CreateMemoryMonitorStream (LStream * inStream)
{
    return (new MemoryMonitor (inStream));
}

MemoryMonitor::MemoryMonitor()
{   // empty
}

MemoryMonitor::MemoryMonitor (LStream * inStream)
    : LWindow (inStream)
{
    previousFree = 0;
}

// Destructor
MemoryMonitor::~MemoryMonitor()
{
    // Remove object from lists of idlers and repeaters
    StopRepeating();
    StopIdling();
}

// FinishCreateSelf
void MemoryMonitor::FinishCreateSelf()
{
    // Save pointer to caption that displays amount of free memory
    FreeMemCaption = (LPane *) FindPaneByID (FREE_MEMORY);
    // Add object to lists of idlers and repeaters
    StartRepeating();
    StartIdling();
}

// FindCommandStatus: used to deactivate menu option while window is on screen
void MemoryMonitor::FindCommandStatus(CommandT inCommand, Boolean &outEnabled,
        Boolean &outUsesMark, Char16 &outMark,Str255 outName)
{
    switch (inCommand)
    {
        case cmd_memory_monitor:
            outEnabled = false;
            outUsesMark = false;
            break;
        default:
            LWindow::FindCommandStatus (inCommand, outEnabled, outUsesMark,
                outMark, outName);
            break;
    }
}
```

Continued next page

Listing 11.2 (Continued) The MemoryMonitor class's member functions

```
// SpendTime
void MemoryMonitor::SpendTime (const EventRecord & inMacEvent)
{
    #pragma unused (inMacEvent) // suppress error messages

    long bytesFree = ::FreeMem ();
    // update only if memory has changed to avoid flicker
    if (previousFree != bytesFree)
    {
        PString stringBytes = bytesFree;
        previousFree = bytesFree;
        FreeMemCaption->SetDescriptor (stringBytes);
        FreeMemCaption->Refresh();
    }
}
```

CHAPTER

12

Printing

Printing from a Macintosh application, while relatively simple for the user, has always been a challenge from the programmer's point of view. Fortunately, one of the things that PowerPlant does well is to simplify programming for printing. For example, PowerPlant takes care of figuring out how to break up a document into pages.

In this chapter we will be looking at the way in which PowerPlant implements printing and in particular at the classes LPrintout, LPlaceholder, and UPrintingMgr. You will see how to create LPrintout objects that contain LPlaceholder objects, how to implement the printing process, and how to add support for the Page Setup and Print dialog boxes.

How PowerPlant Printing Works

Like many parts of PowerPlant, printing functions are managed by a sequence of interlinked functions that belong to more than one class. In this particular case, what the programmer needs to do and what PowerPlant does are very far removed from each other. To help you understand what is happened, we'll first look at what a program needs to do to implement printing. Then we'll explore what PowerPlant does when a program initiates printing.

A Program's Printing Tasks

To print the contents of a PowerPlant window, a program does the following:

- Creates an object of class LPrintout. The printout object contains views created from LPlaceholder.
- Installs views from the window whose contents are being printed into the placeholders on the printout.
- Tells the printout to print itself.
- Deletes the LPrintout object to return the views from the placeholders to their original locations.

Before telling the printout to print itself, a program may also display the Print Job dialog box.

The Printing Process

Before beginning to print, the LPrintout class takes care of dividing the panes or views being printed into pages. The portion of a pane or view being printed that will fit on one page is called a *panel*. In this case, the boundaries of the placeholder into which a view is installed become the view's frame for the time the view resides in the placeholder. A panel is therefore the amount of a view that will fit into the placeholder's frame.

The printing process is actually handled by both LPrintout and either LPane or LView (depending on whether you are printing a pane or a view). When a program calls the LPrintout function `DoPrintJob`, the call initiates the following sequence of actions:

- `DoPrintJob` **obtains the print job information (the range of panels to be printed and the number of copies to print). It then calls** `PrintPanelRange`**, another LPrintout function.**
- `PrintPanelRange` **opens the print manager using the UPrintingMgr function** `OpenPrinter`**. It then calls** `LPrintout::PrintCopiesOfPages`.
- `PrintCopiesOfPages` **contains a loop that repeatedly calls** `LPrintout::PrintPanel` **to print the required number of copies of each panel.**
- `LPrintout::PrintPanel` **calls either** `LPane::PrintPanel` **or** `LView::PrintPanel` **(depending on whether you're printing a pane or view) for each pane and subpane in the LPrintout object panel.**
- `LPane::PrintPanel` **or** `LView::PrintPanel` **takes care of supplying local frame coordinates and then calls** `PrintPanelSelf`**, which by default simply calls** `DrawSelf`.

LPrintout's Limitations

In most cases, you won't need to subclass LPrintout. Its default behavior can handle most printing situations. However, although LPrintout does handle the pagination of multiple-page documents, there are a couple of things that, as a generalized printing engine, it simply can't do. In particular, it can't determine whether the place at which a page breaks is actually appropriate. For example, if you are printing text, LPrintout has no way to know if a panel boundary cuts through the middle of a line of text. In addition, LPrintout doesn't handle nonplaceholder views or panes well. For example, you might want to add a letterhead, graphics, or display text to a printout that doesn't appear on the screen view. However, you usually can't add those elements directly to the LPrintout object and expect them to print properly on a multipage document.

If you need to determine panel boundaries yourself or want to add items other than placeholders to printed output, you will need to create a subclass for the view being printed and override the LPane or LView function `PrintPanelSelf`. Unfortunately, there's nothing simple about figuring out where panels should break. Doing so is very program-dependent and therefore beyond the scope of this book.

Creating LPrintout Objects

The first step in printing is to use Constructor to create an LPrintout object that contains a placeholder for the data to be printed. The simplest LPrintout object used by

Penultimate Videos, for example, handles printing a note. As you can see in Figure 12.1, the object contains only one pane: the LPlaceholder object with the resource ID 1502. In contrast, the LPrintout object for handling a printed customer receipt (Figure 12.2) contains several placeholders, as well as objects of class LPicture and LCaption.

Figure 12.1 The LPrintout object for printing a note

Figure 12.2 The LPrintout object for printing a customer receipt

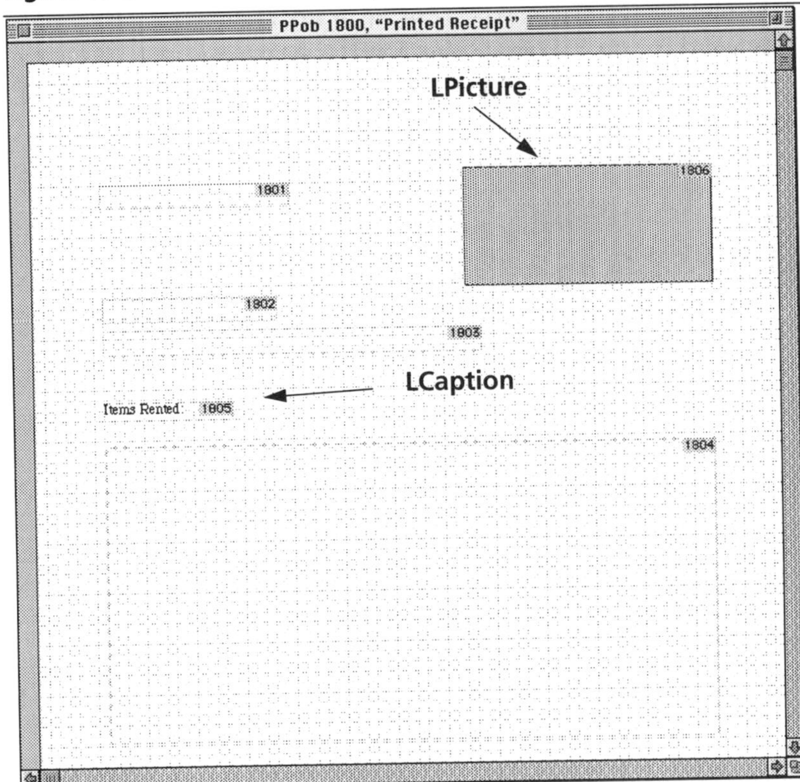

NOTE

Although printing typically doesn't work well when you place objects other than placeholders on an LPrintout object, you can often get away with it if a printout will never be more than one page in size. This happens to be the case for the receipt, which means that the receipt can contain the Penultimate Videos logo and some display text without requiring overriding of the LPane function PrintPanelSelf.

To create an LPrintout object, open Constructor and create a new view of type LPrintout. Then, drag LPlaceholder objects onto the view; resize, number, and move them as needed.

As you can see in Figure 12.3, an LPrintout object has very few properties with which you need to be concerned. By default, the size is set to letter-sized paper in a portrait orientation. However, during the printing process, LPrintout adjusts the size based on the paper size and oriented specified by the user through the Page Setup dialog box.

Figure 12.3 LPrintout properties

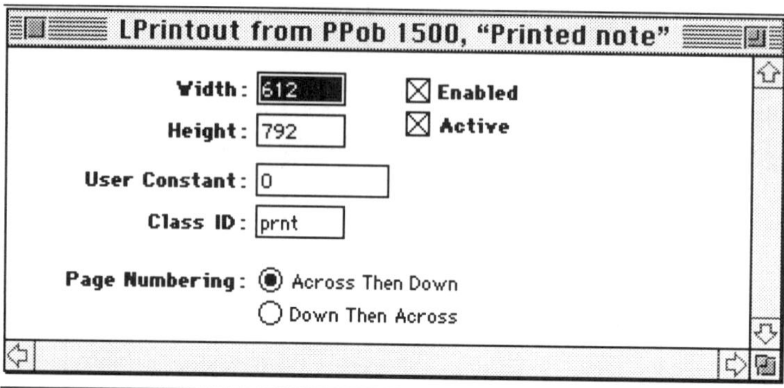

The Page Numbering property refers to the order in which panels are numbered and printed. Assume, for example, that you are printing a large poster containing the image in Figure 12.4. The poster is far too large to fit on one piece of paper. It therefore has been broken up into 18 panels, represented by the heavy lines in Figure 12.4. These panes can be printed across, moving from left to right beginning in the top row, or down, moving from top to bottom beginning with the leftmost column. Use the Page Numbering radio buttons to select the correct panel printing order for your output.

LPlaceholder's properties (Figure 12.5) are primarily inherited from LView. However, the alignment properties at the bottom of the properties window are particularly important. They determine how a portion of a view or pane that is smaller than the panel in which it is installed will be aligned with the panel's frame. The alignment possibilities affect the printed output in the following way:

- No alignment: The pane or view is resized to fit the panel's frame.
- Horizontal alignment but no vertical alignment: The pane or view is sized vertically to fit the panel's height, but the chosen horizontal alignment is used for placing the pane or view within the panel's width.
- Vertical alignment but no horizontal alignment: The pane or view is sized horizontally to fit the panel's width, but the chosen vertical alignment is used for placing pane or view within the panel's height.
- Both horizontal and vertical alignment: The pane or view is not resized, but placed using the horizontal and vertical specifications.

Figure 12.4 Panel "numbering"

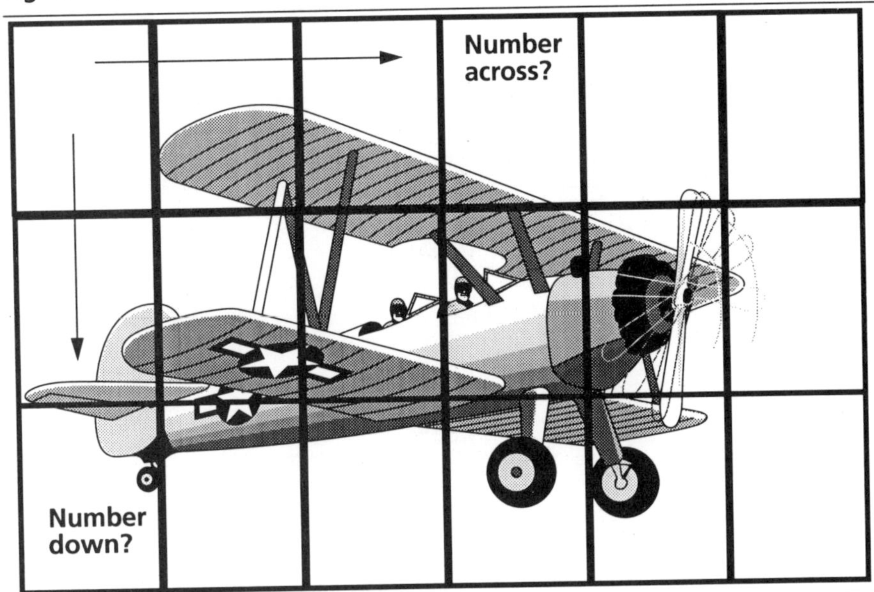

Coding Simple Printing

If you want to print without showing the Print Job dialog box, coding the printing is straightforward. In Listing 12.1, for example, you can see how the Penultimate Videos application object prints a customer receipt in its `PrintReceipt` function. The code uses the same general steps outlined earlier in this chapter.

`PrintReceipt` first creates an object of class LPrintout (`thePrintout`). Next, the function calls `FindPaneByID` to first get a pointer to one of the LPlaceholder objects on the printer. It then calls `FindPaneByID` again to get a pointer to the pane that is to be installed in the placeholder.

To install the pane into the placeholder, `PrintReceipt` calls the LPlaceholder function `InstallOccupant`, passing in the pointer to the pane being installed and a constant that indicates the alignment to be used. (Alignment constants, such as the `atNone` used by Penultimate Videos, can be found in *Icons.h*.) This process—getting the pointers and installing the pane—is repeated for each placeholder on `thePrintout`.

Figure 12.5 LPlaceholder properties

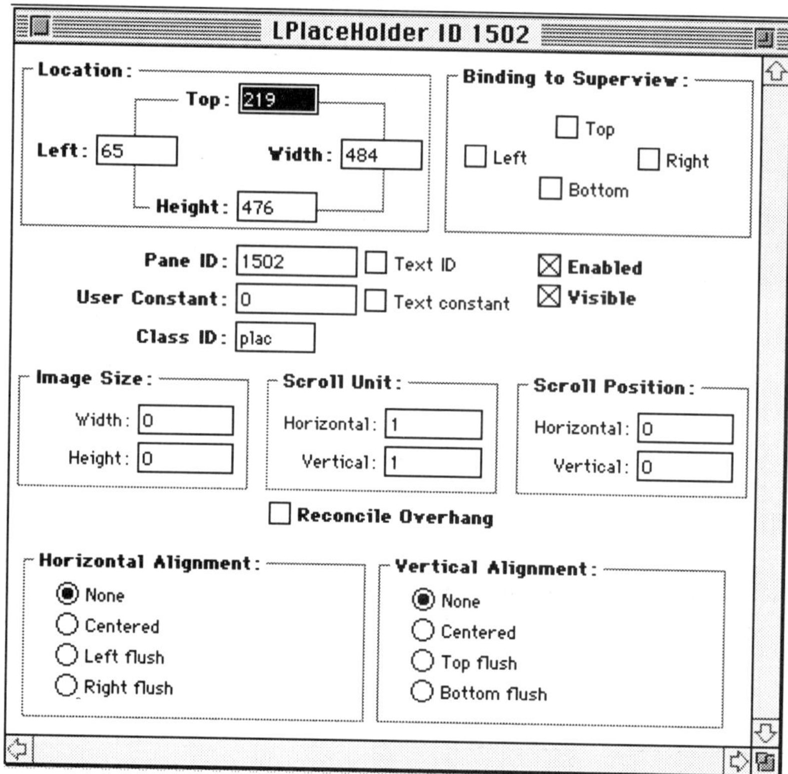

Once all the panes have been transferred to the printout object, `PrintReceipt` calls `DoPrintJob`. As you read earlier, `DoPrintJob` initiates a series of actions that perform the actual printing.

When printing is completed, the panes that were transferred to the printout object need to be returned to their original location. This activity is performed by LPrintout's destructor. A program should therefore delete the printout object.

Listing 12.1 Printing without the Print Job dialog box

```
void CPPVideoStoreApp::PrintReceipt (SDialogResponse * dialogResponse)
{
   // create prinoutout object from resource
   LPrintout * thePrintout = LPrintout::CreatePrintout (WINDOW_RECEIPT_PRINTOUT);

   // get panes in dialog box and install in placeholders
   LPlaceHolder * thePlace = (LPlaceHolder *)
      thePrintout->FindPaneByID (RECEIPT_PRINTOUT_DATE);
   LView * theView = (LView *) receiptDialog->FindPaneByID (RECEIPT_DATE);
   thePlace->InstallOccupant (theView, atNone);

   thePlace = (LPlaceHolder *) thePrintout->FindPaneByID (RECEIPT_PRINTOUT_CUST_NUMB);
   theView = (LView *) receiptDialog->FindPaneByID (RECEIPT_CUST_NUMB);
   thePlace->InstallOccupant (theView, atNone);

   thePlace = (LPlaceHolder *) thePrintout->FindPaneByID (RECEIPT_PRINTOUT_NAME);
   theView = (LView *) receiptDialog->FindPaneByID (RECEIPT_NAME);
   thePlace->InstallOccupant (theView, atNone);

   thePlace = (LPlaceHolder *) thePrintout->FindPaneByID (RECEIPT_PRINTOUT_LIST);
   theView = (LView *) receiptDialog->FindPaneByID (RECEIPT_TABLE);
   thePlace->InstallOccupant (theView, atNone);

   // now, print it; Print Job dialog box doesn't appear
   thePrintout->DoPrintJob();

   // to get the scrolling view back to its window, you must delete the
   // printout to trigger its destructor
   delete thePrintout;

   // close other dialog boxes
   CloseRentWindows (dialogResponse);
}
```

Adding Support for the Printing Dialog Boxes

Although there are some situations in which it is acceptable to print without displaying the Print Job dialog box and without giving the user access to the Page Setup dialog box, in most cases you will want to give users the flexibility those dialog boxes provide. Because both dialog boxes modify a print record, code that supports them must allocate a print record and store a handle to that record.

As an example of supporting the printing dialog boxes, the Note class turns on the Page Setup menu option whenever at least one note window is open; printing a note displays the Print Job dialog box. To provide access to the print record needed to support both dialog boxes, the Note class includes a variable of type THPrint (mPrintRecordH).

Support for Page Setup is usually placed in the ObeyCommand function of a printable object. In our example, it appears in the Note class. However, if every window opened by an application is printable, you may want to place the Page Setup code in the application object's ObeyCommand function.

In Listing 12.2 you will find the Page Setup code from the Note class. The PowerPlant class that forms the basis of this code is UPrintingMgr. The UPrintingMgr class acts as a wrapper for many Printing Manager functions, including such things as creating a new print record, obtaining a handle to the class's print record, and opening and closing a printer driver.

Listing 12.2 Handling the Page Setup dialog box

```
case cmd_PageSetup:
    UDesktop::Deactivate();

    // check for existing print record
    if (mPrintRecordH == nil)
        mPrintRecordH = UPrintingMgr::GetDefaultPrintRecord();

    // display the page setup dialog box
    UPrintingMgr::AskPageSetup(mPrintRecordH);

    UDesktop::Activate();
    break;
```

As you can see in Listing 12.2, to provide the Page Setup dialog box, you call the UPrintingMgr function AskPageSetup, passing it a handle to the print record that should be modified. If a print record hasn't been allocated, the call to AskPageSetup will cause a program crash. Therefore, the code first checks for a valid print record handle and if necessary calls GetDefaultPrintRecord to obtain the class's default print record handle. Notice also that because the Page Setup dialog box is modal, the code deactivates the front window with UDesktop::Deactivate before displaying the dialog box. Once the dialog box has been dismissed, it makes the front window active again with UDesktop::Activate.

As you have read, LPrintout checks a printable class's print record to determine the number of copies and page range to print. To give the user the opportunity to change these values, a Macintosh application displays the Page Job dialog box. A PowerPlant program can do so with the UPrintingMgr function `AskPrintJob`.

The code used by the Note class to print itself appears in Listing 12.3. Notice that this function first creates an LPrintout object. It then determines whether a print record exists. If there is no print record, it creates one by calling `UPrintingMgr::CreatePrintRecord`, which returns a handle to the newly created data structure. Then, it attaches the new print record to the LPrintout object by calling `LPrintout::SetPrintRecord`.

Listing 12.3 Printing with the Print Job dialog box

```
void Note::PrintNote()
{
    // Create the LPrintout object
    LPrintout * thePrintout = LPrintout::CreatePrintout (WINDOW_NOTE_PRINTOUT);

    // Create print record if necessary
    if (mPrintRecordH == nil)
        mPrintRecordH = UPrintingMgr::CreatePrintRecord();

    // Switch the print record
    thePrintout->SetPrintRecord (mPrintRecordH);

    // Create a pointer to the placeholder
    LPlaceHolder * thePlace = (LPlaceHolder *)
        thePrintout->FindPaneByID (RETURN_PLACEHOLDER);
    // Find ID of the pane that scrolls inside the scroller
    LView * theView = (LView *) LTextEditM::FindPaneByID (NOTE_TE);
    // Install pane into place holder in printout object
    thePlace->InstallOccupant (theView, atNone);

    // display Job dialog box
    UDesktop::Deactivate();
    Boolean PrintIt = UPrintingMgr::AskPrintJob (mPrintRecordH);
    UDesktop::Activate();

    if (!PrintIt)
        return; // user cancelled; get out of here

    // now, print it
    thePrintout->DoPrintJob();

    // to get the scrolling view back to its window, you must delete the
    // printout to trigger its destructor
    delete thePrintout;
}
```

`PrintNote` installs the Note object into the LPrintout object's placeholder. At that point, the function deactivates the front window, displays the Print Job dialog box, and then reactivates the front window. At that point, the note is ready to be printed with `DoPrintJob`. The final step is to return the Note to its original superview by deleting the LPrintout object.

Binary Search Trees

Appendix

A *binary search tree* is a data structure that organizes elements in key order to provide fast searches based on that key. Although binary search trees are classic data structures that have been used for many years, the influence of object-oriented programming has introduced new ways of handling these structures.

In this appendix you will first be introduced to the binary tree data structure along with algorithms for inserting, searching for, and deleting items. You will also be introduced to tree traversal algorithms. If you are familiar with classic binary trees, you can skip this first material. The second major portion of this chapter looks at the classes and techniques used to implement binary trees in an object-oriented program. These latter techniques are used to provide the underlying data management for the Penultimate Videos sample program.

The Binary Tree Data Structure

A binary tree is made up of a collection of *nodes*, each of which is usually contains a pointer to an object. It is theoretically possible to store an entire object as a node in a tree. However, more commonly binary trees are viewed like indexes to a book: A book's index contains an ordered list of topics and pointers (page numbers) to where the topic can be found. Using pointers to objects means that the same object can appear in many trees, yet only be stored in memory once. If we extend the example of book indexes, a book can contain an index by topic, another by illustration, and yet another by authors of works cited in the book. In all three cases, the book uses page numbers as pointers to avoid repeating any information in the text.

A binary tree gets its name from its structure. As you can see in Figure App.1, each node points to at most two nodes below it (its left child and right child). Each node also has at most one node above it (its parent).

Figure App.1 A binary search tree

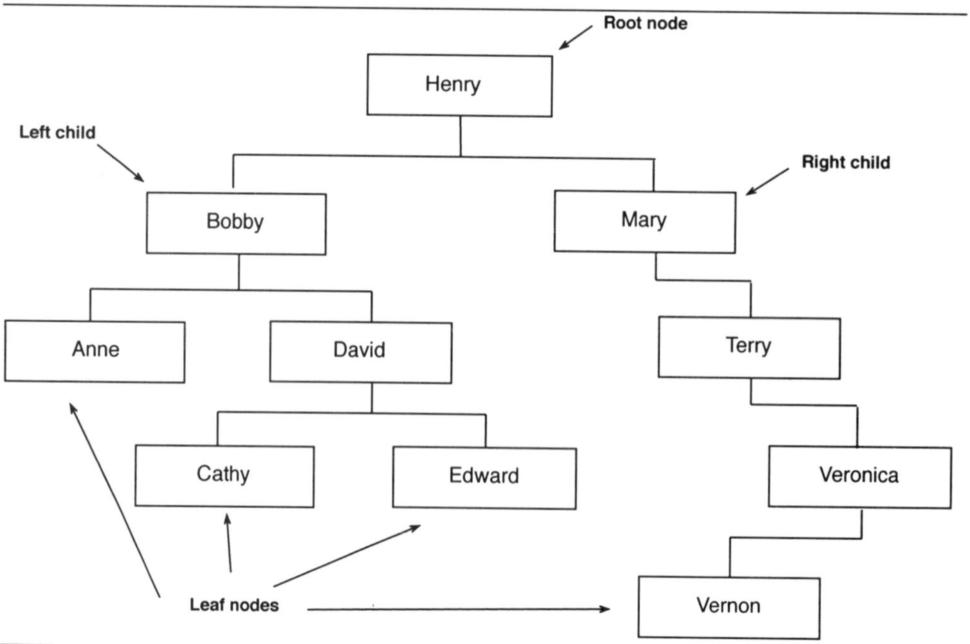

The node at the top of the tree is called the *root*. This is the first node that is placed in the tree and provides the single entry point to the entire tree. It is the only node that doesn't have a parent. Any node that has no children is called a *leaf*.

The tree in Figure App.1 uses a person's first name as the key by which the nodes are ordered. In an actual tree, the keys aren't part of the nodes, but have been included in the illustration to make it possible to identify the way in which the nodes are ordered.

If you look at any given node, you will notice that the key of its right child is greater than the key of the node; the key of its left child is less than the key of the node. This very simple organizing principle enables very fast searching of the tree.

Searching a Binary Tree

The most common reason for using a binary tree is for fast searching. If the 10 nodes of the tree in Figure App.1 were stored in a linked list ordered by name, a program would need to access every node to find Veronica, the alphabetically last node in the list. However, when searching the binary tree, a program only needs to access four nodes to find Veronica. By the same token, an unsuccessful search of a linked list (a search where the key for which the program is looking isn't present in the list) requires searching every element in the list. In contrast, an unsuccessful search of a binary tree will require searching only one node at each level in the tree. This means that in the worst case of an unsuccessful search of the tree in Figure App.1, a program will at most need to consult only five nodes, whereas if the objects were stored in a linked list, the program would need to consult 10 nodes.

The process for searching a binary tree can be summarized as follows:

1. Find the root node and make it the current node.
2. Compare the search key with the key of the current node.
3. If the search key and the current node's key match, the search has been successful.
4. If the search key is less than the current node's key, retrieve the current node's left child. If the current node has no left child, the search is unsuccessful. Otherwise, make the left child the current node and continue with Step 2.
5. If the search key is greater than the current node's key, retrieve the current node's right child. If the current node has no right child, the search is unsuccessful. Otherwise, make the right child the current node and continue with Step 2.

As an example, assume that we are searching for Veronica in Figure App.1. The search then proceeds in this way:

1. Find Henry and make Henry the current node.
2. Compare Henry to Veronica.
3. Veronica is greater than Henry. Therefore, retrieve the right child (Mary) and make it the current node.
4. Compare Mary to Veronica.
5. Veronica is greater than Mary. Therefore, retrieve the right child (Terry) and make it the current node.
6. Compare Terry to Veronica.
7. Veronica is greater than Terry. Therefore, retrieve the right child (Veronica) and make it the current node.
8. Compare Veronica to Veronica.
9. The search key matches the key of the current node. Therefore, the correct node has been found and the search ends successfully.

An example of a function to search a binary tree appears in Listing App.1. This particular function works on a binary tree made up of pointers to Merchandise_Item objects and is organized by item number. To support the tree, the Merchandise_Item class includes pointers for an object's left and right children (the variables `LeftNumb` and `RightNumb`). The class also includes functions to set the pointers (`setLeftNumb` and `setRightNumb`) and retrieve the pointers (`getLeftNumb` and `getLeftNumb`). As you read through this code, compare it to the general algorithm described earlier.

Inserting Nodes into a Binary Tree

To inert a node into a binary tree, a program searches the tree until it finds an unused child pointer that will place the new node in the correct sequence in the tree. The general algorithm is as follows:

1. If the tree is empty, insert the new node as the root node.
2. Otherwise, find the root node and make it the current node.
3. Compare the key of the new node with the current node.
4. If the key of the new node is less than the key of the current node, retrieve the current node's left child. If there is no left child, insert the new node as the current node's left child. Otherwise, make the left child the current node. Continue with Step 3.
5. If the key of the new node is greater than or equal to the key of the current node, retrieve the current node's right child. If there is no right child, insert the new

Listing App.1 Searching a binary tree

```
Merchandise_Item * MerchTree::find (ANSIstring iTitle)
{
    Merchandise_Item * current;

    if (root) // make sure there is at least one node
    {
        current = root;
        while (current) // as long as there's a pointer
        {
            if (strcmp (current->getTitle(), iTitle) == 0)
                return current; // send back pointer to merchandise item object
            // if less, go down right side
            if (strcmp (current->getTitle(), iTitle) < 0)
                current = current->getRightName();
            // if greater, go down left side
            else
                current = current->getLeftName();
        }
    }
    return 0; //  not found
}
```

node as the current node's right child. Otherwise, make the right child the current node. Continue with Step 3.

As an example, assume that we want to insert a new node with a key of Tammy into the binary tree in Figure App.1. A program performing the insertion would proceed in this way:

1. Determine that the tree is not empty because a root node exists.
2. Make Henry the current node.
3. Compare Tammy to Henry.
4. Because Tammy is greater than the current node, retrieve the current node's right child (Mary).
5. Because a right child exists, make it the current node.
6. Compare Tammy to Mary.
7. Because Tammy is greater than the current node, retrieve the current node's right child (Terry).
8. Because a right child exists, make it the current node.
9. Compare Tammy to Terry.
10. Because Tammy is less than the current node, retrieve the current node's left child.

11. Because no left child exists, insert the new node as the left child of the current node.

A function to insert an object into the tree that orders objects of classes derived from Merchandise_Item by item number appears in Listing App.2.

Listing App.2 Inserting a node into a binary tree

```
void MerchTree::Insert (Merchandise_Item * newItem, ANSIstring iTitle, Boolean
file_flag)
{
    Merchandise_Item * current, * child;

    if (root) // if root node exists
    {
        current = root;
        while (current) // keep going while there's a pointer
        {
            if (strcmp(current->getTitle(), iTitle) < 0)
            {
                // go down right side
                child = current->getRightName();
                if (!child) // if no right child, insert
                {
                    current->setRightName (newItem);
                    break;
                }
            }
            else
            {
                // go down left side
                child = current->getLeftName();
                if (!child) // if no left child, insert
                {
                    current->setLeftName (newItem);
                    break;
                }
            }
            current = child;
        }
    }
    else
        root = newItem;
    if (!file_flag)
        Item_count++;
}
```

DELETING ELEMENTS FROM A BINARY TREE

Unlike searching and inserting, both of which are relatively simple, deleting nodes from a binary tree is somewhat challenging. A program can't just remove the node; if a node isn't a leaf, the space left by the node must be filled with something.

The general algorithm is as follows:

1. Find the node to be deleted, using the search technique discussed earlier in this appendix.
2. If the node is a leaf, set the pointer of its parent to zero. This deletes the node from the tree, without removing the object from memory.
3. If the node is not a leaf, determine whether the node has children.
4. Determine whether the node is the left or right child of its parent.
5. If the node has a left child but no right child, make the node's left child the child of the node's parent.
6. If the node has a right child but no left child, make the node's right child the child of the node's parent.
7. If the node has both a right child and a left child, find the lowest right node in the node's left child tree. Replace the node to be deleted with the lowest right node in the left child tree.

The trickiest part of the delete algorithm occurs when the node to be deleted has both right and left children. To see what must happen, assume that you want to delete Bobby from the tree in Figure App.1. The program first finds Bobby and identifies the node as the left child of its parent. Then the program finds the lowest right node in the left child tree. In this case, the left subtree consists of only one node, Anne. (If Anne had a right child, that program would use that child rather than Anne.) To finish the delete, the program makes Anne the left subchild of Bobby's parent (Henry).

An implementation of the delete algorithm for the MerchTree class can be found in Listing App.3. Notice that this function uses a find function that returns two values: a pointer to the node to be deleted and a pointer to its parent.

NOTE

If the value of a node's key value changes, a program must delete the node from the tree and reinsert it using the new key. Otherwise, the tree will no longer be in the correct order. Because the Penultimate Videos program maintains a tree by item title and by customer name (first and last), this procedure must be used whenever a user modifies the title/name data of either type of object.

Listing App.3 Deleting a node from a binary tree

```
Boolean MerchTree::Delete (Boolean deleteCopies, Merchandise_Item * forDeletion,
CopyTree * Copies)
{
    Merchandise_Item * theItem, * parent, * rightChild, * leftChild, * parentRightChild;
    char * iTitle, * iSystem;

    iTitle = forDeletion->getTitle();
    if (forDeletion->getItem_type() == GAME)
    {
        Game * theGame = (Game *) forDeletion;
        iSystem = theGame->getSystem();
        find (iTitle, iSystem, theItem, parent);
    }
    else
        find (iTitle, theItem, parent);

    if (theItem == 0)
        return FALSE; // item not found

    if (deleteCopies) // remove all copies from copy tree
    {
        Item_copy * currentCopy, * oldCopy;
        int copy_numb;
        currentCopy = forDeletion->getFirst();
        while (currentCopy)
        {
            copy_numb = currentCopy->getInventory_numb();
            Copies->Delete (copy_numb);
            oldCopy = currentCopy;
            delete currentCopy; // remove copy from memory
            currentCopy = oldCopy->getNext();
        }
    }

    rightChild = theItem->getRightName();
    leftChild = theItem->getLeftName();
    parentRightChild = parent->getRightName();
        // used to figure out which side of parent node is on

    if (rightChild == 0 && leftChild == 0) // node to be deleted is a leaf
    {
        if (parentRightChild == theItem)
            parent->setRightName (0);
        else
            parent->setLeftName (0);
}
```

Continued next page

Listing App.3 (Continued) Deleting a node from a binary tree

```
    else if (rightChild == 0) // node to be deleted has left child but no right
    {
        if (parentRightChild == theItem)
            parent->setRightName (leftChild);
        else
            parent->setLeftName (leftChild);
    }
    else if (leftChild == 0) // node to be deleted has right child but no left
    {
        if (parentRightChild == theItem)
            parent->setRightName (rightChild);
        else
            parent->setLeftName (rightChild);
    }
    else // node to be deleted has both right and left children
    {
        Merchandise_Item * current = theItem;
        Merchandise_Item * stack[20];
        int stackPtr = -1;

        current = current->getLeftName(); // get left child
        while (current) // slide right while right child
        {
            stack[++stackPtr] = current;
            current = current->getRightName ();
        }

        // replace node to be deleted with node at top of stack
        stack[stackPtr]->setRightName (rightChild);
        stack[stackPtr]->setLeftName (leftChild);
        if (parentRightChild == theItem)
            parent->setRightName (stack[stackPtr]);
        else
            parent->setLeftName (stack[stackPtr]);
        stack[stackPtr - 1]->setRightName (0);
            // parent of rightmost child no longer has child
    }
    Item_count--;
    return TRUE;
}
```

Tree Traversals

The primary reason for creating a binary search tree is to facilitate fast data retrieval. However, there are also times when you need to retrieve the data stored in the tree in order. This is known as *traversing* the tree.There are three general traversals:

- In-order traversal: Nodes appear in whatever ordering is used to construct the tree. In the example in X, an in-order traversal would produce a listing in alphabetical order. To implement an in-order traversal, a program processes a node's left subtree, the node itself, and then the node's right subtree.
- Pre-order traversal: A pre-order traversal processes the node first, followed by its right subtree and then its left subtree.
- Post-order traversal: A post-order traversal processes a node's right subtree, its left subtree, and finally the node itself.

The Penultimate Videos program uses in-order traversals to populate scrolling lists. However, it uses a pre-order traversal when writing data to a file. The in-order traversal would produce an alphabetical list in a file. When the file was read back into memory, the resulting tree would be no better than a linked list. (If you don't believe this, create an alphabetical list of a half dozen names and insert them, in order, into a binary tree.)

The In-Order Traversal

To perform an in-order traversal, a program needs to keep track of the nodes it visits as it travels down a right or left subtree. Therefore, in-order traversal algorithms typically use a stack to store nodes as the program visits them. The basic process is as follows:

1. Find the root node and make it the current node.
2. Push the current node onto the stack.
3. Make the current node's left child the current node.
4. Repeat steps 2 and 3 until you encounter a node without a left child. This slides all the way down the left subtree.
5. Process the node on the top of the stack.
6. Pop the top node from the stack and make it the current node. If the stack is empty (no node left to pop), stop the traversal.
7. Retrieve the current node's right child and make it the current node. Go to step 3.

8. If there is no right child, the current node becomes the node at the top of the stack.
9. Go back to step 5.

To see how this works, trace through Figure App.2, which graphically illustrates the process for the sample tree in Figure App.1.

THE PRE-ORDER TRAVERSAL

As you read earlier, a pre-order traversal processes the node first, followed by its right subtree and its left subtree. Like the in-order traversal, the pre-order traversal uses a stack to contain nodes to be processed. The algorithm—which is considerably simpler than that for the in-order traversal—can be generalized as follows:

1. Push the root node on the stack.
2. Process the node on the top of the stack.
3. Pop the node from the top of the stack, making it the current node. If there is no node to pop (the stack is empty), the traversal is complete.
4. If the current node has a left child, push that left child onto the stack.
5. If the current node has a right child, push that right child onto the stack.
6. Go back to step 2.

To see a pre-order traversal in action, trace through Figure App.3, which graphically illustrates the process for the tree in Figure App.1.

Object-Oriented Binary Trees

The object-oriented way of handling data structures is considerably different from that used in traditional structured programs. In this section you will learn how object-oriented trees are managed and how tree traversals are performed. To understand how tree traversals work, you should be very comfortable with operator overloading.

Figure App.2 An in-order tree traversal

Step	Action	Stack
1.	current = Henry	
2.	Push Henry	Henry
3.	current = Bobby	
4.	Push Bobby	Bobby Henry
5.	current = Anne	
6.	Push Anne	Anne Bobby Henry
7.	Process Anne	
8.	Pop Anne current = Bobby	Bobby Henry
9.	Process Bobby	
10.	Pop Bobby current = Bobby	Henry
11.	Push David	David Henry
12.	current = David	
13.	Push Cathy	Cathy David Henry
14.	Process Cathy	
15.	Pop Cathy current = David	David Henry
16.	Process David	
17.	Pop David current = David	Henry
18.	Push Edward	Edward Henry

Continued next page

Figure App.2 (Continued) An in-order tree traversal

19. Process Edward

20. Pop Edward
    current = Henry

    Stack: Henry

21. Process Henry

22. Pop Henry
    current = Henry

    Stack: (empty)

23. Push Mary

    Stack: Mary

24. Process Mary

25. Pop Mary
    current = Mary

    Stack: (empty)

26. Push Terry

    Stack: Terry

27. Process Terry

28. Pop Terry
    current = Terry

    Stack: (empty)

29. Push Veronica

    Stack: Veronica

30. Push Vernon

    Stack: Vernon, Veronica

31. Process Vernon

32. Pop Vernon
    current = Veronica

    Stack: Veronica

33. Process Veronica

34. Pop Veronica
    current = ?

    Stack: (empty)

Traversal stops because there's no node to pop to make current

Figure App.3 A pre-order tree traversal

Step	Action	Stack
1.	Push Henry	Henry
2.	Process Henry	
3.	Pop Henry	(empty)
4.	Push Bobby	Bobby
5.	Push Mary	Mary Bobby
6.	Process Mary	
7.	Pop Mary	Bobby
8.	Push Terry	Terry Bobby
9.	Process Terry	
10.	Pop Terry	Bobby
11.	Push Veronica	Veronica Bobby
12.	Process Veronica	
13.	Pop Veronica	Bobby
14.	Push Vernon	Vernon Bobby
15.	Process Vernon	
16.	Pop Vernon	Bobby
17.	Process Bobby	
18.	Pop Bobby	(empty)

Continued next page

Figure App.3 (Continued) A pre-order tree traversal

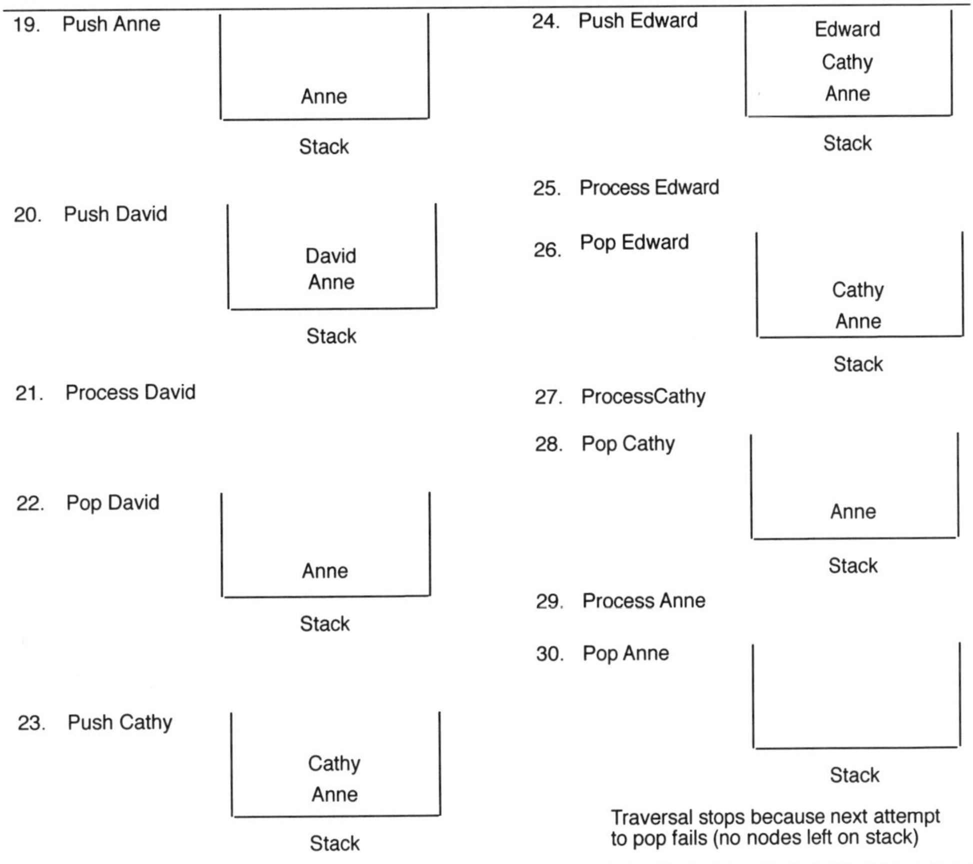

TREE CONTAINER CLASSES

Object-oriented programs use container classes to manage data structures. A *container class* is a class designed specifically to "contain" access to a data structure. The code that you have seen in this appendix for inserting, deleting, and modifying elements in a binary tree has all come from a container class.

A container class usually doesn't contain the actual data that make up the data structure. Instead, it contains just enough information to access the data structure. For example, a container class that manages a linked list would contain a pointer to the first element in the list; a container class that manages a tree would contain a pointer to the root node of the tree. The pointers that link elements in the data structure (pointers to the "next" element in a list or to the left and right children in a binary tree) are part of the objects whose pointers make up the data structure.

The container class for a binary tree actually needs no other variables beyond the address of the root node. However, as you can see in Listing App.4 (the MerchTree class, which organizes items alphabetically by title), the container class also holds a count of the items in the tree and the last item number used. Until the program deletes a merchandise item, the count of items and the last item number used will remain the same. However, even when items are deleted, the item numbers continue to increment as new items are added; item numbers for deleted items are not reused.

Listing App.4 A container class for a binary tree

```
class MerchTree
{
    private:
        Merchandise_Item * root;
        int Item_count, lastTitle_numb;
    public:
        MerchTree (int, int); // base constructor
        void Insert (Merchandise_Item *, ANSIstring, Boolean);
        Merchandise_Item * find (ANSIstring); // find
        Game * find (ANSIstring, ANSIstring); // used just for games (based on title and
system)
        // Flag indicates whether copies should be deleted along with the title
        Boolean Delete (Boolean, Merchandise_Item *, CopyTree *);
        void find (ANSIstring, Merchandise_Item * &, Merchandise_Item * &); // for videos
        void find (ANSIstring, ANSIstring, Merchandise_Item * &, Merchandise_Item * &);
// for games
        int getItem_count();
        void setItem_count (int);
        int getlastTitle_numb ();
        int inclastTitle_numb ();
        Merchandise_Item * getRoot();
};
```

The container class contains all functions needed to maintain the tree, including inserting new items, deleting items, and searching for items. It also provides functions that return container class values. However, notice that the container class does not perform tree traversals. That is left to a special type of class known as an interator.

TRAVERSAL ITERATORS

An *iterator* is a class that performs a traversal of the objects organized by a data structure. In the case of a linked list, an iterator provides access in first/next or last/prior order. A binary tree iterator is written to handle one of the three traversal orders (pre-order, post-order, or in-order). Whenever a program needs to traverse a binary tree, it creates an iterator object to manage the process.

To understand how an iterator works, let's first look at some code that uses one. In Listing App.5, for example, the Penultimate Videos application object is performing an in-order traversal of the merchandise item tree (an object of class MerchTree named Items) to display titles in a list box object.

Listing App.5 Using an iterator object

```
:
    MerchItr traversal;
    int Type, row = 0;
    Merchandise_Item * currentOne;
    char * Title;
    Cell theCell, * theCellPtr;
        // a cell (row & column number) and a pointer to the variable
    theCellPtr = &theCell;

    for (traversal.Init (Items); !traversal; ++traversal)
    {
        currentOne = traversal();
        Type = currentOne->getItem_type();
        if (Type == item_type)
        {
            Title = currentOne->getTitle();
            ::LAddRow (1, row, theListHandle); // add a row to the list
            ::SetPt (theCellPtr, 0, row++);
                // initialize the coordinates of the cell just added
            ::LSetCell (Title, strlen(Title), theCell, theListHandle); // add the data
        }
    }
:
```

The program first creates an iterator object (`traversal`, from the class `MerchItr`). Then it uses a `for` loop to perform the traversal. The first portion of the `for` initializes the iterator with the root node of the tree being traversed and slides all the way left to find the first node that should be processed. The termination condition (`!traversal`) stops the process when an attempt to pop a node off the iterator's stack fails. The increment (++traversal) moves to the "next" node in the tree. Meanwhile, in the body of the loop, traversal() returns a pointer to a node for processing.

An In-Order Traversal Iterator

The iterator class that performs an in-order traversal (Listing App.6) maintains a stack, a stack pointer, and private functions to push items onto and pop items off the stack and to slide left until a node without a left child is found. The public functions include the function that initializes the iterator and the overloaded operators that are used by a program performing a traversal.

Listing App.6 An iterator class for an in-order traversal

```
class MerchItr
{
    private:
        Merchandise_Item * stack[25], * root;
        int stackPtr;
        void push (Merchandise_Item *); // push onto stack
        Merchandise_Item * pop (); // pop from stack
        void goLeft (Merchandise_Item *);
    public:
        MerchItr ();
        int Init (MerchTree *);
        int operator++ (); // find node
        int operator! (); // check for end of traversal
        Merchandise_Item * operator() (); // return pointer to current object
};
```

The member functions for the MerchItr class can be found in Listing App.7. First take a look at the Init function. Notice that it retrieves the root of the tree being traversed and then calls the goLeft function, which pushes nodes onto the stack until it reaches a node that has no left child.

The goLeft function works in conjunction with the overloaded ++ operator to provide the traversal. To see how this happens, take a look at the function for ++. It first pops the top node off the stack. Then it checks to see if the node just popped has a right child. If it does, then the function uses goLeft to slide all the way down the right child's left subtree.

Listing App.7 An iterator class's member functions for an in-order traversal

```
int MerchItr::Init (MerchTree * tree)
{
    stackPtr = -1; // set stack as empty
    root = tree->getRoot(); // initialize current node to root
    goLeft (root); // go down left side of tree
    return stackPtr >= 0; // is stack empty?
}

int MerchItr::operator++ ()
{
    Merchandise_Item * parent, * child;

    if (stackPtr >= 0)
    {
        parent = pop();
        child = parent->getRightName();
        if (child)
            goLeft (child);
    }
    return stackPtr >= 0;
}

Merchandise_Item * MerchItr::operator() ()
    { return stack[stackPtr]; }  // current node is top of stack

void MerchItr::goLeft (Merchandise_Item * Item)
{
    while (Item)
    {
        push (Item);
        Item = Item->getLeftName();
    }
}

int MerchItr::operator! ()
    { return stackPtr >= 0; } // check for end of traversal

void MerchItr::push (Merchandise_Item * Item)
    { stack[++stackPtr] = Item; }

Merchandise_Item * MerchItr::pop ()
    { return stack[stackPtr--]; }
```

Notice that a pop occurs only in the ++ function. When the program asks for a node to process, the ( ) function sends back the contents of the top of the stack, without removing it from the stack.

A Pre-order Traversal Iterator

A class to perform a pre-order traversal is very similar to the class to perform an in-order traversal. In fact, as you can see in Listing App.8, the only difference between the MerchItrPre class and the MerchItr class is the absence of a `goLeft` function, which the pre-order traversal doesn't need.

Listing App.8 An iterator class that performs a pre-order traversal

```
class MerchItrPre
{
    private:
        Merchandise_Item * stack[25], * root;
        int stackPtr;
        void push (Merchandise_Item *); // push onto stack
        Merchandise_Item * pop (); // pop from stack
    public:
        MerchItrPre ();
        int Init (MerchTree *);
        int operator++ (); // find node
        int operator! (); // check for end of traversal
        Merchandise_Item * operator() (); // return pointer to current object
};
```

The differences between the two iterators becomes clearer when you look at the member functions (Listing App.9). Notice first that the `Init` function simply pushes the root node onto the stack to start the traversal, rather than pushing all nodes that are in the left subtree as is done with an in-order traversal.

To move to the "next" node, the ++ function pops the top node from the stack, just like the in-order traversal. However, after this point the process changes. The function looks to see if the node just popped has a left child. If so, it pushes the node on the stack. It then repeats the procedure for a right child.

NOTE

The beauty of iterators is that the programmer who uses one doesn't need to be concerned about the internal workings of a traversal. If you look at the code in the Penultimate Videos program—in particular, if you compare the code in the application class's Unload function to the code in any function that builds a list of titles—you'll notice that both in-order and pre-order iterators are used in exactly the same way. The only difference is the class from which the iterator object is created.

Listing App.9 An iterator class's member functions for a pre-order traversal

```
MerchItrPre::MerchItrPre()
{
    stackPtr = 0;
    root = 0;
}

int MerchItrPre::Init (MerchTree * tree)
{
    stackPtr = -1;
    root = tree->getRoot();
    if (root)
        push (root); // place root on stack to get traversal started
    return stackPtr >= 0; // is stack empty?
}

int MerchItrPre::operator++ ()
{
    Merchandise_Item * parent, * child;

    if (stackPtr >= 0)
    {
        parent = pop(); // remove current node from stack
        child = parent->getLeftName();
        if (child)
            push (child); // push left child, if any
        child = parent->getRightName();
        if (child)
            push (child); // push right child, if any
    }
    return stackPtr >= 0;
}

Merchandise_Item * MerchItrPre::operator() ()
    { return stack[stackPtr]; } // returns note at top of stack for processing

int MerchItrPre::operator! ()
    { return stackPtr >= 0; } // check for empty stack and end of traversal

void MerchItrPre::push (Merchandise_Item * Item)
    { stack[++stackPtr] = Item; }

Merchandise_Item * MerchItrPre::pop ()
    { return stack[stackPtr--]; }
```

Glossary

Action: Something that can be undone.

Active: A property of a pane; any pane in an active window.

Application framework: A shell program that provides basic program services and is customized and expanded by a programmer.

Attachment: A class that modifies the behavior of another class while a program is running.

Broadcaster: An object that sends a message that another object (a listener) must act upon.

Chain of command: The ordering of commanders that determines the order in which events are passed to commanders for handling.

Commander: A class that listens and responds to messages generated by keystrokes and menu choices.

Container class: A class that manages a data structure, such as a tree, list, or array.

Enabled: A property of a pane that means that a pane can respond to mouse clicks.

Frame: The rectangle that forms the border of an object.

Idler: An object that receives attention after every idle event.

Iterator: A class that manages the traversal of objects in a data structure such as a linked list or binary tree.

Listener: An object that listens for a message sent by another object (a broacaster).

Node: An element in a binary tree.

Pane: An area in which a program can draw. A pane also can respond to clicks of the mouse pointer.

Pane descriptor: A Pascal string describing some major property of a pane, such as its contents.

Pane value: The integer equivalent of the pane descriptor.

Panel: The portion of a pane or view being printed that will fit on one page.

Periodical: A class whose objects receive attention at regular intervals, either after every event (repeaters) or after every idle event (idlers).

PowerPlant object: A resource that can be used as the basis of an object created from a PowerPlant class.

PPob: A PowerPlant object resource.

Registering classes: The action that occurs when a PowerPlant program builds a table of class IDs and names of constructors to use when creating objects from external data sources (usually resource files).

Repeater: An object that receives attention after every event.

Root node: The single node at the top of a binary search tree.

Subcommander: Objects below a commander in the chain of command.

Subpane: A pane that is contained within a view.

Supercommander: An object above a commander in the chain of command.

Superview: The view containing a specific pane.

Synthetic commands: Items for menus such as the or Font menu where the menu items can't be specified before the program is run.

Target: The single object that is available to listen for and handle a command.

Traverse (a binary tree): Access the nodes in a tree in some known order.

Value message: The message sent by a broadcaster.

View: A container for panes.

Index

WARRANTY DISCLAIMER

METROWERKS AND METROWERKS' LICENSOR(S), AND THEIR DIRECTORS, OFFICERS, EMPLOYEES OR AGENTS (COLLECTIVELY METROWERKS) MAKE NO WARRANTIES, EXPRESS OR IMPLIED, INCLUDING WITHOUT LIMITATION THE IMPLIED WARRANTIES OF MERCHANTABILITY AND FITNESS FOR A PARTICULAR PURPOSE, REGARDING THE SOFTWARE. METROWERKS DOES NOT WARRANT, GUARANTEE OR MAKE ANY REPRESENTATIONS REGARDING THE USE OR THE RESULTS OF THE USE OF THE SOFTWARE IN TERMS OF ITS CORRECTNESS, ACCURACY, RELIABILITY, CURRENTNESS OR OTHERWISE. THE ENTIRE RISK AS TO THE RESULTS AND PERFORMANCE OF THE SOFTWARE IS ASSUMED BY YOU. THE EXCLUSION OF IMPLIED WARRANTIES IS NOT PERMITTED BY SOME JURISDICTIONS. THE ABOVE EXCLUSION MAY NOT APPLY TO YOU.

IN NO EVENT WILL METROWERKS AND METROWERKS' LICENSOR(S), AND THEIR DIRECTORS, OFFICERS, EMPLOYEES OR AGENTS (COLLECTIVELY METROWERKS) BE LIABLE TO YOU FOR ANY CONSEQUENTIAL, INCIDENTAL OR INDIRECT DAMAGES (INCLUDING DAMAGES FOR LOSS OF BUSINESS PROFITS, BUSINESS INTERRUPTION, LOSS OF BUSINESS INFORMATION, AND THE LIKE) ARISING OUT OF THE USE OR INABILITY TO USE THE SOFTWARE EVEN IF METROWERKS HAS BEEN ADVISED OF THE POSSIBILITY OF SUCH DAMAGES. BECAUSE SOME JURISDICTIONS DO NOT ALLOW THE EXCLUSION OR LIMITATION OF LIABILITY FOR CONSEQUENTIAL OR INCIDENTAL DAMAGES, THE ABOVE LIMITATIONS MAY NOT APPLY TO YOU. Metrowerks liability to you for actual damages from any cause whatsoever, and regardless of the form of the action (whether in contract, tort (including negligence), product liability or otherwise), will be limited so as not to exceed the cost of the replacement of the media on which the software is distributed.

SOFTWARE LICENSE

PLEASE READ THIS LICENSE CAREFULLY BEFORE USING THE SOFTWARE. BY USING THE SOFTWARE, YOU ARE AGREEING TO BE BOUND BY THE TERMS OF THIS LICENSE. IF YOU DO NOT AGREE TO THE TERMS OF THIS LICENSE, PROMPTLY RETURN THE UNUSED SOFTWARE TO THE PLACE WHERE YOU OBTAINED IT AND YOUR MONEY WILL BE REFUNDED.

1. License. The application, demonstration, system and other software accompanying this License, whether on disk, in read only memory, or on any other media (the "Software") the related documentation and fonts are licensed to you by Metrowerks. You own the disk on which the Software and fonts are recorded but Metrowerks and/or Metrowerks' Licensor retain title to the Software, related documentation and fonts. This License allows you to use the Software and fonts on a single Apple computer and make one copy of the Software and fonts in machine-readable form for backup purposes only. You must reproduce on such copy the Metrowerks copyright notice and any other proprietary legends that were on the original copy of the Software and fonts. You may also transfer all your license rights in the Software and fonts, the backup copy of the Software and fonts, the related documentation and a copy of this License to another party, provided the other party reads and agrees to accept the terms and conditions of this License.

2. Restrictions. The Software contains copyrighted material, trade secrets and other proprietary material. In order to protect them, and except as permitted by applicable legislation, you may not decompile, reverse engineer, disassemble or otherwise reduce the Software to a human-perceivable form. You may not modify, network, rent, lease, loan, distribute or create derivative works based upon the Software in whole or in part. You may not electronically transmit the Software from one computer to anoth-

er or over a network.

3. Termination. This License is effective until terminated. You may terminate this License at any time by destroying the Software, related documentation and fonts and all copies thereof. This License will terminate immediately without notice from Metrowerks if you fail to comply with any provision of this License. Upon termination you must destroy the Software, related documentation and fonts and all copies thereof.

4. Export Law Assurances. You agree and certify that neither the Software nor any other technical data received from Metrowerks, nor the direct product thereof, will be exported outside the United States except as authorized and as permitted by the laws and regulations of the United States. If the Software has been rightfully obtained by you outside of the United States, you agree that you will not re-export the Software nor any other technical data received from Metrowerks, nor the direct product thereof, except as permitted by the laws and regulations of the United States and the laws and regulations of the jurisdiction in which you obtained the Software.

5. Government End Users. If you are acquiring the Software and fonts on behalf of any unit or agency of the United States Government, the following provisions apply. The Government agrees: (i) if the Software and fonts are supplied to the Department of Defense (DoD), the Software and fonts are classified as "Commercial Computer Software" and the Government is acquiring only "restricted rights" in the Software, its documentation and fonts as that term is defined in Clause 252.227-7013(c)(1) of the DFARS; and (ii) if the Software and fonts are supplied to any unit or agency of the United States Government other than DoD, the Government's rights in the Software, its documentation and fonts will be as defined in Clause 52.227-19(c)(2) of the FAR or, in the case of NASA, in Clause 18-52.227-86(d) of the NASA Supplement to the FAR.

6. Limited Warranty on Media. Metrowerks warrants the diskettes and/or compact disc on which the Software and fonts are recorded to be free from defects in materials and workmanship under normal use for a period of ninety (90) days from the date of purchase as evidenced by a copy of the receipt. Metrowerks' entire liability and your exclusive remedy will be replacement of the diskettes and/or compact disc not meeting Metrowerks' limited warranty and which is returned to Metrowerks or a Metrowerks authorized representative with a copy of the receipt. Metrowerks will have no responsibility to replace a disk/disc damaged by accident,abuse or misapplication. ANY IMPLIED WARRANTIES ON THE DISKETTES

AND/OR COMPACT DISC, INCLUDING THE IMPLIED WARRANTIES OF MERCHANTABILITY AND FITNESS FOR A PARTICULAR PURPOSE, ARE LIMITED IN DURATION TO NINETY (90) DAYS FROM THE DATE OF DELIVERY. THIS WARRANTY GIVES YOU SPECIFIC LEGAL RIGHTS, AND YOU MAY ALSO HAVE OTHER RIGHTS WHICH VARY BY JURISDICTION.

7. Disclaimer of Warranty on Apple Software. You expressly acknowledge and agree that use of the Software and fonts is at your sole risk. Except as is stated above, the Software, related documentation and fonts are provided "AS IS" and without warranty of any kind and Metrowerks and Metrowerks' Licensor(s) (for the purposes of provisions 7 and 8, Metrowerks and Metrowerks' Licensor(s) shall be collectively referred to as "Metrowerks") EXPRESSLY DISCLAIM ALL OTHER WARRANTIES, EXPRESS OR IMPLIED, INCLUDING, BUT NOT LIMITED TO, THE IMPLIED WARRANTIES OF MERCHANTABILITY AND FITNESS FOR A PARTICULAR PURPOSE. ACADEMIC PRESS DOES NOT WARRANT THAT THE FUNCTIONS CONTAINED IN THE SOFTWARE WILL MEET YOUR REQUIREMENTS, OR THAT THE OPERATION OF THE SOFTWARE WILL BE UNINTERRUPTED OR ERROR-FREE, OR THAT DEFECTS IN THE SOFTWARE AND THE FONTS WILL BE CORRECTED. FURTHERMORE, ACADEMIC PRESS DOES NOT WARRANT OR MAKE ANY REPRESENTATIONS REGARDING THE USE OR THE RESULTS OF THE USE OF THE SOFTWARE AND FONTS OR RELATED DOCUMENTATION IN TERMS OF THEIR CORRECTNESS, ACCURACY, RELIABILITY, OR OTHERWISE. NO ORAL OR WRITTEN INFORMATION OR ADVICE GIVEN BY ACADEMIC PRESS OR AN ACADEMIC PRESS AUTHORIZED REPRESENTATIVE SHALL CREATE A WARRANTY OR IN ANY WAY INCREASE THE SCOPE OF THIS WARRANTY. SHOULD THE SOFTWARE PROVE DEFECTIVE, YOU (AND NOT ACADEMIC PRESS OR AN ACADEMIC PRESS AUTHORIZED REPRESENTATIVE) ASSUME THE ENTIRE COST OF ALL NECESSARY SERVICING, REPAIR OR CORRECTION. SOME JURISDICTIONS DO NOT ALLOW THE EXCLUSION OF IMPLIED WARRANTIES, SO THE ABOVE EXCLUSION MAY NOT APPLY TO YOU.

8. Limitation of Liability. UNDER NO CIRCUMSTANCES INCLUDING NEGLIGENCE, SHALL ACADEMIC PRESS BE LIABLE FOR ANY INCIDENTAL, SPECIAL OR CONSEQUENTIAL DAMAGES THAT RESULT FROM THE USE OR INABILITY TO USE THE SOFTWARE OR RELATED DOCUMENTATION, EVEN IF ACADEMIC PRESS OR AN ACADEMIC PRESS AUTHORIZED REPRESENTATIVE HAS BEEN ADVISED OF THE POSSIBILITY OF SUCH DAMAGES. SOME JURISDICTIONS DO NOT ALLOW THE LIMITATION OR EXCLUSION OF LIABILITY FOR INCIDENTAL OR CONSE-

QUENTIAL DAMAGES SO THE ABOVE LIMITATION OR EXCLUSION MAY NOT APPLY TO YOU.

In no event shall Metrowerks' total liability to you for all damages, losses, and causes of action (whether in contract, tort (including negligence) or otherwise) exceed that portion of the amount paid by you which is fairly attributable to the Software and fonts.

9. Controlling Law and Severability. This License shall be governed by and construed in accordance with the laws of the United States and the State of California, as applied to agreements entered into and to be performed entirely within California between California residents. If for any reason a court of competent jurisdiction finds any provision of this License, or portion thereof, to be unenforceable, that provision of the License shall be enforced to the maximum extent permissible so as to effect the intent of the parties, and the remainder of this License shall continue in full force and effect.

10. Complete Agreement. This License constitutes the entire agreement between the parties with respect to the use of the Software, the related documentation and fonts, and supersedes all prior or contemporaneous understandings or agreements, written or oral, regarding such subject matter. No amendment to or modification of this License will be binding unless in writing and signed by a duly authorized representative of Metrowerks.

Become a CodeWarrior now!

Order the commercial version of Metrowerks CodeWarrior!

Metrowerks CodeWarrior delivers three times a year. When you buy CodeWarrior and register with Metrowerks, you will receive free updates throughout the year.

CodeWarrior Gold
(For Power & 68K Macintosh, Win32/x86, MagicCap, Be, Java) **$399**

Discover Programming for Macintosh
(For 68K Macintosh development) **$79**

Discover Programming with Java
(For Java development) **$99**

METROWERKS WORLDWIDE
http://www.metrowerks.com

**Metrowerks CodeWarrior.
The world's best-selling
Macintosh development tools.**

Metrowerks is continually adding new features and products.
Check our website for the latest products, prices and Geekware.

[cut here]

About the CD-ROM

The CD-ROM that accompanies this book contains the source code, supporting files, and project files for the Penultimate Videos program in a folder named *Penultimate Videos*. To compile and run the program, first make sure that you have PowerPlant installed. (See the last paragraph of this section if you don't own CodeWarrior already.) Also be sure that you have QuickTime in your Extensions folder and, if you are working on a PowerMac, the QuickTime PowerPlug. The PowerPlug is required to run QuickTime from native PowerPC code.

Copy the *Penultimate Videos* folder to your hard disk. Then, move the files *PP_VidSHeaders* and *PP_VidSHeaders (68K)* from the *Penultimate Videos* folder to the Precompiled Headers folder (inside the PowerPlant Folder, which is inside the MacOS Support folder, which is inside the Metrowerks CodeWarrior folder). At this point, you can open the appropriate project file (68K or PPC) and go.

NOTE

If you have a lot of fonts, the Penultimate Videos program may take a while to launch because it must build a font menu.

If you don't yet have your own copy of the CodeWarrior development software, install CodeWarrior Lite that comes on the CD-ROM. This version of CodeWarrior will allow you to run and view the sample programs. However, the text editor's Save option has been disabled so that you won't be able to save any changes made to source code files.